6th Battalion
the Cheshire Regiment
in the Great War

6th Battalion the Cheshire Regiment in the Great War

A Territorial Battalion on the Western Front
1914–1918

John Hartley

Pen & Sword
MILITARY

First published in Great Britain in 2017 by
PEN & SWORD MILITARY
an imprint of
Pen and Sword Books Ltd
47 Church Street
Barnsley
South Yorkshire S70 2AS

ISBN 978 1 47389 758 8

A CIP record for this book is available from the British Library

Printed and bound in England
by CPI Group (UK) Ltd, Croydon, CR0 4YY

Typeset in Times New Roman by Chic Graphics

Pen & Sword Books Ltd incorporates the imprints of
Pen & Sword Archaeology, Atlas, Aviation, Battleground, Discovery,
Family History, History, Maritime, Military, Naval, Politics, Railways,
Select, Social History, Transport, True Crime, Claymore Press,
Frontline Books, Leo Cooper, Praetorian Press, Remember When,
Seaforth Publishing and Wharncliffe.

For a complete list of Pen and Sword titles please contact
Pen and Sword Books Limited
47 Church Street, Barnsley, South Yorkshire, S70 2AS, England
E-mail: enquiries@pen-and-sword.co.uk
Website: www.pen-and-sword.co.uk

Contents

Introduction

Back in the late 1990s I started to research the names on four local war memorials. I wanted to find out what I could about these men who had died so many years ago and who had been pretty much forgotten by their communities. I wanted to discover not just who they were but what had happened to them. Of course I knew that they had died in the First World War – or Great War, as I came to know its other name. Their names would not otherwise be on the memorials. The next decade saw me expand the original interest to include the names on all the civic war memorials in the borough of Stockport – nearly 3000 of them. In general I was able to identify them and discover the circumstances of their deaths. Many of the names were men who had served with the 6th Battalion, Cheshire Regiment – the local Territorial Force unit which recruited in Stockport, as well as the neighbouring towns of Hyde, Stalybridge and Glossop.

My interest in the Cheshires grew and I knew that, at some point, I would want to write their story. These were working class men, who worked in the local cotton and hatmaking industries. They were poorly paid, worked long hours in dangerous conditions and lived in the small terraced houses of the towns, often in poor health. But, once a week, they put on a uniform and became part-time soldiers. It gave them camaraderie and status. And annual training camp effectively meant a paid holiday at the seaside with your mates.

Few of the young men will have considered that they might actually have to go and fight. But all that changed on 4 August 1914, when the 6th Cheshires were mobilised on the outbreak of war. They were considered to be well trained and the Battalion was amongst the first of the territorials to leave Britain to go on active service. By November 1914 they were in France and, within a few weeks, took part in the famous Christmas Truce.

Over the next four years, they were regularly in action, involved in the heavy fighting at the Battle of the Somme in 1916 and at Ypres the following year. They suffered badly during the German offensives in the spring of 1918 before taking part in the final successful Allied advances in the summer and autumn. For much of the war the Battalion retained its recruitment links with north Cheshire until the need for reinforcements meant that men started to come from the wider area of the county and, later still, from across the country.

My research for this book started with the aspect that most interested me – the men themselves. Who were they? Where did they live? What was their work? Were they married? What happened to them once they joined the army? And, for the survivors, what happened after they returned home? I slowly built up a database of nearly 4500 men who passed through the Battalion's ranks during the war. Surviving records are incomplete – it is thought only 30% of service files survived a fire in the 1940s – so for many of the men there is scant information. For others there is a wealth of detail. However, it is a sad fact that much of this detail comes from newspaper obituaries after a man's death in action was reported. These cotton mill workers were not great letter writers or men who would keep a diary or later write their wartime memoirs. But there are sufficient first-hand accounts, from both officers and men, to be able to tell some of the Battalion's story in their own words.

The basis for the history of the Battalion comes from official records – mainly the war diary, which was a document written up daily by one of the officers. But local newspapers are a superb resource to get additional details and I would want to thank staff at local libraries for their assistance – Glossop Library, Stockport Local Heritage Library and Tameside Local Studies Library and the staff at libraries across the country who responded to my emails asking if it would be possible for them to look up their local newspapers to see if Private X had an obituary. A few declined, citing pressure on staff resources, and that is understandable, but most were only too pleased to help. The Regimental Archives has also been most helpful, allowing me access to the documents and photographs in its care. There are others, too numerous to mention by name, who have assisted – descendants of the men who have allowed me to include family accounts and photos; and members of the Great War Forum who, as usual, have answered my most obscure queries, often within minutes.

I have enjoyed the research and have enjoyed the writing. I hope the book does justice to the men it remembers.

John Hartley
Autumn 2017

CHAPTER 1

The Men of 1914

When the part-time soldiers of the 6th Battalion, Cheshire Regiment, were mobilized to report to their respective drill halls on 4 August 1914, it was the culmination of over a century of tradition of voluntary military service. Now that Britain was at war with Germany, their role was to defend the country against invasion.

For a few of the Battalion's oldtimers, this was not the first time that they had put on their uniform with the intent to fight if need be. Colour Sergeant Frank Naden had seen service in South Africa during the Boer War and may well have thought 'Here we go again'. He was born in 1878, at Hartington in Derbyshire, close to the border with Staffordshire. Details of his early life are uncertain but, by the closing years of the nineteenth century, he had moved to the Stockport area and joined the Cheshire Regiment's 4th Volunteer Battalion. This was the unit that, a few years later, would become the 6th Territorial Battalion. The Regiment's 2nd Battalion, part of the regular army, had sailed for South Africa on 7 January 1900. Reinforcements from the Volunteer Battalions followed six weeks later. Naden was part of this first contingent, which included another thirty eight of his comrades from the 4th Volunteers.

Sergeant Naden joined the Royal Marines from six to ten years back and was in the Ashantee and Brass expeditions. He also took part in the bombardment of Zanzibar. He subsequently joined the Bechuanaland Mounted Police and was in the famous Jameson raid, his horse being killed under him in the first battle. Sergeant

Frank Naden.

Naden managed to effect his escape when many of his comrades in arms were taken prisoners. He is familiar with the country from Capetown to Bulawayo and speaks the Boer language, which should serve him in good stead.

(Cheshire Observer, 3 February 1900)

Naden wrote home in the spring, saying he had been in action on a number of occasions. He gave no details but the Cheshire Regiment is known to have been part of an attack on Boer positions at Karee Siding in March. There was another attack, on Boer defenders of a crossing point on the Zand River, in the May. He returned to Stockport in 1901, where he married Hannah Edge soon after arrival. His occupation at the time was given as police constable – believed to have been a position with the Johannesburg police force. He may have returned to South Africa at some point but, by 1914, he was carrying on business as a greengrocer on Wellington Road North. He was a skilled soldier and a brave man and both of these talents would be recognised over the four years of what was to become known as the Great War, with the award of several gallantry medals and promotion through the ranks to lieutenant colonel.

Over a hundred years before Naden went to South Africa, Stockport men had come together to defend against the possibility of an invasion. In 1794, they established the town's Loyal Volunteers; the threat came from the French forces led by Napoleon. They paraded in January 1795, Captain Holland Watson receiving their new colours, a gift from Lady Warren. The *Chester Courant* reported that, *The horrors of a foreign invasion and those arising from civil war, were portrayed in lively colours, the blessings from concord were also admirably depicted.* It was a time of some considerable political unrest in Britain, with the government passing two bills, known as the convention bills – the Seditious Meetings Act, which restricted public gatherings to fifty people and the Treason Act which, amongst other things, made it a crime to even imagine doing harm to the King. The protests resulted in one member of Stockport's Loyal Volunteers being drummed out, as reported by the *Leeds Intelligence*, in February 1796.

Not for exercising his opinions respecting war and the convention bills but upon his own declaration – that if necessity should require the exertion of the corps, he would march with it and the moment he had the opportunity he would quit the ranks and join the malcontents in their measures.

With peace being negotiated in 1801, the Volunteers disbanded. The officers met for a final dinner in February 1802, presenting their commander, now Major Watson, with a *large and very elegant silver cup, lined with gold and richly ornamented*, which the *Chester Courant* reported was inscribed as presented by the officers *as a tribute of their esteem and to convey the high sense they entertain of his loyalty and patriotism.* There was a further presentation to Watson from the rank and file Volunteers, although not until January 1803. These were four cups, similarly decorated and engraved. After the speeches, Watson ordered *a hogshead of stout old ale to be tapped which was plentifully distributed among the volunteers.*

The peace was shortlived and Britain and France were again at war (1803). A National Defence Act was promulgated which encouraged the formation of volunteer units and a number of these were created in north Cheshire. These remained in existence until Napoleon Bonaparte was defeated in 1815. His nephew, Napoleon III, would present the next perceived threat of invasion to Britain. Although France and Britain had been allies during the Crimean War, the French Emperor embarked on an expansionist policy in its aftermath. In 1859 the French defeated Austria, then in control of much of northern Italy, and the British government feared that the country might become his next target. Once again there was a call for volunteer infantry units to be created to defend the nation if invasion occurred.

A meeting in late November 1859 decided to form the Stockport Volunteer Rifle Corps.

The members who have signified their intention of joining this corps number about 300 and large bodies are waiting to see the uniform before following the example. The committee have decided upon the uniform; it is to cost about £4 and is to be made by Messrs Whitley & Roberts of Chester. It is of light grey and consists of a loose buttoned-up surtout, with dark braid on the collar, breast and sleeves, bronzed buttons on the coat, trousers bordering on the peg-top style, and a peaked cap. One employer has undertaken to equip 70 volunteers.

(*Cheshire Observer*, 24 December 1859)

In the early part of the nineteenth century, a volunteers group had been formed in the Glossop area and there had been a fine record of military service. A meeting was held in 1859 to form a Rifle Corps, as urged by the Government; but it was opposed by a number of men, including the pastor of Littlemoor Chapel. He was reported to have said,

Glossop in the early twentieth century.

> *The present system of the formation of Rifle Corps would be destructive of the morals of young men, and if the vast commercial establishments in Manchester were carried on by some who led semi-military lives they would wither and decay as fast as they have grown up.* The proposal was defeated by 26 votes to 16.

Another attempt to form a Rifle Corps was made in 1875 and this now met with much approval from Glossop's young men, over 150 registering their interest. Several months later a notice appeared in the local newspaper, asking men to attend the Town Hall on 10 January 1876 to be enrolled and on the following Saturday to take the oath of allegiance. They became the 23rd Derbyshire Rifle Volunteers. It had already been decided that the Glossop men would throw in their lot with the Cheshire Regiment units from Hyde, Stalybridge and Stockport, rather than their own county regiment. By agreement between the Regiment and the Nottinghamshire & Derbyshire Regiment (the Sherwood Foresters), there would be a reciprocal arrangement whereby the Foresters would recruit in Whaley Bridge, then partially in Cheshire. It was, presumably, a simple matter of geographical convenience. After taking the oath, the men were formed up to receive their first drill under the direction of their instructor, Sergeant Major Hiney, assisted by his counterparts from the three Cheshire units.

The Cheshires' drill hall at Stalybridge. Photo: Tameside MBC Image Archive

Stockport's Armoury had been built in 1862 at a cost of £4000 and included a spacious drill hall, sixty yards long and twenty yards wide, with a separate band room, storage facilities for the rifles, offices, etc. The Hyde detachment had premises at Mottram Road, whilst the Stalybridge troops paraded at their drill hall, built in 1880, on the corner of Astley Street and Walmsley Street. In Glossop, the market hall had been divided and, by 1882, half of it had become a drill hall.

The close links between the part-time troops of the four towns were formalised and they became a single entity in 1880, with the official title of the 4th Cheshire (Cheshire & Derbyshire) Rifle Volunteer Corps. In

1887, it became the 4th Volunteer Battalion, Cheshire Regiment, and would remain as such until 1908.

The Battalion at the turn of the century reflected the class structures of Victorian and Edwardian society. The rank and file were working class men, mainly employed in the area's cotton mills, hatworks and factories. Their sergeants, like Frank Naden, were the foremen or small business owners; whilst the officers exclusively came from the upper echelons of the community.

Like Naden, Captain Herman Hesse had served as a part time soldier for a considerable time, having been commissioned as a second lieutenant in December 1896. As his name suggests, he was born to two German immigrants, in 1869, who were then living in Chorlton-cum-Hardy. It is possible that, as a young man, he spent time in Germany, as he does not

Herman Hesse.

appear on census returns for the latter part of the nineteenth century. If so, he had returned to the Manchester area by 1894, when he married Beatrice Heginbotham. In a sign of his growing financial success, the couple moved to Cheadle Hulme, living on Station Road and, later, at 16 Queens Road. The 1901 census suggests the family had all the trappings of middle class life, including the employment of a live-in servant. At that time Hesse was in business as a button manufacturer and, later, as a manufacturer's agent dealing in lace.

For men such as Hesse and Naden, life in the early twentieth century was relatively comfortable. Conditions for the majority of the population were also improving. Like Stockport, the smaller towns of Glossop, Hyde and Stalybridge were industrial in their nature and the dominant industry was cotton. It was hard work and conditions were often hazardous. The north west was the centre of the worldwide industry and Manchester was affectionately called Cottonopolis, with many of the major traders having offices and warehousing in and around what is now known as the Northern Quarter. Although trade would take place in the city centre, the actual production of cloth was in mills in the outlying towns. There were also the thriving associated factories – companies who would bleach and then dye the cloth. There had been setbacks to the growth of the industry, most notably the 'cotton famine' of the 1860s when, during the American civil war, the ports of the Confederacy were blockaded by Union ships to prevent trade. The industry's heyday was reached in the 1890s, when Stockport alone had over fifty cotton mills. Some of them were relatively small scale operations, with no more than a few hundred spindles – a rotating spike fitted to the machines used to twist the cotton fibres into yarn before weaving it into cloth. For example, Peter Crossley Ltd operated just 516 spindles at premises at Hope Carr Mills. The company made wicks for candles and lamps. At the other end of the scale there were several very large scale operations with over a hundred thousand spindles. Stockport's largest was probably Palmer Mills; at the time of the war it had about 180,000 spindles and employed several hundred.

William Bennett, from Stockport. Mortally wounded and taken prisoner in July 1917.

William Bennett worked at Palmer Mills, in Portwood, as a piecer. It is a precise job title. Bennett would have worked with the man in charge of minding the spinning mule, which usually operated over 1000 spindles. Both of them would be keeping their eyes open for breaks in the cotton thread. Bennett would then go underneath the machine to 'piece' together the fibres – a potentially hazardous task underneath moving machinery. It was the work of seconds but, with several breaks occurring every minute, he must have been exhausted after a day's work. But, in spite of this, he found time to train with the Cheshires, which he had joined in about 1911. At that time he was living at home at 30 Hanover Street, Portwood – a short walk from work. His father, John, worked as a cotton spinner and it is very probable that William worked with him. His older brother, John, had been a regular soldier but, in early 1914, he returned to the Stockport area. He had been working as a nursing orderly at an army hospital in India and this, no doubt, helped him get a job at Cheadle Royal Hospital. As an army reservist, he was recalled to the colours in August 1914. The oldest brother, Herbert, married in 1909 and was now living at Peak Street, also working at the mill as a piecer.

All three brothers would die during the war. John was wounded in July 1916 and, returning home for treatment, died on 1 September. He is buried in the graveyard of St Paul's Church, Portwood. Herbert died of pneumonia in 1918, probably after catching the Spanish Flu – a worldwide pandemic which killed millions. He is buried at Basra, in Iraq. At some point after 1911 William married and the couple are believed to have lived at 23 Ratcliffe Street. He was badly wounded during the 6th Cheshires' attack on 31 July 1917 and was taken prisoner. He died on 28 August 1917 and is buried in Hamburg.

Stockport's second industry was hat making. The town had had a skilled workforce for centuries but this was on a small scale. Industrialisation brought in larger companies with Christy's, a well known London firm, opening a factory in the town in 1826. By the 1840s it had become the world's largest hat making factory. In 1890, it employed around 4,500 people and was exporting over six million hats a year, as well as very many sales within the UK. The Mad Hatter is a popular character in Lewis Carroll's *Alice in Wonderland* and there is a factual basis for the phrase 'mad as a hatter'. Men working in the industry would use a mercuric nitrate solution in making fur felt hats and, of course, would breathe in the fumes. Over time this could cause a range of problems – slurred speech and loss of co-ordination, as though a man was drunk, as well as memory loss, depression and anxiety attacks. In 1899 poisoning from mercury was made a notifiable disease under the health and safety legislation of the Factories Act and, from 1906, workers were entitled to be compensated if they became ill from the poisoning. These steps did not outlaw the use of the compound, although usage reduced, so it is inevitable that a number of the part time soldiers would have been affected.

Born in Hyde in 1869, Thomas Long is thought to have been employed in the hatting industry all of his adult life. He married Mary Jane in 1894 and the couple lived at 2 Nelson Street in the town. He worked as a felt hat blocker – a skilled job but one that was hard work as the process was done by hand, even in the industrial age. He would take a hood shaped piece of felt, pulling it over a block of wood, fashioned to the right size and shape for the desired hat. He would tie it down and shrink it to shape using steam. Men would suffer from the effects of the steam and buckets of water were kept at hand to cool down their hands but there would still be regular scalding. Long had been a part time soldier for several years – he would rise to the rank of company sergeant major before being discharged from the army in 1916 due to illness. Although the details of his illness are not known, there is nothing to suggest that the hazards of his civilian occupation had caught up with him.

There were no such occupational hazards for Captain Samuel Hill-Wood. He was educated at Eton and ran the cotton business founded by his father. The family home was at Park Hall, Hayfield but at the time of the 1911 Census he was living at 12 Grosvenor Place, London. An indication of his very considerable wealth is suggested in the census by his employment of eighteen servants, including a butler, footmen, cook, housemaids and grooms. He first served with the Volunteers, as a second lieutenant, between 1889 and 1902. The years around the turn of the century were significant for him. He played cricket for Derbyshire, captaining the county side between 1899 and 1902. He also married in 1899. The following year, Wood (as he was then known) stood successfully as the Conservative candidate for the St James ward of Glossop Council. It was the start of a political career that would see him elected to Parliament, in 1910, for the local High Peak constituency. He changed his name to

Captain Samuel Hill-Wood.

Hill-Wood in 1912. He had a lifelong interest in football, owning the Glossop North End club before the war and, in the 1920s, becoming chairman of Arsenal. With the outbreak of war, he reapplied for a commission, becoming a captain and, later, major with one of the Regiment's home service reserve battalions.

Conditions for the majority of the population living in the towns from which the Cheshire Regiment drew its men had gradually improved in the late 19th century but the environment remained generally unhealthy, with smoke and soot from the many factories, mills and homes that used coal for heating. Respiratory disease shortened many a life. In his annual report for 1902, Stockport's medical officer noted that infant mortality in the borough amounted to 197 per 1000 registered births. Dr Young commented that it was an *appalling figure, implying as it does that one-fifth of the children born die off before completing twelve months of life, leaving only four-fifths of the infant population to struggle for existence and to be further reduced by the ever present and terrible dangers attending child life in a densely populated manufacturing town.* By 1913, the Medical Officer was able to report that the mortality rate had been all but halved and was the lowest ever recorded, at 109 deaths per 1000. He attributed this to the high rainfall and low temperatures in the summer of 1912.

The residents of the other towns experienced similar problems but they were not always taken as seriously as they had been by Dr Young. In May 1909, the Stalybridge Town Council considered a report from Cheshire County Council which noted that the borough had the highest death rates, for adults and infants, in the county. Alderman Simpson commented that it was an industrial town and they had appointed a lady health visitor. He did not that think the figures were alarming.

A number of practical steps had been taken over the years to improve conditions. Many Victorian slums had been cleared. They were often a building surrounding a small yard, with a single toilet for the use of the many families crammed into the rooms. They were replaced with the terraced housing that we still see today in the older parts of towns. By comparison they were spacious and quite luxurious, with each having its own toilet in an outhouse in the backyard.

From 1861 water for the Stockport area was supplied by the privately owned Stockport & District Waterworks Company, headed by William Legh, of Lyme Hall. In 1899 Stockport Corporation acquired the company and set about a programme of improvements. Most notable of these was to create a new reservoir at Kinder, near Hayfield. It took nine years to build and, on completion in 1912, was reported to have the world's largest dam. By the time of the war, people in the area had a reliable and safe source of clean water.

It was a time of great civic pride and local councils involved themselves in many aspects of day-to-day life, operating enterprises which, today, are in the hands of private companies. It, perhaps, reflects the growing numbers of those eligible to vote. Men could vote but only if they were over the age of twenty one and were householders, paying rates to the council. Although it would not be until 1918 before some women gained the vote for parliamentary elections, they were enfranchised for local elections if they were also of age and householders. This obviously excluded married women whose husband, as the householder, would be the only one permitted to vote.

Stockport had been a county borough since 1894, carrying out the full range of local government responsibilities. It had absorbed the area of the Reddish Urban District Council in 1901, followed by the area of the Heaton Norris Council in 1913. As the war loomed, its population was nearing 135,000. By comparision, the Cheshire Regiment's other recruitment areas were much smaller, with Hyde and Stalybridge having populations in 1911 of around 30,000 each and Glossop with around

Stockport Armoury. Photo: Gwyneth M Roberts.

21,000. These smaller boroughs were dependent on the Cheshire and Derbyshire County Councils for the provision of major services but there was no less pride in what they could do.

Stockport's full range of services included water supply as mentioned and also gas and electricity as well as its own police force. From the early part of the twentieth century it also operated the new electric trams, which allowed people to move around the area much more easily than the horse drawn trams they replaced. It meant that workers no longer needed to live very close to their places of employment, although the vast majority had little option but to remain in their small, low rent homes. But, for some, it contributed to the development of the town's suburbia. It also meant that people could enjoy their leisure time more fully – there are accounts of families catching the tram from Stockport to Gatley, then still a semi-rural village, for a walk in the countryside.

The smaller sizes of the other towns meant they had to band together to provide services. For example, Stalybridge joined with Ashton under Lyne and Dukinfield to form a waterworks committee; whilst its partners providing a tram service were Hyde, Mossley and Dukinfield. However the borough ran its own combined police force and fire brigade. It also built a number of elaborate buildings, not least of which were the municipal baths, opened in 1870.

The building, which is in the Italian style, comprises a swimming bath, with a clear water area of 70 feet by 28 feet and, on each side, are dressing boxes, thirty two in number…..There is also another swimming bath with a clear water area of 60 feet by 24 feet and of less depth. There are twenty private baths and a complete set of Turkish baths. (Kelly's Directory, 1914)

Shortly after the start of the 20th century, public criticism of the Volunteer movement started to grow. It was felt that the officers were treating it as a social club rather than instructing the rank and file in military matters. In consequence, the soldiers were becoming increasingly 'inefficient', particularly with regard to musketry skills. In 1904 a Royal Commission was established to enquire into the continued suitability of the Volunteers and the other auxiliary forces of the Militia and the Yeomanry cavalry. The *Manchester Courier*, in its edition of 21 May 1904, asked,

Is the Volunteer Force as at present constituted equal to the strain that would devolve upon it in the event of an invasion? That is the question which will shortly be answered by the Commission. The reply will, of course, be in the negative. What then are the desiderata? A uniform standard of fighting efficiency, a smaller and more efficient force, every branch of which is equipped with modern weapons, better musketry and signalling, machine gun detachments well trained, higher bearer organisation and complete transport.

The Commission reported later in the year and, whilst giving a nod in the direction of reform, failed to make any root and branch proposals for change. Richard Haldane was appointed Secretary of State for War in 1905 and embarked on a further exercise, in which he quickly concluded that the way forward for the army was for the regular forces to be regarded as an expeditionary force, with the Militia acting as its reserve, whilst the Volunteers and Yeomanry would be merged into a new single Territorial Force for home defence purposes. Legislation was passed and the changes came into force on 1 April 1908.

The *Manchester Courier* reported that the Cheshires' Stalybridge Company said 'farewell' to the old organsation at a dinner in the drill hall on Saturday, 4 April, whilst welcoming the new one.

There was a full muster of officers and men. Colonel Gimson, who presided, supported by Colonel Johnston, said the Volunteers after

Princes Street, Stockport.

fifty years service could claim to have done good and patriotic service. It was the duty of all to now make the new scheme a success. There had been a good deal of hostile criticism directed against it but personally he failed to see much difference between the old and new – the only difference really being a compulsory camp. Both Colonel Gimson and Colonel Johnston advised the men to give the new force a twelve months trial.

With that, the men now found themselves members of the 6th Territorial Battalion. Or, to be precise, would be when they had formally volunteered for the new unit. Two men who were, almost certainly, there enjoying dinner were Charles Robinson and George Fowden. Both men had already officially joined the territorials, having signed up on 1 April. Twenty year old Robinson was a Yorkshireman by birth but had lived in the area for some time. His army service records indicate that he served in the army in South Africa in 1902 during the Boer War, presumably as a boy soldier. A few years later, at the time of the Great War, he was married and living at 105 Market Street with Mary and their two sons. He worked as a carter for the council. Fowden was three years older than Robinson and, when he sat down to the meal at the drill hall, had got married to Ethel just a few weeks before. He was employed at one of the local cotton mills, where he worked in the cardroom. This was a low skilled job, minding a carding machine. This equipment combed the cotton fibres to align them for ease of making a stronger thread. Even by the standards of mill work, the carding room was an unpleasant place to work and men would go home covered in fluff and would regularly be breathing in the fine particles that were in the atmosphere. Both of them would go on active service with the battalion in 1914. Fowden found himself in trouble even before he had fired a bullet – in November, he was fined eight days' pay for using threatening language towards one of the Non-Commissioned Officers. Both men would return to Britain when their contracted time with the territorials expired in early 1916. Fowden may well have had some explaining to do to Ethel – in January 1916, he received medical treatment for gonorrhoea and was away from duty until almost the time when he was due to return to the UK to leave the army. His pay may have been suspended or reduced during this time, as the army would often regard sexually transmitted diseases as self-inflicted injuries.

The Stockport Volunteers also marked the formation of the new Battalion with a hotpot supper at the Armoury. The band played and the disbanding of the Volunteers was commemorated by the sounding of the Last Post and Lights Out. The new territorial battalion was ushered in by Reveille being played and the flags unfurled. As at Stalybridge, there were speeches urging men to sign up and, over the coming days, many did so.

The new Battalion was organised into eight companies. Two companies, A and B, drilled at Stalybridge with one each at Hyde (C) and Glossop (D). The other four companies, E – H were Stockport based, drilling at the Armoury, which also housed Battalion headquarters. Enlistment into the territorials was for four years and was open to those aged between seventeen and thirty five and existing terriers would be able to rejoin until they were forty. Recruits had to be at least five feet two inches tall – a requirement that excluded a goodly number of adult men, until the regulations were changed in late 1914. An examination of surviving service records suggest that the average height of the 6th Battalion men was five foot six inches. By comparison, their middle class officers averaged five foot eight inches. The difference reflects the better living conditions, diet and general health of the middle classes.

They would be trained as though they were regular soldiers, although the training would inherently have to be piecemeal due to their part-time nature. It would include foot drill, rifle drill, weapon handling, musketry, bayonet practice and signalling, as well as general physical training. There would be lectures and demonstrations; for example, how to dismantle and reassemble a machine gun which they would then need to undertake themselves. The members of the Battalion band would also have music practice. When on active service the band members usually undertook the role of stretcher bearers, so would also receive instruction in first aid. A new recruit had to attend forty drill sessions in his first year but, thereafter, it could reduce to twenty. The enabling legislation provided that the territorials would be mobilized on the outbreak of war and would have a primary role in home defence. Once mobilized, there would be additional training for war and it was envisaged that, after six months, they could be called upon to volunteer for overseas service, supporting the regular army. It would be left to each individual soldier to decide whether to volunteer.

The organisation within the Cheshire Regiment was now such that there were two regular army battalions, as before – the 1st and 2nd. One would always be overseas on Imperial duty, whilst the other was on home duties somewhere in Britain, which then included Ireland. When war was declared in 1914, the 1st Battalion was stationed in Londonderry, whilst the 2nd was in India, garrisoned at Jubbulpore. There were four territorial battalions, as well as the 6th, the 4th with headquarters at Birkenhead, the 5th at Chester and the 7th at Macclesfield. As far as has been established, all six battalions were understrength in 1908 and would remain so until after war was declared. As mentioned earlier, the old Volunteer movement had not been well thought of in its final years and, it is fair to say, that the new Territorial Force did not find much favour either with the politicians or the general public. Their nickname, the 'Saturday Afternoon Soldiers', was not intended as a compliment.

Administrative control of the territorial battalions would lie with County Associations, which would be responsible for recruitment, provision of buildings and other facilities and, amongst other matters, the arrangements for annual training camps. They would not, however, exercise any responsibility for the actual training programmes at camp, nor any general supervision of military matters. Although annual training camps had been a feature of the Volunteer movement, attendance at them was now enshrined in the legislation governing the Territorial Force.

For the army, camps provided the opportunity for training in ways that better replicated conditions on active service that simply could not be achieved in the confines of an urban drill hall. A battalion could operate as a single unit, bringing together its eight companies and working with other battalions in its brigade. Large scale manoeuvres would permit, for instance, mock battles to be fought.

For the majority of the north Cheshire men who worked in the mills and factories, the weekly attendance at the drill hall gave them some escape from the routine of daily life with, perhaps, some pride in being able to walk

Stalybridge A Company at annual camp in about 1912. Photo: Tameside MBC Image Archive

through town in their distinctive uniform of blue trousers, scarlet jacket and peaked helmet, similar to the ones traditionally worn by policemen.

Annual camp put the icing on the cake. This was often regarded as a paid holiday, usually at the seaside, with your mates, away from parental gaze and away from the cramped conditions at home, where several children might occupy one bedroom in a two up, two down terraced house. And there would be better food as well. At camp, the men would be having meat every day for their main meal – served in the middle of the day and then always called dinner – and often bacon for breakfast. This would contrast with their normal daily lives, where meat would be eaten on only a minority of days and the diet was generally poor. A survey, conducted by the Rowntree family in York in 1901, found that in many working class families women would regularly go without food so that their husbands and children would not go hungry. The army had also been forced to reject many recruits for service in the Boer War for reasons of malnutrition. These and other studies helped to bring in legislation which, in 1906, provided for schools to establish canteens and, in certain circumstances to provide free meals for the poorest children. But inadequate diet remained a defining difference between the Battalion's officers and men.

The early part of 1908 saw weeks of industrial unrest in the north west's cotton industry. The trade union had sought an increase in wages but this had been completely rejected by the employers. A strike was inevitable and it would be a bitter one, lasting several weeks. Amongst the strikers were the employees of Ashton Brothers in Hyde. Its managing director, Thomas Gair Ashton, had previously been the MP for the town but now represented Luton. He was reported as saying that *a great principle is at stake…and they are not prepared to accede to operatives' demands*.[1] By July, the Glossop, Hyde and District Cotton Employers Association were discussing actually reducing wages by 5%. When the trade unions would not agree, the employers closed the mills, locking the men out. The dispute was not resolved until 1909, when poverty forced the men to accept the employers' demands, reducing their pay. They would lose one shilling per week from wages that averaged around £1 5s.

Walter Murray was one of the employees of Ashton Brothers. Born in 1891, he had probably left school when he was twelve and gone straight to work at the mill. His first job would have been as a scavenger, collecting up the bit of fibres that had fallen to the floor. It was not until 1911 that he joined the territorials, going overseas with them in November 1914. However, his war would be over within hours of his first visit to the trenches, when he was wounded by shrapnel on 12 December. After treatment in France, he was back in Britain by the middle of January 1915. He was never fit enough to return to duty and was discharged on 1 May 1916.

Men attending camp were paid at the rate of one shilling per day. However, few worked for employers who would give them paid leave to go. For young single men, this may not have been a big issue, although there would obviously be a reduction in the family income. It was a much bigger problem for the married men who had families and a home to support. They would be losing around 70% of their weekly income in order to attend camp. It meant that many simply could not afford to attend and, in consequence, could not be regarded officially as 'efficient' soldiers. A few weeks after creation of the territorials, Colonel Gimson wrote to Stalybridge Council requesting that it pay the difference between what a man would usually earn and the one shilling a day army payment. The request was rejected.

Camp in 1908 was held at Conway, a popular destination for the Cheshire Brigade. They had been there, or to neighbouring Deganwy, nine times since 1886. As usual, it was held over the fortnight around the Whit Monday holiday. As well as the manoeuvres, there were inter-battalion competitions in presentation, drill and musketry and, as had happened on several prior occasions with the Volunteers, the winning unit amongst the four battalions was the Stalybridge A Company.

Mottram Road, Stalybridge. Home to several members of the Battalion.

The end of June 1908 was the last day former Volunteers could elect to join the Territorials for one year or more. New recruits would now have to undertake to serve for four years. Although some 80% of the Volunteers had transferred, the Battalion was seriously understrength. The establishment was 1060; but actual numbers were only 660. The end of the year saw the companies hold prize-giving events, the Glossop gathering being held on 30 December:

> *A large company was present at the Victoria Hall, Glossop when the annual gathering, dance and distribution of prizes took place in connection with the Glossop detachment of the 6th Battalion, Cheshire Regiment. Major F G Knowles, officer commanding the detachment, stated the Glossop detachment had the honour of being the strongest company in the Battalion up to the present time, only about seven more men being required to complete the establishment…. A vote of thanks was accorded to Lord Howard who provides for the detachment free use of a handsome drill hall and rifle range and, in his reply, Lord Howard urged the necessity of an efficient standing army.*
>
> *The silver cup presented for shooting, by Mr O Partington, MP, was won by the Glossop team; the physical drill cup (given by A Profumo) by Sergeant Darwent's Glossop team; the bayonet fighting competition by the Hadfield team; and the ambulance cup (presented by Surgeon-Captain R B Sidebotham) by Private S Mills for the second year in succession.*
>
> (*Manchester Courier*, 31 December 1908)

The Battalion was slowly moving away from being a social club towards taking its responsibilities for home defence more seriously. In 1909 it started to run weekly classes in Stockport for married women in how to attend to the wounded in case of invasion. It was hoped to run around twenty classes. At the end of March 1909, the *Manchester Courier* reported that a public meeting had been held at Stockport Town Hall in support of the Territorial Movement and as a recruiting drive for the 6th Battalion. It was addressed by General Sir Charles Burnett, then the senior officer in Western Command, Major General Lloyd, commanding the Welsh Division, and Colonel Bromley Davenport.

> *A number of Socialists were present and constantly interrupted the speakers with cries of 'What about the unemployed?' and 'What price an Englishman's home?'. One of the Socialists asked whether in the event of a strike riot, the Territorials would be called on to shoot down their shopmates. Colonel Bromley Davenport replied 'No, they would not'. General Sir C Burnett said that if people of this country were not prepared to protect themselves, the same fate would overtake the country which overtook many of the old world empires. The only way to avoid national disaster was to have behind the regular army and navy an organised Citizen Army prepared and ready to defend the country against foreign invasion. An appeal was made by the speakers for men to join the 6th Cheshires, which is about 200 short of establishment."*

The early months of 1914 were as quiet and normal as those of previous years. The events of the coming summer were far away. Recruitment was still a problem for the Battalion. At the annual prize giving in Stalybridge, Colonel Sykes hoped that local employers would encourage their staff to join up and would allow them to attend annual camp. If ever there was a list of the great and the good of the Stockport area, Alan John Sykes would be near the top of it. Born in 1868, he joined the Freemasons when he was at Oxford University. He had then joined the family firm – the Sykes Bleaching Company, which had been established in 1792 in Edgeley. He became a director of the Bleachers' Association, actually a commercial

Lieutenant Colonel Alan Sykes.

operation which grew by taking over many bleaching companies. He was also interested in agriculture, managing the family estates in Saskatchewan, albeit from the far side of the Atlantic. Outside of business, Sykes was a keen cricketer and also hunted with the Cheshire hounds. He had been a Justice of the Peace, treasurer of the Infirmary and a governor of the Grammar School. He was an active Conservative politician and had served as Stockport's mayor in 1910/11 and, in 1910, was elected as MP for the Knutsford constituency. He had been active in the Volunteer movement from 1904 and, on being promoted to lieutenant colonel in March 1911, took command of the 6th Battalion. The following year, Sykes extended his influence in the community when he gained control of the Stockport Advertiser newspaper group.

Annual camp for 1914 took place between 31 May and 13 June. The Stockport men formed up at the Armoury early on the Sunday afternoon and marched to Edgeley Station for the train to Rhyl. A large crowd lined the streets to cheer them on. They were led by the band which played a selection of tunes that included 'Old Comrades' and 'The March of the Cheshires'. They marched from Rhyl Station to a field between the town and Abergele where their first job was to peg down their tents on what was a windy, wet and cold late afternoon. It is an area still used for camping, although it is now in modern chalet type caravans. There were church parades later in the day.

Towards the end of the first week, the four Cheshire territorial battalions paraded to be inspected by the brigade commander at 8.30am on 5 June. After they were dismissed, there was a short march to warm the men up after standing in the cold and they then practised digging trenches. The next day there was company training in the grounds of Bodelwyddan Castle. A large army camp was based nearby, at Kinmel, during the forthcoming war and the grounds continued to be used for training throughout it. The parish churchyard contains a number of burials of soldiers who died from natural causes, together with several who were shot when over-enthusiastic barrack guards opened fire when trying to quell a drunken riot in 1919.

There were strong winds in the early hours of 8 June and the officers' mess hut nearly blew down. It had been a miserable time for the men of several companies who had been out all night on a training exercise. They arrived back at dawn and were given hot coffee and allowed to sleep through the morning. At midday the Battalion paraded for field firing training.

Pay day at annual camp near Rhyl in June 1914. Photo: Stockport Express

The men are supposed to be under fire from the enemy. The men run to take up their positions and, so as not to become too prominent targets for the enemy, spread out and lie down. The target cannot be seen by the naked eye, as would be the case in warfare, when the enemy would be lying down hidden. The section commander locates the enemy with the aid of field glasses and then gives verbal instructions to the men where to concentrate their fire. Five men are in the hospital with minor complaints, largely due to the cold weather.

(*Stockport Advertiser*, 12 June 1914)

As always, each battalion nominated one of its companies to represent it in the annual competition. The 6th Battalion again picked the Stalybridge men of A Company, which had won every year except 1909 and 1913. As before, the companies would compete in inspection, company drill, extended order drill, musketry and protection. There would be a maximum of 200 points. The competition was again won by the 6th Battalion, which amassed 141 points, just beating their usual close rivals from the 4th

Battalion, which scored 137. The 7th and 5th Battalions were somewhat behind, with 129 and 124.

The men packed up camp on the morning of 13 June and left the area in two trains – one for the Stockport companies and the other for the remaining half of the Battalion. The Stalybridge men were back in their home town at 3.15pm .

Here a large crowd had assembled to welcome the local Terriers and, as they emerged from the station, carrying the Deputy Lieutenant's Cup – which "A" Company has won five times during the last seven years – they were accorded an enthusiastic welcome. All along the route to the Drill Hall, large numbers of people had assembled. Captain Leah was in charge. There were also present Captain Kirk, Lieutenant Underwood, 2nd Lieutenants Innes, R Norman and C Norman and drill instructor Sergeant Murray.
(*Stalybridge Reporter*, 20 June 1914)

Second Lieutenant Cyril Norman.

Captain Frederick Leah was 35 in 1914 and, although commanding the Stalybridge company, was a Stockport man. He had been in the Volunteers since 1893 and had held his current rank since 1903. He was outranked by his older brother, George, who was one of two men with the rank of major in the Battalion. The 1901 census indicates Leah was studying to be a doctor but he does not appear to have continued with that career and, in 1911, was not employed in any capacity.

Second Lieutenant Ronald Norman.

Whilst the Stalybridge men might be regarded as the local territorials' crack shots, there was a significant lack of musketry skill in many units throughout the country. It was not for the want of effort. Even before a new recruit could undertake target practice, he had to go through a course of instruction, which included lectures in the care of arms and the principles of rifle firing and several drills practicing firing an unloaded rifle. To pass the standard test for a soldier, a man would have to fire twenty three rounds at targets at distances varying from 100 to 500 yards, of which eight had to be rapid fire. However, for soldiers in an urban area, regular rifle practice on the range was difficult.

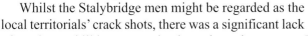

The Battalion did have one on farmland near Chapel-en-le-Frith but this could obviously only be used occasionally for actual testing. The solution for many battalions was to adapt the Lee Enfield rifle. This would be done by inserting into the barrel what was known as a "Morris Tube". This reduced the diameter of the barrel, allowing a much less powerful .22 bullet to be fired safely on a thirty yard indoor range in the drill hall. It allowed men to get used to holding their rifles, taking aim and firing. In spite of all the efforts, over 30% of Territorials failed their test in the 1909/10 period. The situation had barely improved in 1912, when some 58,000 men either failed the test or did not present themselves for testing.

With camp over for another year, the men returned to their normal lives with no indication of the events that were about to overtake them. Just over a week after the *Stalybridge Reporter* wrote of the Cheshires returning from Rhyl, a young Bosnian Serb nationalist, Gavrilo Princip, assassinated Archduke Franz Ferninand, heir to the throne of the Austro-Hungarian empire. Within a month, the Austrians had declared war on Serbia and had invaded it. Over the coming days a series of treaty obligations led one country after another to mobilize their armies. But in Britain hardly a thought seems to have been given in the newspapers that the country might also have to fight. The feeling was that this was a 'European matter' with little to do with Britain, except wondering how trade might be maintained or if it offered new opportunities for profit. Life, for the vast majority of the population, carried on as normal.

The *Manchester Courier*, in its edition of 1 August, gave notice that the 6th Battalion's band would be playing at the Warrington Agricultural Society Show, at Walton Park in the town on 6 August. The same day as the newspaper report, Henry Stafford joined the territorials. He was a thirty seven year old married man, living at 83 Great Egerton Street, Stockport. Stafford married Elizabeth in 1900 and worked as a carter for a horse slaughterer. As many before him, he had probably joined up for social reasons – a 'hobby' giving him something to do in his spare time when he was not dealing with dead horses and for the camaraderie. Perhaps he had heard how enjoyable camp was. In place of these pleasures, Henry Stafford woke up on the morning of 4 August to find he was about to be at war with Germany.

CHAPTER 2

Mobilization

In spite of intense diplomatic manoeuvring, the international situation rapidly continued to deteriorate. On the day that Henry Stafford joined the territorials, Germany declared war on Russia. The next day, 2 August, it started an invasion of France and Poland. The Germans also wrote to the Belgian government, indicating that they intended to violate the country's neutrality by crossing through it to continue their attack on France. Belgium responded the next day, rejecting the German demand of unmolested passage across the country, and asked Britain to assist with safeguarding its neutrality in accordance with treaty obligations between the two countries dating back to 1839. That was followed by Germany issuing formal declarations of war on both Belgium and France.

During the evening of 3 August, the Foreign Secretary, Sir Edward Grey, spoke to the House of Commons. *I would like the House to approach this crisis in which we are now from the point of view of British interests, British honour, and British obligations, free from all passion as to why peace has not yet been preserved.* He went on to conclude that honour, interest and obligations would demand that Britain would be *forced, and rapidly forced, to take our stand on these issues.* War now seemed almost inevitable. There would be last minute diplomatic appeals to the Germans but, during 4 August, the British army was mobilized and put on a war footing. The official declaration of war was not until 11pm but it had already been a busy day for the troops, both regular army and territorials.

During the day, the King issued a proclamation to embody the territorials – formally calling them up for service. By early evening, notices started to appear on the north Cheshire town halls, drill halls and other buildings.

Stockport town hall was officially opened by the Prince of Wales in July 1908.

NOTICE OF MOBILISATION

6ᵀᴴ BATTALION CHESHIRE REGIMENT

Orders have been received for the mobilisation of the above Territorial Battalion. All officers, NCOs and men are required under the provisions of the Territorial & Reserve Forces Act to assemble without delay for actual military service to report themselves at once in marching order.

Under the provisions of the Territorial & Reserve Forces Act, if any officer, NCO or man, not incapacitated by infirmity for military service, refuses or neglects to assemble or march, he shall be deemed a deserter and dealt with under the provisions of the Army Act.

Alan J Sykes, Lt. Colonel
Commanding 6ᵗʰ Cheshire Regiment

There was a prompt response from the men. Within an hour many had arrived at Stockport's Armoury dressed in uniform. As each arrived, they were greeted with cheers from a gathering crowd. Shortly afterwards, Sykes arrived in the town by train, having been in Parliament earlier in the day. There was a brief parade and the men were then sent home, being told to report back the next day, when there would be a medical inspection.

There were similar scenes at Glossop and Stalybridge. At Hyde's Armoury on Mottram Road, *as each man arrived, he was relieved of his bayonet and these were taken by motor car, along with several officers' swords, to a local works where they were ground and sharpened.....Towards dinnertime, the crowd thinned somewhat, many of the women no doubt remembering that dinner had to be prepared.*

Inside the Armoury, a vigorous examination was proceeding, each man being separately and thoroughly examined by Surgeon-Lieutenant John Morris. The men were lounging in all sorts of positions. After continually being on their feet since eight o'clock, they were feeling a little tired. Some were seated, others standing in little groups and others stretched full length on the floor, with their kit bags for pillows.

One matter which appears to be troubling some of the Territorials is the fact that they will be separated from their lady friends for an indefinite period. Private Horsfield had arranged to be married on Saturday but, being anxious to get it settled before leaving the town, had the knot tied on Wednesday morning.

(*North Cheshire Herald*, 8 August 1914)

At Stalybridge, almost all the men from the two companies had reported to the drill hall. After a parade the men were sent home until the following morning. They were back at 8am, all in uniform. *The drill hall became the centre of a scene of great activity and large crowds assembled to watch the Territorials arrive. At times, the crowd was very great, at other times somewhat slacker.* (*Stalybridge Reporter*, 8 August 1914). There was a

Hyde market place.

medical inspection and, with two exceptions, all were reported fit. Surgeon-Captain McCarthy noted that one of the two exceptions should be fit for duty within a couple of days.

On Saturday, 8 August, the men from Glossop and Stalybridge prepared to join their comrades at Stockport. Similarly, the Hyde men were also on the move, as recorded by the *Hyde Reporter*.

> *About 5 o'clock, they marched out of the drill hall and formed up outside. After the salute, the Mayor, Alderman Hinchcliffe Brook, expressed the great privilege of being present. He was proud to see they had in Hyde an army that could be pulled together at such short notice. The Hyde Detachment, wherever they would go, would show they were well drilled and knew their duty. When duty called, he hoped they would respond like Englishmen. He hoped they would have good health and return back to their old home and be citizens of the town in which they would always be held in great respect. He was proud to hear that every man had received five pounds. He asked them to see their wives got some of the money to fall back on while they were away. He hoped they would never be short and their wives would never be the same.*

The company, numbering about 140, then marched along Mottram Road to Godley Station, the watching crowd often cheering them past.

> *The scene at the station was most enthusiastic. As the Territorials boarded the train, there were many handshakes and partings and, as the train left the station at 6 o'clock, amidst great cheering, one could see many people, very probably relatives, wives and sweethearts of the Territorials, much affected by their departure.*

Colour Sergeant Arthur Taylor on board the mobilisation train at Godley station. He served as a Company Quartermaster Sergeant for most of the war, joining a company of the Labour Corps in the summer of 1917.

The Cheshires undertake a route march in 1915. The man on the left of the third row is Private James Briggs, who joined up in February 1915. Photo: Tameside MBC Image Archive

During the day the Battalion's colours were left at St George's Church, in the custody of the vicar, Rev. Thorpe, who was the Battalion's chaplain. They would remain with him until 1919. The men from the smaller towns were accommodated overnight at the Armoury, the Stockport men having been allowed home for a few hours. The Cheshires were still under strength and a recruiting officer was appointed, who immediately started an appeal for 200 men to join up and fill the vacancies

The full Battalion paraded again at 4.30am on Sunday and left for Edgeley Station in two parties – one at 6am and the other at 8am. Their destination was Shrewsbury. The train journey took several hours and they then had a two mile march to their billets. They stayed there until the 22nd, mainly undertaking fitness training and route marches. The Battalion then moved to Church Stretton, putting up their tents in the rain. They stayed there until the 31st and, by all accounts, had a miserable time due to the weather.

Whilst they were in Shropshire the government started to consider how the Territorial Force might be deployed overseas. Lord Kitchener, the newly appointed Secretary of State for War, was the man with the task. In the middle of the month a number of newspapers published the same report on his thinking.

> *By one means or another, the land forces available for overseas service must be increased and as a large part of the Territorial Force is able and willing to go abroad, Lord Kitchener desires to render it capable of going. But he has no idea of asking the Force to volunteer en masse for foreign service. It would be a very unfair demand to make for it was not enlisted for this purpose. (He) proposes to divide the Territorial Force into two categories – namely those able and willing to serve abroad and those whose business or occupations absolutely preclude them from doing so. There is no idea in Lord Kitchener's mind of flinging half-baked troops into the war furnace....There will be a distinction in the degree of training to be given to those ready to serve abroad and to those who serve at home. The former will be thoroughly trained and will be raised as soon as practicable to the standard required for fighting with regular troops.*

As with most territorial battalions, when it was put to them, almost all the officers of the 6th Cheshires volunteered for overseas service, as did 80% of the men. Their state of readiness was such that they were identified as a battalion that could go into action sooner rather than later. The 5th Cheshires would not go to France until February 1915 and it would not be until July 1915 before the 4th and 7th Battalions left Britain to join the ill-fated campaign at Gallipoli. There were further medical examinations of the men while they were in Shropshire to ensure that they were sufficiently fit for the rigours of war. Perhaps fortunately for his long term future, Colonel Sykes did not pass the medical and he had to remain in Britain, resigning his commission within a few days. In 1916, he was again holding a commission when, in the November, he was appointed as a lieutenant colonel commanding a local battalion of the newly created Cheshire Volunteer Regiment. The Volunteer Regiments were similar to the Home Guard in the Second World War, formed of those under or over age for the regular army or the territorials. They would be trained in drill and rifle shooting.

In Sykes' absence, command now passed to Captain George Heywood. Heywood was a partner in the family wholesale newsagency business in Manchester and was a fairly wealthy man in his own right. He married

Evelyn Platt in 1903 and, at the time of the 1911 census, the couple were living with her father in Hadfield. Edward Platt was a cotton manufacturer and employed seven live-in servants at the house. Heywood had joined a Volunteer battalion of the Manchester Regiment in 1900 but had later transferred to the Cheshires. He was promoted to a commanding officer's rank of lieutenant colonel in October 1914.

On 31 August the four Cheshire battalions in the brigade moved to Northampton, where training for war properly started, as Lord Kitchener had indicated. In the initial days this was all about building up fitness for which regular route marches, in full kit, were the key. It is worth noting that full kit weighed sixty pounds. The marches gradually increased in length to fifteen miles and, at one point, the whole of the Welsh Division undertook a twenty mile

Lieutenant Colonel George Heywood.

march. On 11 September one of the marches was to the village of Quinton, about five miles south of Northampton. The *Manchester Evening News* reported that food was cooked en route. They camped here for several nights and, during the first evening, the men were issued with new boots and were paid. During their time there a local man came into camp to donate sixty rabbits that he had shot.

The days were long and tiring for the men, as described by the *Northampton Mercury* on 4 September.

> *Twelve hours a day is given to hard work. At half past five, the men turn out of bed or get up from the floor in less hospitable homes. An hour later they have arrived at the points where they parade and then, with top coat, a hundred rounds of ammunition and all the impediments that a soldier carries on active service, they go for an hour's march. About an hour for breakfast is allowed on the return; work of all kinds from nine till one and again in the*

Battalion cooks at Northampton. Photo: Stockport Express

*afternoon. At half past six, work for the day is over except for those
going on sentry go and special duty and, at half past nine, tired out,
they go to their temporary homes for eight hours sleep.*

The Battalion was generally welcomed by the people of Northampton and,
in particular, trade boomed for the town's small businesses. A confectioner
commented to a reporter from the *Stockport Express, I'm doing very well,
thanks to the troops. If it were not for them, I might shut down. I hope they
stay here twelve months.*

It was not only the troops who were spending money, as a local
dressmaker commented.

*Trade is positively booming. So many ladies have come to me and
ordered dresses for evening wear. They have officers billeted with
them, they say, and can't come down in the same dress every night.
They all insist on the dresses being made quite plain and simple but
they must have new ones.*

With the day nearing when they would go on active service, a number
of the men took the opportunity to marry their sweethearts. Like his father,
Lieutenant Thomas Gibbons was a dental surgeon in civilian life. He lived
at home on Heaton Moor Road. He married Effie Mary Douglas at All
Saints Church, Northampton on 30 September. She had worked as a shop
assistant in her father's drapery business on Manchester's Rochdale Road.

Lieutenant Thomas Gibbons and his new wife, Effie, on their wedding day. Photo: Northampton Mercury

Within a couple of weeks Gibbons was promoted to captain and given command of one of the companies.

There were other marriages during this time. Alfred Smith was a lieutenant with the Glossop company. He married his fiancée, Edith, at Northampton. He was also promoted to captain at around this time, taking command of the company. Private George Hemmings was another to tie the knot in Northampton, marrying Mary Rowlands. He had been unable to get leave to travel back to Stockport, so she had come to him. Hemmings was an upholsterer by trade, living in Heaton Mersey. He would survive the war and return to the Stockport area, where he died in 1941, aged 57.

Sergeant Arthur Spedding almost certainly met his future wife, Ethel, while the Cheshires were in Northampton. Unusually for the 6th Cheshires, Spedding was not a manual worker. He was educated at Manchester College of Technology (later UMIST) and worked as a chemist's assistant. In his spare time he had been a member of the territorials since its creation and had been with the Volunteers before that. He remained in Britain for most of the war, training new troops, and married Ethel in 1916. By then he was a second lieutenant and only went on active service to France a few weeks before the end of the war.

Back in north Cheshire, charity fund-raising was under way. Whilst the soldiers were receiving pay, together with allowances for wives and children, it was much less than the average wages in the mills. And, for many of the companies, orders had dried up due to the conflict. The firms had no option but to go on short time. Relief Committees sprang up across the area and were soon making emergency payments to families from their limited funds. Schools were quick to help, offering free breakfasts and midday dinners to the children of the poor.

Friends and relatives were also keen to set up soldiers' comforts committees to send gifts to the men. The speed of mobilisation had, in part, out-stripped the arrangements necessary to provide for the men, as indicated by an anonymous letter to the Stalybridge newspaper:

> *I would like to know the reason why the men who enlist in the 6th Battalion, Cheshire Regiment Territorials have to find their own kit, yet the men who join the Manchester Territorials have their kit found free. Also, they have an allowance of 3d per day, for the use of their civilian clothes. I know they can have them provided but it*

At Northampton.

is stopped out of their pay, also I know they are allowed 10/- but this does not meet all the requirements, which cost something like 50/- .

The matter of the men's clothing was also on the mind of Lieutenant Henry Cooke and he wrote to the *Hyde Reporter:*[2]

It has occurred to me that perhaps some people of Hyde have been making articles of clothing for the troops, such as shirts, and sending them to headquarters, such as Manchester. It would be more satisfying to them to know where the articles are going and as Hyde has a Company of its own, some ninety per cent of whom have volunteered for active service abroad and each man must have two shirts and a change of socks which the men must buy for themselves, that somebody in Hyde might be able to do something for the men by collecting these articles and sending them on for distribution to the Company.

There had already been gifts for the Hyde men. Fred Wellerman, a local building contractor, had bought 1500 Gold Flake cigarettes and sent them off to Northampton.

As mentioned earlier, when the Cheshires left Stockport in the middle of August they were under strength and a recruitment drive was started. At the beginning of November a hundred of these new recruits, hurriedly trained, left Stockport to join their comrades,

This morning, a contingent of the 6th Cheshires, 100 strong, left Stockport to join the Battalion at Northampton. These men, with 125 others, were recruited after the outbreak of the war for active service and will take the places of those who have not volunteered to go abroad. They include many lacrosse players who were unable to get into the 6th and 7th Manchesters.

Before leaving the Armoury, the men were addressed by the Mayor, Councillor T W Potts, who said the people of the town were proud that such a fine body of men came forward to serve their country. The Mayor presented the men with cigarettes. A very large crowd witnessed the march of the contingent through the street to the station, headed by the bugle band. Lieutenant Underwood was in command.

(*Manchester Evening News*, 2 November 1914)

Men from F Company outside their billets at Northampton. Photo: Stockport Express

Amongst this group was Ernest Battey, a photographer from Glossop. His service file describes him as 5' 7" tall, with a fresh complexion, blue eyes and brown hair. He would be evacuated home in early 1915, suffering from rheumatism, but returned to the front to serve with other battalions of the Cheshire Regiment. Battey was wounded in 1917 and, as a result, discharged from army service. His discharge papers indicate that he was a 'steady, sober, honest, industrious man'.

Joseph Wilson was already at Northampton. He had joined the territorials towards the end of 1913, or early 1914. He now found his father joining him. William Wilson joined up on 8 August and was part of the group travelling from Stockport. The two men came from Tintwistle. As far as is known, the younger man fought with the Regiment throughout the war. His father, however, was wounded by shrapnel on 26 January 1915. It was at first thought to be a comparatively minor wound but he was not able to return to duty and was discharged from the army in May 1916.

With the new arrivals, the Battalion was ready to finalise its arrangements to go on active service. Stockport's Mayor and Colonel Heywood exchanged telegrams, the Mayor writing, *I hear that the 6th Cheshires are*

Battalion signallers in October 1914. Photo; Stockport Express

about to leave for foreign service. Please convey to them congratulations of Stockport people on honour given to our battalion and wish them God-speed and good luck. Heywood replied, *All ranks of the 6th Cheshire Regiment thank you for your congratulations and good wishes. They hope to deserve the honour they have received.*

Before leaving Britain, Heywood prepared a report for his superior officers, which is contained with the Battalion's official war diary:[3]

Notes on mobilization, Organisation, Education, Training, Equipment, etc

Mobilization proceeded smoothly according to the programme. Pay books and identity discs should be kept up to date. The name of a clerk should be registered for use on mobilization and he should be partially trained in military work.

The transport was a weak point. The civilian transport was generally unsuitable. No remedy can be suggested for this except the provision of military transport.

Much might have been done in the time available for training had not the Battalion been frequently been moved from place to place. As it was, the training was thrown back several months.

Had the Battalion been encamped, rather than in billets, it would have been much better in the interests of training and discipline and would have inured the men to service conditions. Much useful elementary knowledge can only be taught in barracks.

The cleaning of rifle and equipment has not hitherto been a sufficiently important part of the training. It should be the duty of every man to keep his own rifle and bayonet clean.

The number of compulsory drills has not been sufficient. Weekend camps should be more frequent and compulsory.

The equipment was very old. It was replaced only five days before leaving England. The men did not know the rifle, the pull off of which was different. The rifles being new required use, practice with dummy cartridges and many minor adjustments before they could be considered thoroughly serviceable.

The first issue of boots was very bad. It appears essential that boots should be kept as an article of mobilization stores, and the turn over arranged for at the annual training.

A far greater percentage of Regular establishment is badly needed to ensure the smooth working of discipline and interior economy. The fact that all ranks are drawn from the same district militates against perfect discipline.

William Lister Read. Joined the Battalion at Northampton, as a second lieutenant. Read was promoted to lieutenant in 1915 and transferred to the 1ˢᵗ Cheshires at the end of that year. Wounded in July 1916, he was posted to 1/5ᵗʰ Welsh on recovery. Killed in action, 10 March 1918, Read is buried in Jerusalem War Cemetery.

Sergeant Robert Morton. Photo: Jon Thornley

The men were mainly young and of only moderate physique. A far stricter medical examination would have been advisable.

The methods under which National Reservists were enrolled appears to be in need of revision.

The unequal treatment (financially) of men who rejoined the colours caused much dissatisfaction.

Captain Claude Gossett was the Battalion's only regular army officer and was posted to the Cheshires as its adjutant – the officer responsible for administrative matters in the unit. For reasons not recorded, he was not going to go overseas with the Battalion and was posted to 19th Signal Company, Royal Engineers, with which he was serving when he died in France of pneumonia on 14 February 1916. His place was taken by Captain John Diggles. Born in 1880, in Bramhall, he still lived there with his sister. Diggles worked as a cloth agent and had been a territorial officer since 1908.

Captain Claude Gossett.

There was a full parade on Saturday, 7 November, in front of Major General John Lindley, the GOC of the Welsh Division. There was a large crowd and many friends and relatives had travelled from Cheshire to say goodbye to their loved ones and wish them good luck. About twenty of the soldiers would not be going overseas immediately. They would remain to help with training new recruits.

The Cheshires paraded again on Monday morning but this was to form up to march to the station. They were loudly cheered by local people lining the route. They carried with them a mascot of a horseshoe, the gift of a local woman, decorated with red, white and blue ribbons and a note: 'Real good luck to the Cheshires.' The train took the Battalion to Southampton, where they boarded the *SS Honorius*. They numbered twenty six officers and 794 other ranks – still considerably understrength despite all efforts.

Second Lieutenant Charles Brockbank had only joined the Battalion in recent days. The twenty year old had been living in West Didsbury and working as an invoice clerk. He applied to become an officer on 14 September and, as with many applications from young middle class men at that time, was commissioned within weeks. He became an officer on 14 October.

We left Northampton today by train for Southampton, after a wonderful scene of activity, organised confusion, when boarding the train. From an onlooker's point of view it would seem impossible to straighten out the seeming confusion but it all comes right in the end. We went on board the troop ship "Honorius" this evening, wondering what would befall us next as we were badly overcrowded & I had to sleep up on the bridge (by permission from the skipper) behind the canvas dodgers. I was bitterly cold. Too cold to be sick.

(Second Lieutenant Charles Brockbank. Diary entry, 9 November 1914[4])

Second Lieutenant Charles Brockbank. Photo: Regimental museum

Brockbank had described the *Honorius* as a troop ship but it was, in fact, a ship fitted out to carry cattle across the Atlantic. It had been requisitioned by the army in the early weeks of the war. Needless to say, the conditions for the men were poor and most decided to stay on the outside decks to avoid the smells. It was, however, a minor discomfort in comparison with the privations the men would endure in the coming months and years.

SS Honorius.

CHAPTER 3

Into Action

Sergeant James Boardman was one of the stretcher bearers. He was another man who kept a diary during the war.[5] Apart from the smells, he noted the ship had a lot of rats. *We played cards, sang and slept (if we could).*

Another soldier wrote to the *Stockport Advertiser*:

Three transports left (censored) together and one had a bodyguard of four cruisers, two destroyers and two submarines. We sailed under a blaze of light, the searchlights from the cruiser sweeping the sea for miles and I shall never forget the sight. We went very slowly in places, having to be on the lookout for mines. The sea was very rough. On arrival, we were not allowed off the boat and expect to sail again for (censored) from which we will have a five mile march to the rest camp.

In fact, they had reached their destination port of Le Havre. The normally short voyage had taken sixteen hours.

We were marched to a Rest Camp on the top of the cliffs, where we arrived in darkness, and found to our horror we were to be in tents. It was my first experience of tents, but I learnt a lot very quickly, as it began to rain & blow a gale. By midnight I felt the water coming into my valise so had to go out and stem the flood. After digging a really good ditch to drain away the water, the tent almost blew down & we spent a very miserable time till breakfast. I hated the sight of a tent.

(Second Lieutenant Charles Brockbank)

The harbour at Le Havre during the war.

The Battalion parades shortly after arrival in France. Photo: Regimental Museum

There was another lengthy and tedious journey on the 13th, to the town of St Omer. Brockbank wrote that it took from 8.30am until midday on the following day. Sergeant Boardman jokingly reckoned he could have walked it in the time. The train stopped at the town of Abbeville and the men were told they could get off for about an hour while the horses were fed and rations issued. However, after thirty minutes, the train started to move off and about 250 of the men, who had been strolling about could not get back on. Many had left their greatcoats on the train. They were stuck there for two hours before they were able to catch another train, arriving at St Omer some ten hours after their comrades.

Everyone was quartered in an old French regular army barracks where most of the windows were broken. William Davies was one of the new recruits and had joined up only on 8 August. He wrote home to Stalybridge, saying the barracks were a good place for sleeping. *We get good food and we are taking no harm.*

St Omer was a very busy town as it was the General Headquarters for the British Expeditionary Force. One of the Cheshires commented[6]

> *What a sight it was when we detrained. There were buses, motor wagons and motor cars rushing hither and thither with supplies. Aeroplanes are quite common. We can hear the heavy guns distinctly here. If we do, as I hope, get in touch with the Germans, you may rely upon it that the Cheshires will not disgrace themselves.*

Field Marshals of the British Army never formally retire from active service, which explains why 82 year old Frederick Roberts, the 1st Earl Roberts, was in France in November 1914. Much of his army service had been in India and Afghanistan and he was awarded the Victoria Cross for

St Omer, a town with a strong historical connection with Britain.

his bravery during the Mutiny there in 1858. He had been appointed the honorary Colonel-in-Chief of the Indian Corps and had insisted on going to France to welcome the Corps' first arrivals on the Western Front. On his tour of the various units he insisted on getting out of his car on what was a bitterly cold day to speak to the troops. He caught pneumonia and died on 14 November. On the 17th a detachment from the Battalion, under the command of Major Rostron, formed part of the procession escorting his coffin. The remainder of the Battalion lined the streets of St Omer whilst the cortege passed.

> *They fired a nineteen gun salute for him and his motor was escorted by English cavalry & French Lancers, while seven of our planes flew overhead. It was a very striking event and one that I am not likely to forget for many years.* (Second Lieutenant Charles Brockbank)

The next day, Brockbank and his men were busy digging trenches.

> *I was terribly cold with just standing about watching the men dig, so took off my coats and took a hand at it. I worked hard for a fair time because I noticed the men did not like to do less than I, and also I had to get warm. It would not surprise me if I find myself too stiff to bend tomorrow when I get up. Whilst we worked, aeroplanes were continually passing above us on their way to the line or else circling round and going back to the drome. I aired my mongrel French on some French soldiers tonight.*

He was not the only one feeling the cold. Writing to his parents at Gee Cross, Tom Mather asked if *you can send me a good big wrap to put around my neck and a pair of gloves. The weather is very wintry and snow is falling, but when you send these, I shall want for nothing else.*

One Stockport man, serving with another unit, went to visit friends in the Cheshires.

> *Every one of them spoke of the good meals they were having. Machonochie rations (enough for two men) but they had one apiece and would have given francs for more. Bacon, posy, bread and cheese. That's not bad. I went up one night to the quarters and took them some Woodbines. You should have seen the scramble. I*

thought Machonochie was grand but the good old potato pie wants some beating. Just fancy – potato pie being served out to the Cheshires. The casualties would never be known in the rush.[7]

During the final days in England, a number of officer promotions had taken place and, as well as Lieutenant Colonel Heywood, the group now comprised:

Majors Herman Hesse and Robert Rostron.
Captains Henry Cooke, John M Diggles,
William D Dodge, Thomas Gibbons, Richard
Kirk, Frederick Leah, Alfred W Smith and
Charles F White.
Lieutenants George E Haworth, James C Hoyle,   *John Diggles.*
William B Innes, James E Johnston, Cyril
Norman, Ronald Norman, Ellis E Spence and Francis White.
Second Lieutenants Stephen A Alexander, Harold B Burgess,
Robert R Cooke, Charles E Brockbank and William L Read.
Honorary Major and Quartermaster John Rawlinson.

The medical officer, attached from the Royal Army Medical Corps, was Lieutenant John Morris. Morris qualified as a doctor in 1904 and initially worked as a house surgeon at Denbigh Infirmary. In 1909 he moved to Hyde to establish a medical practice and became the local police surgeon. He joined the territorials in 1912. He would not return home. Promoted to major and serving with another unit, Morris was killed in action on 7 October 1918.

Quartermaster John Rawlinson had been a regular soldier in his younger days. He left the army in 1905, with the rank of colour sergeant, and had taken up a job with the South Lancashire Regiment. Later, he became quartermaster of the Cheshire's old Volunteer Battalion. It was army tradition that this position would held by someone who had been a sergeant or sergeant major. They would hold officer's rank but the position was an honorary one and Rawlinson would never have been expected to lead troops into battle.

On the 20th the Battalion moved to new billets in the village of Helfaut, about four miles to the south of St Omer. There had been three inches of snow overnight and the roads were all but impassable for the horse drawn transport. The village was on top of a low hill and the only way the wagons could be got up was to hitch more horses to each, together with ropes on which the men also pulled. It took them over seven hours to move the four miles. The next day the transport had to make a round trip to draw rations and it was, again, a problem getting the wagons up the hill. It was a trying time for the transport officer, recently promoted Lieutenant Ellis Spence, in civilian life a chemist working for the family firm, which manufactured colours and other chemicals, with premises at Manchester Road, Stockport.

One soldier wrote to the *Stockport Express*:

We are sleeping in a hayloft which is overrun with rats. We have a lively time in the night chasing them. We have a good dining hall and have to pass through a cow shed and past a pig sty to get to it. So we have rather restrained appetites. We are having the usual cold stew.[8]

On Sunday, 22 November, there was a tobacco issue for the first time since they arrived, was the result of gifts sent from home. One man wrote,

It was indeed a treat. If the generous donors could only have seen us amidst the snow and ice devouring our weeds, they would have felt amply repaid for their generosity.

The same man noted that their languages skills were improving and they could now order drinks correctly and be able to get the right change.

During the time at Northampton, Sergeant Frank Naden was billeted near the vicarage of All Saints Church and had become friendly with the vicar, Canon Jones. He now wrote to Jones:

No doubt you will think I have forgotten you so soon, but such is not the case. We are restricted in the despatch of letters owing to strict censorship. It is Sunday and everything is quite peaceful here, the ground covered with snow. The bells are ringing for church and only for the sound of the guns, fourteen miles away in the firing line, one could imagine oneself in some rural village in England.

We left General [sic] French's HQ last Thursday with all its bustle. It is there that one realises and to such an extent, what war is. Motor buses and wagons by the thousand and, nearly every

moment of the day, five or six aeroplanes are to be seen above reconnoitring. We are forming at present a unit of the reserves for the firing line and, at any moment, we may be drafted there.

The health of everyone is very good and we have all that can be desired under the circumstances, the food being excellent and plenty of it……everyone is satisfied and, when you think of it, the number of men and horses to be fed, it is really astonishing how it is done. The only thing we seem to be short of is news. We know little of what is going on, beyond the big guns booming all day and night, we know nothing.

Kind regards to all.[9]

The following days were spent training in what Charles Brockbank described as 'Art-Form' – artillery formation, in army jargon. It was the way groups of men, even whole companies or battalions, might advance across, say, a No Man's Land between opposing trenches. Effectively, it meant the groups or units would advance in a rough diamond or arrowhead shape, keeping distance one from another, so that casualties from artillery fire might be minimised. A whole company of 250 men might advance in an area 300 yards wide by 200 yards deep. It was easy going for the first day or so but then a thaw set in.

We could only do a little more "Art-Form" today as the fields are soggy beyond all my imagination & it is fearfully hard work marching about on them, when you sink into the ground at every step for about three or four inches the jest gets beyond a joke.
(Second Lieutenant Charles Brockbank.
Diary entry, 25 November 1914)

A couple of days later, Brockbank was thoroughly fed up with having to constantly practise the 'Art-Form' in the rain. He hoped for some variation. It came the next day, Sunday 29 November.

We had to get up at 6.30 this morning and march the eight miles to dig trenches like last week. We got into a filthy state as it poured with rain the whole time, the trenches were a foot deep in water that we had to bail out with shovels, & the ground is all clay. I was very glad when we started for the billet again, but was a good deal more glad when we arrived there.

He was able to have a rest on the Monday with no training to be undertaken.

> *Had an awful time with a man mad drunk with rum. We had to tie his legs, spreadeagle him & put a stick between his teeth to stop him biting us. He was over it by morning but felt much the worse for wear.*

This was probably Private Harry Massey who, on 22 December, faced a court martial for being drunk on active service. He was fined ten days' pay and also sentenced to twenty eight days Field Punishment No. 1. This consisted of him having to undertake hard labour each day and also being tied to a fixed object, such as a fence post or wagon wheel, for two hours on each of the days. It was intended to be a public act of humiliation.

Over the coming days, the Battalion undertook bayonet practice – something they could do in the dry, as bales of straw were hung up in the barns that were being used as billets. Brockbank enjoyed himself: *It feels more satisfactory than pulling a trigger at something hundreds of yards away.*

On 8 December orders arrived instructing the Battalion to start to march towards the front line the next day. They left the village at 8.30am to make their way to Hazebrouck, where they would stay overnight in barns. It was a hard march along roads made of cobbles but Brockbank said what was worse were the motor vehicles passing them, which meant they had to regularly step off the road into the mud. The barns had been previously been used by British soldiers, as Sergeant Boardman noted they were littered with empty jam and bully beef tins.

Before they set off the next morning, they were paraded into a field where they were addressed by General Horace Smith-Dorrien, commanding the British II Corps. He praised the territorials for being so well turned out and ready to get to the front. He then spotted Sergeant Peter Tanner, in the ranks wearing his medal ribbon from the Afghan War. Tanner, then a regular soldier with the Manchester Regiment, had taken part in the march from Kabul to Khandahar and subsequent battle in September 1880. A specific medal had been issued for the march. Smith-Dorrien spoke to him, saying it was a great honour to have such a man in the ranks. According to Brockbank, Tanner was aged 62. His service number, 1820, suggests that he was one of the men who enlisted just after war was declared, on 8 August. He must have been very persuasive to convince the recruiting officer that he should be allowed to join up at that age – the official maximum was 45.

The next overnight billet was at Bailleul. The men had had an increasingly difficult time, as their feet had been wet for much of the past week. Charles Brockbank had the job of following the march to round up stragglers who could not manage to go any further and try to get them moved by lorry. The billets were in a large 'grapery', with greenhouses each three hundred yards long but no grapes were being grown.

> *My word, wasn't it cold! Fancy living in glass houses with no heat in them in the depths of winter.*
> (Sergeant James Boardman, diary entry)

There was a short march the next morning to a position described in the war diary as a crossroads 2.25 miles south west of Neuve Église. They were billeted about a kilometre from the village near an estaminet called 'Aux Deux Nations'. Brockbank wrote that it was near the border and half the Battalion were in France and his half in Belgium and was only a short distance behind the front line. The estaminet still exists, on the Rue de Lille, now called L'Estaminet de Deux Pays. Almost immediately after their arrival, orders were issued for half the Battalion to undertake a brief tour of duty in the front line, under the guidance of the regular army troops from the brigade to which they were now attached. The other half would take their place two days later.

The Estaminet Aux Deux Nations, now renamed and (in 2016) for sale. Photo: author

We tossed up as to who should have the honour of being first in action and B, C, G and H companies won. Colonel Heywood and the adjutants, Captains Clarke and Diggles, went off earlier than the companies to the trenches, so they were really first to be under fire.

(Captain Thomas Gibbons, *Stalybridge Reporter*, 26 December 1914)

The Cheshires going into the trenches were commanded by Major Hesse. B and H Companies would be under the supervision of the 2nd Manchesters, while C and G would be with the 1st Duke of Cornwall's Light Infantry. Both of these battalions were very experienced, having been in action since the Battle of Mons, back in August.

We set off with full packs up to about a mile past Neuve Eglise when we were met by a guide and had to take to the fields. We slipped all over the place when trying to keep up with the leaders as the fields were all under watery mud from 3 inches deep on the level to three feet deep in the ditches. It was an awful job, everyone haunted by the fear of getting lost from the man in front of him, heaving a sigh of relief at every check. It poured with rain the whole time. We arrived at our destination about 11.30 p.m. and then discovered our cooks had got lost, so I was detailed to go back and find them. We were in a ruined farmhouse near the trenches, one company was to be here and one in the line, ours was to be the reserved one. The guide told us there were some dugouts in the field for us so we went to find them. We could not see any until a man went in up to his waist in water & the guide said "There you are, just bale 'em out & you will be O.K". My idea of a dugout was an underground room about 30 feet long, 6 foot deep and about 10 foot wide, these were 6 foot long 4 foot broad & about 2 foot deep, made "safe" with a gate or similar thing with some straw & earth on top. It was a moment of horrified disillusionment. We went up into the "trench" proper later on which was merely a series of "grouse butts" joined together, with a narrow trench behind, filled with water, for when they started shelling. I got my bit of trench baled out first thing.

(Second Lieutenant Charles Brockbank)

The man who had fallen into a hole was Harry Barrow, an eighteen year old from Dukinfield. He commented, *I had to do my turn shivering in wet clothes and a biting wind.*

James Boardman was faring no better in his part of the trench line.

There were very few trenches. The defences were simply sandbags built up into a parapet. Whenever there was any shelling there were some narrow trenches behind to get in, but these were full of water. I shall never forget my first night in the line. Every now and then there would be a burst of rifle fire, and everyone would open out, not knowing what he was firing at. At daybreak I saw my pal, Johnny Bennett, all covered with blood. I asked him what was the matter with him, and he told me he had only been laid in a pool of blood where someone had been killed the previous day. During the day the enemy sent over a few Jack Johnsons and coal boxes. Of course, we had the wind up, as this was our first taste of shell fire, and they were dropping too near to be comfortable.

When daylight came, Brockbank was surprised that they were so close to the Germans, who were only 150 yards away. During the night, the Cheshires had lost their first man, Brockbank noting he had been shot through the head through the parapet. *He was crouched up against the parapet and I thought he was asleep so shook him. There was no mistake about his being dead.* The dead man was nineteen year old Walter Williamson from Gee Cross, near Hyde. He had been a member of the local Boys Brigade and was working as a piecer at Ashton Brothers' cotton mill before mobilization. Williamson had been a territorial since the previous year.

Private Walter Williamson, the first of the Battalion to be killed in action.

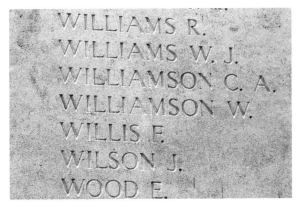

Walter Williamson has no known grave and is commemorated by this inscription on the Menin Gate Memorial to the Missing.

Other men were wounded during this initial exposure to the reality of war. As mentioned in Chapter 1, Walter Murray was hit within hours of arriving at the front line.

It was about 4.30, just about dusk, when I got hit. In taking turns to watch, we had to stand up. They opened a heavy fire on us and one of the bullets caught me in the foot and another went in the side and came out the other. I did not know I was wounded really, as I was bleeding so much and I felt an awful pain in my side. I lay there for five and half hours and they brought me out.

Second Lieutenant Brockbank records Murray's wounding in his diary, noting he was hit while walking about to try and keep warm. Brockbank would have another day in the trenches before he could get back to relative safety.

We were relieved today & had to march back to 'Aux Deux Nations', I was in charge of the Coy, & some job it was too, we were all dead-tired, fighting against sleeping & feeling the reaction of the nervous tension. We had to keep stopping to allow stragglers to catch up, then found half the men were asleep. By the time I arrived home I was all-in and hardly able to realise where I was. When I got into the billet I just slumped onto the floor with my kit still on & went to sleep. They woke me in about ten minutes to have some food, real nice hot soup, but I was so tired I could hardly keep awake to finish it. Felt much better after it and went up into the attic, climbed into my valise & went to sleep. There were five of us in the one room and I woke late in the night, imagined I was still in the trenches, found Cooke was asleep so woke him & told him 'they are asleep down on the left'. He was under the same misapprehension as I was so woke Alexander. In the end all five of us were awake, not realising we were in the billet. I was not popular when someone realised what fools we were, but all had to laugh at the idea of us doing such a thing.

(Second Lieutenant Charles Brockbank.
Diary entry, 13 December 1914)

Brockbank's comrades were Second Lieutenants Robert Cooke and Stephen Alexander. Like Brockbank, they had only recently been commissioned as officers. Nineteen year old Cooke came from the

Stockport area. Alexander was the oldest of the three. Born in Runcorn in 1891, he had been working in London in the flour milling industry before joining the army.

The other half of the Battalion now took over in the front line and would spend seventy two hours there. William Hughes, from Hyde, had a lucky escape:

> *I had been in about seventeen or eighteen hours when a shell struck the dugout. The concussion was terrible. The dugout collapsed and the weight of the earth and the shock from the shell caught me in the back, crushing it. I was dug out after about an hour and remained there through the night until I was taken to hospital.*[10]

Hughes' luck continued to hold throughout the war until he was discharged back to civilian life on 6 March 1919. His final year's army service was with the Labour Corps, probably in Britain.

During this time of accustoming the Battalion to trench warfare, there was a re-organisation designed to bring the unit into line with the regular army in having four, not eight, companies. Each of the Stockport companies would join with one of the others as follows:

A and E Companies became the new A, officered by Captains F Leah and T Gibbons, together with Lieutenants C Norman and G E Haworth

B and H became B, with Captains Kirk and J E Johnston, together with Lieutenants R Norman, S A Alexander and H B Burgess

C and G became C, with Captains W Dodge and H Cooke, together with Lieutenants J C Hoyle and W R Innes and Second Lieutenant C Brockbank

D and F became D, with Captains A W Smith and C F White, together with Lieutenant R R Cooke and Second Lieutenant W L Read

The weather continued to be a problem; Sergeant Albert Lowe wrote home to his wife, Mary, in Stalybridge.

> *We have been ordered to get new boots and to get a size bigger so that we can get a couple of pairs of socks on as protection against*

frostbite for it is bitterly cold here at present and, in the trenches, there is very little room to move. They are narrow as a protection against heavy German artillery.[11]

The position eased a bit when a donation of 800 pairs of khaki woollen gloves arrived as an early Christmas present from the Stockport & District Tobacco Committee. It was one of the several fundraising groups in the area which sent comforts to the troops and, presumably, had decided that gloves, rather than cigarettes, would be more welcome.

It was dangerous enough in the front line but, around this time, two of the men from Hyde tested their luck. They had fallen out over whose turn it was to return a food dixie. In the narrow confines of the trenches, they decided to get out of them and square up to each other. The fight was quickly brought to a halt when the Germans opened fire on them. Both were shot, although both wounds were minor – one being nicked on the forehead, the other on the cheek.

Joseph Bardsley was an experienced territorial from Hyde, having joined up in 1913. But carelessness can affect anyone. On 15 December his platoon was away from the front line and there was a rifle inspection. Foolishly, he pulled his rifle towards him, barrel first, and something caught the trigger. The rifle was cocked and loaded so it went

Sergeant Albert Higgs.

off, the bullet blowing off his trigger finger and passing between three men, fortunately without further injury, before burying itself in a wall. Sergeant Albert Higgs bandaged it up and took him back to the aid station. It was fortunate that there were witnesses to the accident as the army could view self-inflicted injuries such as this as a deliberate attempt to avoid active service.

In his letter home, Higgs recounted that 'first blood to us' was drawn by John Redfern, who *got a sniper, a German crack shot. He bowled him over fine.[12]*

On 17 December, the Battalion was formally attached to 15 Brigade and withdrew to billets in Neuve Église. It would now fight alongside the regular troops of the 1st Cheshires, as well as the 1st Norfolks, 1st Bedfords and 1st Dorsets. They were very much the junior partners. The next day

Colonel Heywood was admitted to hospital, suffering with a problem with his eyesight. He was evacuated back to Britain, where he returned to his home in Hadfield. The *Glossop Chronicle*, 24 December 1914, reported *His eyes were heavily bandaged, the affliction to his eyesight being due to severe strain and the effect of work in the trenches.* Heywood never returned to duty and he was discharged from the army in September 1916. Major Hesse took command of the Battalion.

The men returned to the trenches on the 18th. Over the next few days half of each platoon would be in the front line, the other half remaining in the billets. They would change over at approximately forty eight hour intervals. When in the trenches, the men from A and D companies were attached to 1st Dorsets, B to 1st Bedfords and C to 1st Norfolks.

Aged just seventeen, William Holt was the Battalion's second youngest soldier. The family lived at Muslin Street, Hyde. His older brother, Herbert, had enlisted into the 6th Battalion the previous month and would serve overseas with it after finishing his training. He later transferred to the 11th Battalion, with which he was killed on 2 August 1917.

> *I had the most terrible shock I have had in all my life. I had just got up to fire at a sniper in a farmhouse at the back of the German trench, when my rifle was literally torn out of my hands. A bullet had ripped my rifle in two. It was a miracle I was not killed. About 12 o'clock, I went down for rations in the officers' trench and Captain Cooke looked at me and said 'Holt, do you expect to get back alive? I would not give tuppence for your life now.' He was right, for I was open to enemy fire all the way back.*

Holt's letter home was published in the *Hyde Reporter* on 17 April 1915. By then, he had returned home *having had a physical breakdown.* He recovered and, towards the end of 1917, returned to duty, serving with the Labour Corps and the Army Service Corps.

Wilfred Platt was less lucky than Holt and did not escape the enemy artillery fire. At some point during 18 December he was wounded by shrapnel in the abdomen. The stretcher bearers were called and Privates Harry Bailey and William Cooper went to his aid. Bailey was later invalided home with frostbite and gave an interview to the *Ashton Reporter,* saying they carried Platt out of the *trenches, the German snipers firing all the time. We got him back to the dressing station and then, as we were coming back, Private Cooper nearly lost his life. We were on the road leading to the trenches and I told Cooper to go on, but he stopped and just as he stopped a bullet grazed his eyebrow but fortunately did him no injury.*

Platt, a nineteen year old cotton piecer, from Stalybridge, was evacuated away to a military hospital. However, it was a mortal wound and he died during the early hours of 24 December. Within a few days his mother received a letter from one of the nursing sisters.

> *From the first, there was little hope of recovery, but there was just a chance. The doctors here did all in their power to save him and he was seen by several surgeons but, in spite of all that, God has taken him out of all further trouble. He was assisted by the chaplain several times and told him to tell you not to worry and to give you his love. They are sending you a ring he had on his little finger. I am sorry for you. God alone can comfort you. This terrible war is too awful.*[13]

Private Wilfred Platt. Died of wounds on Christmas Eve.

William Holt and his comrades in 9 and 10 Platoons were relieved by 11 and 12 Platoons on the 20th. Charles Brockbank was commanding one of the incoming platoons. They had been back to the village of Wulverghem to collect rations before setting off for the trenches. They were under artillery fire during this time. Once they were there, Brockbank went to the officers' dugout and lay down *fagged out. I could not sleep owing to the cold and also to the rain coming through the roof.*

Ben Turner was a little way along the front line, with A Company and the men from the Dorsets. He was sitting on a box in the trench, well under cover, when a bullet hit an iron loophole above him and deflected downwards. It went through his cheek and neck, severing the jugular vein. He died almost instantly. The eighteen year old was from Stalybridge and had

Benjamin Turner, killed in action on 20 December.

worked for iron manufacturers, John Summers & Sons Ltd. A committed Christian, Turner had worshipped at the Holy Trinity Mission Hall. Joseph Price, an eighteen year old from Stockport, died from a 'clean' gunshot through the head. He was buried in the churchyard at Wulverghem, the village just behind the front line, but his grave and a number of others, were destroyed by artillery fire later in the war.

Harry Mullins, from Mount Street, Hyde, was the Battalion's youngest soldier. He had just turned 16. Mullins was too young to enlist in the regular army but, as a trained territorial, who had volunteered for overseas service and had that request approved by the commanding officer, it was entirely within regulations, if he was regarded as a drummer or bugler. Writing home around this time, Mullins thanked his parents. *I am very pleased with the way you have made me up a Christmas parcel and I can assure you the contents will not be needlessly wasted. Let all know that I am doing as well as can be expected.*

The British front line was in a difficult position. In front of them, the ground rose towards the small town of Messines (now Mesen). This meant the Germans could easily look down on them and great care was needed, particularly during the daylight hours. One unknown Glossop man wrote to the local newspaper on Christmas Eve.

Private Harry Mullins. Aged 16, he was the Battalion's youngest soldier. He would not return home.

It was an infinitely better trench for it gave much more protection than the others and every six yards or so there was a part roof over to make a sort of dugout. Moreover, there was straw in the bottom which, even if damp, is better than none. The dugout I was in wasn't at all bad, except the roof dripped water all the time. Of course, it was beastly cold – your feet got absolutely frozen. The Germans had a most excellent trench on a hill above us. You could not put your head above the parapet in daylight. Two orderlies came to our trench just about dawn and started back together, one a 6th Cheshire, the other of the Dorsets. Well, the sniper dropped the Dorset in no time with a bullet in the thigh, but the Cheshire chap

December 1914. The German view over the Cheshires' positions from the Messines Ridge. Stinking Farm can be seen on the left and, on the right, the road to Wulverghem. Photo: author

> *stuck to him bravely, although all the Germans potted away at them and he managed to drag the wounded man back to the trench. In front of us is a ruined barn, a stream and then the slope up to the wire entanglements of the Germans, about seventy yards in front. If a man got hit in the daytime, he has to lie in the trench till night because it is quite impossible for anyone to approach to remove him till night.[14]*

The 'Cheshire chap' was Private James Cropper, a nineteen year old hatter from Bredbury. In a letter published by the *Hyde Reporter* on 9 January 1915, he recounted the story.

> *I went with a message to some other trenches and just as I delivered it, another messenger was leaving the trench. Before I had gone far, the Germans opened fire on us and I heard the other messenger shout. I ran back to him but the Germans kept up a heavy fire on us. I must have borne a charmed life for one shot passed through my coat but never harmed me. The bullets were dropping all around and one scarred my finger. The other messenger's thigh was shattered and he could not move. We were about forty yards from the trench and I turned him over and straightened his leg and, between us, we managed to get under cover. The Germans are cowards. They fired at us till I got him in the trench.*

Cropper was recommended for a gallantry award. It is not known if it was for this action or another later act of bravery but, on 11 October 1916, he was awarded the Military Medal. He was also rising through the ranks and, by 1917, was a company sergeant major. He was then selected to train to become an officer, serving as a second lieutenant with another battalion of the Cheshires; he survived the war.

Around this time, Second Lieutenant Brockbank undertook an act of bravery, as recounted by Regimental Sergeant Major Walter Wormington to the *Manchester Evening News*[15].

> *One man sent forward from the front trench on a listening patrol got hit through the pack. The bullet travelled right through his pack and braces and lodged on the buckle of his belt. The shock knocked him into an unused trench and, although it was dangerous to lift a finger, Second Lieutenant Brockbank jumped out of his trench and went forward to assist him. Fortunately, both returned uninjured.*

Charles Brockbank and his men were relieved from the front line on the night of 20/21 December. *They turned a machine gun onto us and sent up flares so that we all had to flop down in the mud. Very exciting and very wet, but nobody was hit.* They returned during the night of 22/23 December, when he records that he was sharing a dugout with officers from the Norfolks. They gave him bacon and sausage and he enjoyed regular drinks of tea and cocoa during the day. *Our trenches had 28 shells in a 50 yard circle. No-one was hit, which seems extraordinary. Plenty of close shaves.*

Christmas Eve was relatively quiet for most of the day, although John Carruthers and Henry Roberts were both killed during the morning. Tom Wadsworth, a wheelwright from Tintwistle, was fortunate to escape injury and wrote home to tell what had happened:[16]

Private John Carruthers, from Stockport. He is remembered on the town's war memorial.

> *We were together in a dug-out. Henry, E Harrop, H Mitchell and myself, when shells started coming. Several dropped round the trench and, when one dropped in front, shrapnel flew, hit Henry and a man named Carruthers and killed them straight out. Then it threw*

earth on them and buried them, Ellis and a corporal got wounded but we managed not to get hit. We had to let them stay there until dusk and then we had to bury them at night. We were with the 1ˢᵗ Cheshires. Tom Boucher was with us and he helped us to bury him. We made as nice a grave as we could under the circumstances and we were shot at several times whilst digging the grave. The awful event happened about 10 o'clock in the morning. I must say, it fairly knocked the heart out of us, seeing a dear pal killed and then having to bury him.

Over the course of the war, the location of the two burials was lost, or the graves were destroyed by subsequent artillery fire. The two men are now commemorated on the Menin Gate Memorial to the Missing at Ypres.

William Seed was serving with A Company, attached to the Dorsets. He had been a member of the Stalybridge Territorials since 1912 and worked as a piecer at Alger Mill in Ashton under Lyne. As dusk fell, he and three of his comrades were sent out to a listening post hidden in No Man's Land about a hundred yards from the trench. Needless to say, they had to keep very quiet and avoid making any noise by moving about. There was deep water and mud in the shell hole that formed the post.

I was practically three hours in one place. It was freezing very hard and, when I came to get my boot out, I found it frozen into the ground. In struggling to get free, I must have fractured my ligament, but I did not feel it so very bad, with my foot being numbed with the frost. [17]

Private William Seed.

Seed reported sick on Christmas Day and, after treatment in France, was evacuated back to Britain on 1 January. He had suffered significant and, presumably, permanent damage, as he was discharged from the army at the end of January. It was, however, late in the day when Seed reported to the medical officer. Before that, he was going to be part of one of the most extraordinary events of the whole war and one which is still talked about today, most recently during the centenary commemorations in 2014.

> *I spent the most agonising night, I ever remember, owing to the cold. It was freezing terribly hard & as we were in support trenches were not allowed fires. I was so cold & my feet so painful that I got out of the dugout & walked about, there was not much danger, stamping my feet till 4.30 A.M. then was so fagged out I fell asleep but kept on waking owing to the pain of my feet, I quite thought I was frost-bitten. 7.0 A.M. it was beginning to grow light but as there was a lot of mist I told the men they could light fires. They did not need telling twice.*
>
> (Second Lieutenant Charles Brockbank. Diary entry, 25 December 1914)

George Blease was another trained soldier but one ordinarily underage for overseas service. He was serving alongside his older brother, Leonard. Both lived at the family home at Chatham Street, Stockport.

> *It was very foggy, so we were able to have a short run on top of the trenches to get warm. Eventually, the fog lifted and our men, as well as the Germans, were exposed to fire. None took place.*[18]

There was a deserted farmhouse a little way behind the front line. It was known to the Tommies as 'Stinking Farm', because of the number of animal corpses killed by shellfire that were lying around. There was still livestock from the farm wandering around the whole front line area. Brockbank and two of his men went back to the farm to see if they could catch some chickens.

> *They fly like pheasants so took some catching & in about ten minutes there were about 60 men in the hunt. The fog lasted till about mid-day so we had good fun, getting in all eleven hens, one of which I brought back for tomorrow's dinner. Now for the extraordinary incident.....*

The incident was being repeated up and down the sector. Troops were calling out to the men on the other side of No Man's Land, wishing them Happy Christmas. Little Christmas trees were appearing on the tops of German trenches. The sound of hymns being sung could be heard in

English and German. Soon after daybreak, someone in the British lines played 'Christians Awake' on a mouth organ. The Germans responded with 'Come Over Here' – a popular song of the times.

The British continued to fire at the German trenches but there was no reply. At about 2.30pm, Brockbank recounts that the Germans started to shout 'Come out and have a drink'. Shortly after, one of them got out of the trench, without any weapon and started to walk slowly towards the British trench. The official report on the day, from the Cheshires' brigade commander, Brigadier General Edward Gleichen, said that the man, an officer or NCO, was holding up a box of cigars. The Cheshires and Norfolks shouted at him to stop but he kept walking. So, one of the British soldiers got out and started walking to meet him in the middle of No Man's Land. It was the start in this sector of what has become known as the 'Christmas Truce'. The two men met and shook hands and that seems to have been the signal for most of the troops in the sector to leave their trenches and come into No Man's Land. Soon, several hundred men were shaking hands and swapping souvenirs. There were more Germans than had been thought holding their trench. The Cheshires' machine gunners were ordered to remain at their posts 'just in case'. Brockbank recorded that he

> *got a cap-badge, belt buckle, whistle, rifle cartridge purse & tea tablets, not to mention getting about four Germans' names and addresses in their own handwriting on field service postcards, as a positive proof that it all really did happen, because it will naturally sound a very tall story when it gets told in the billets.*

Sergeant Thomas Knott found the Germans ...

> *thinly clad in a grey uniform with the number 35 on their collars, which I took to be 35th Regiment Landsturm. They were all elderly men, between 45 and 55 years of age. They were all friendly disposed and they all seemed to wish urgently for peace. Cigarettes were exchanged for cigars and the Germans handed cough drops all round. Both sides parted with much hand shaking after about an hour's conversation.[19]*

William Seed had still not been to the medical officer and, like his comrades, was out in No Man's Land. One of the German soldiers saw him limping and asked if he had been hit. When he told him what had happened, the German gave him a cigar and a cigarette, both of which he took back to Britain as souvenirs.

As reported by the *Cheshire Observer*, 9 January 1915, John Higham said he was a bit timid but ...

I shook hands with about sixteen Germans. They gave us cigars and cigarettes and toffee. They told us they didn't want to fight, but they had to. Some could speak English as well as we could and some had worked in Manchester. All the Cheshires and Germans were now together by this time and we sang 'Tipperary' for them and they sang a song in German for us.

There was nobody better than the Cheshires to be singing 'It's a Long Way to Tipperary'. It was a very popular song in 1914 and the men would have been proud that it had been written in Stalybridge on 30 January 1912 and first performed the next day at the town's Grand Theatre.

Frank Naden, now a company sergeant major, was also in No Man's Land. Shortly after New Year he returned to Britain on leave and gave an interview to the *Evening Mail*, the local newspaper in Newcastle under Lyme.

We fraternised, exchanging food, cigarettes and souvenirs. The Germans gave us some of their sausages, and we gave them some of our stuff. The Scotsmen started the bagpipes and we had a rare old jollification. The Germans expressed themselves as being tired of the war and wished it was over. They greatly admired our equipment and wanted to exchange jack knives and other articles.

The Scotsmen mentioned by Naden were possibly the 2nd Seaforth Highlanders who, at only two kilometres away, were the nearest Scottish unit to him.

The Battalion's later report to Brigade noted that the Germans were aged between forty to fifty and were big and healthy men, well fed, well clad and clean. An officer said that they were from the 5th Konigslieber Landwehr Infantry Regiment, from Berlin. Several of the men had the number 20 on their shoulders, while others had 35, confirming what Thomas Knott had said. The Landwehr were second line militia troops, comprising older, less fit men than the main German army.

Men from Charles Brockbank's unofficial foraging party had caught a pig as well as the chickens. That was cooked in No Man's Land and shared out with the Germans. There was also an opportunity to bury a number of French soldiers who had been lying dead for some considerable time. Before returning to their own trenches, the men sang hymns in their own languages. The Germans said they were not intending to fire for the following three days and expected the war to be over within two months (although there is no record of them saying who they expected would have won it).

My word! The Germans can't half sing songs…. When the time of parting came, we shook hands and saluted each other, each party going back to the trenches. (Private George Blease)

Of course, it was only half of the Battalion who were in the front line who were able to participate in the truce. Sergeant James Boardman wrote

I spent my Christmas Day in the Priest's House at Wulverghem. We had a young pig between eight of us, and also plum pudding and plenty of rum.

One of the enduring stories of the Christmas Truce is of a football match being played in No Man's Land between teams of Britons and Germans. The story often has the Germans winning 3 – 2. And yet there is no hard evidence that any such game took place. Although battalion war diaries often refer to the truce, some describing the day in detail, none mention football. Although there are numbers of letters written home mentioning a football match being played, these are all hearsay – no one writes saying they played in a match or even watched a match, but they had heard of one being played. There are accounts of matches between the two sides being discussed, perhaps to take place on Boxing Day or New Year's Day, if another truce could be arranged – but none of these actually took place. There is, of course, evidence of football being played behind the lines by British troops, but only amongst the British. It is probable that a combination of these aspects led to the creation of the myth about a match being played. If so, it is a myth that has struck a chord in the public imagination.

What of something less formal than a match as we might understand it, with a marked out pitch and goals at each end, a referee and eleven a side?

Here there is contemporary evidence and corroboration that there was a kickabout involving the Cheshires. Second Lieutenant Charles Brockbank wrote of it in his diary on Christmas Day. *Someone produced a rubber ball so, of course, a football match started.* And this was not just amongst the Cheshires, Frank Naden confirming in his account in the *Cheshire Observer* in January 1915 that the Germans joined in.

Late in his life, Ernie Williams recounted his experiences of the day in a television interview. He had been a territorial since 1911.

> *The ball appeared from somewhere. I don't know where, but it came from their side – it wasn't from our side that the ball came. They made up some goals and one fellow went in goal and then it was just a general kickabout. I should think there were about a couple of hundred taking part. I had a go at the ball. I was pretty good then, at nineteen. Everybody seemed to be enjoying themselves. There was no sort of ill-will between us. There was no referee and no score, no tally at all. It was simply a melée – nothing like the soccer you see on television.*

Frank Naden recalled that, on Boxing Day, orders came *that all communication and friendly intercourse with the enemy must cease, but we did not fire at all that day and the Germans did not fire at us.* Naden's memory is slightly awry. The two opposing infantry units may not have fired but the German artillery was active and, during the day, Frank Croft was badly injured in the stomach and thigh. Croft, aged 19, was a machine fitter from Stalybridge. He was evacuated to a hospital on the Channel coast, where he died on 7 January.

Most of the men who had been in the front line over Christmas were relieved and moved back to billets where they had a quiet couple of days as, seemingly, did the men who replaced them. However, when the troops paraded prior to setting off for the trenches and were just about to march off, the village was shelled by the Germans. No-one was killed but three men were wounded, one badly. Frank Croft, from Stalybridge, was taken to the dressing station, only 200 yards away, where he received immediate attention. The nineteen year old died at the base hospital in Boulogne on 7 January.

On the 28th the whole Battalion was relieved from the front line area and marched back the seven miles to rest billets at Bailleul. It had been a very trying time. Over 120 men had been admitted to hospital in their time in the trenches. The days of standing in icy mud had taken a terrible toll and most of those men suffered from frostbite or rheumatism. Many others were suffering from 'trench foot' – a painful complaint caused by poor blood supply. It caused loss of feeling in the feet, swelling and open sores and, in extreme cases, could lead to gangrene, necessitating amputation. There was no effective treatment, except keeping the feet dry and exercising to try to stimulate the blood flow. In civilian life Allen Whitehead was a cotton spinner from Stalybridge. He had been in the territorials since 1908 and at the end of the month he was back home. He had been transferred from a hospital in France. *My feet were lead. I couldn't feel them but they would be alright when I got out of the trench. When I did get out, I could hardly walk. They began to swell and we were told to go to the hospital a mile or so in the rear.* The thirty three year old recovered in due course and returned to duty, serving with the Royal Welsh Fusiliers and the Suffolk Regiment before the war ended.[20]

Whilst the men had been in the trenches, the medical officer had started to inoculate them against enteric fever (typhoid). He completed the remainder at the rest billets. Charles Brockbank got his inoculation on the 30th which left him feeling groggy for much of the day. He was still feeling '*very cheap*' on New Year's Eve, with a bad head and painful arm. He did not recall in his diary how he viewed the passing of 1914.

CHAPTER 4

Back Home

By early January 1915 there was a steady stream of men from the Cheshires returning to Britain for medical treatment. Some of them had been wounded but more were returning with medical complaints directly related to the poor conditions in which they had been serving – frostbite, rheumatism, trench foot, etc. Even at this relatively early stage of the war, medical facilities in Belgium and France were well developed. A man would report sick to his unit's medical officer, such as the Cheshires' Lieutenant Morris. He would undertake a cursory examination to make a preliminary diagnosis, dealing with it if it was minor. Alternatively, he would send the man to the Field Ambulance. This was not a vehicle but a medical unit situated a mile or so behind the front line, staffed by doctors, stretcher bearers, etc. Whilst the Field Ambulance could undertake some emergency treatment of a wounded man, its main role was to stabilise his condition sufficiently for him to be evacuated to a casualty clearing station (CCS), perhaps twenty miles to the rear, in relative safety. The CCS were

A typical tented casualty clearing station, located several miles behind the front line.

large tented field hospitals with reasonably sophisticated surgical facilities. If a casualty survived long enough to reach a CCS, then he was unlikely to lose his life because of the injury.

From there he would probably be further evacuated to one of the base hospitals that had been established on the Channel coast, around Boulogne and Calais. John Morrow, a cotton mill worker from Hawk Green, Marple, reported to the medical officer in early January.

> *When I was taken in the base hospital, the doctor stroked a lighted cigarette along the sole of my foot and I never felt it. It began in my big toe which swelled up tremendous. Then it went down my feet into my legs. My legs swelled and my feet got so big I couldn't put my boots on. The doctor said there was a danger of gangrene setting in.[21]*

Morrow returned to Britain on 1 February to convalesce at Hawk Green. He probably just had time to say goodbye to his older brother, Alfred, who had joined the Cheshires at the end of September and was just about to go overseas to join them. Both men would survive the war, but both would be discharged early due to wounds. John Morrow returned to duty in the late summer of 1916, when he was transferred to the 1st Cheshires. Three weeks later he was badly wounded in the left knee. It was necessary to amputate his leg. Alfred was also wounded in 1916 and, in 1917, was hospitalised for seven months when he was accidently hit on the knee with a spade when trench digging.

From a hospital in France, a man could be further evacuated to Britain. Further surgery might be needed on a wounded man but for the Cheshires with frostbite it was a slow process of recovery. There would be no guarantee that a man would be hospitalised in or near his home area, although it seems some efforts were made. By early 1915 there was a rapidly expanding network of military hospitals. Within days of war being declared, the Army's 2nd Western General Hospital was established at the High School on Whitworth

John Cousil worked at Summers Ironworks in Stalybridge before joining the Battalion in September 1914. Wounded in 1917, he was posted on recovery to 7th Cheshires, then fighting in Palestine. On his way there, his troopship was sunk but he was rescued and continued his journey. He was killed in action on 14 December 1917 and is buried at Jerusalem.

Street in Manchester's city centre. It was ideally located to receive casualties arriving by train. As the need for military hospitals grew, they were established in wards of existing hospitals and, often, schools were converted. Naturally, this created problems for the children's education. A school might be amalgamated with another that was not being used as a hospital. The children would then be taught only on a part-time basis – one school having use of the premises in the morning, the other in the afternoon. It was not long before 2nd Western General Hospital was overseeing the work of over twenty smaller facilities spread round what is now Greater Manchester. At its peak, the total number of beds being overseen from Whitworth Street was in excess of 16,000, including a specialist neurological unit at Brinnington, treating soldiers with shellshock.

Harold Platt, who had joined the Territorials in 1912, wrote home in early January, from hospital in Whitstable. He was another evacuated because of frostbite. The condition of his feet was improving but he was still in a bad way. *The pain is terrible and I've not slept since Christmas. They give us all kinds of drugs at night to make us sleep but it's no use.*[22] It is not known if Platt ever returned to duties with the Battalion but, by the middle of 1917, he was in a non-combat role with the Labour Corps. His records do not indicate if this was at home or overseas.

When Platt and Morrow had gone overseas in November, they had left a number of comrades behind. They numbered about a hundred and were the men who, for whatever reason, had not volunteered for overseas service. In addition, there were men who had been recruited between August and November who had not been sufficiently trained to go on active service. They would form a new reserve unit that would undertake the territorials' original role in home defence, as well as acting as a training unit that would send men overseas to join the Cheshires. It would be known as the Second Sixth. Arrangements were formalised and the new 2/6th Cheshires were established on 7 September 1914, with Captain William Dodge initially in command. Dodge was needed with the 6th Battalion and a permanent commander of the new battalion was soon in post. Major George Leah was a prewar territorial officer who reached his rank in 1910 and had been second in command of the 6th Battalion. He was the older brother of Frederick Leah, who was a company commander with the Cheshires. In civilian life George Leah

Major George Leah.

was in business as a wine and spirits merchant in Stockport. He would prove to be a less than successful commanding officer. Leah was still in command in 1917 but his superior officer, Brigadier General Sloman wrote a report in which he commented that he was *not fit for his present appointment as his disciplinary methods are not adequate.* Promoted to lieutenant colonel to command the 2/6th Cheshires, within weeks of Sloman's report he found himself reduced to his substantive rank of major and posted overseas to a now unknown battalion of the Regiment.

The second in command of the new battalion was Captain, later Major, Fred Rivett, another long serving officer with the prewar Battalion and another officer who would not impress his superiors. In 1915 he was promoted to lieutenant colonel and given command of 46th Provisional Battalion, a home service coastal defence unit. In July 1916, General Hamilton, commanding the Northern District in the UK, inspected the 46th Battalion, reporting on Rivett that *This officer did not make a good impression on me when I inspected the battalion and I consider that if a suitable man can be found a change would be in the interests of the service.* It would appear that a change was quickly made and Rivett reverted to his substantive rank of captain; but it is not known to what post he was sent. At some point after this

Captain Fred Rivett.

he was on sick leave and, in 1917, was serving with the King's Shropshire Light Infantry. He was under consideration for a promotion to major but his commanding officer, Colonel Appleyard, could not recommend it.

> *I do not consider he is sufficiently energetic and zealous in his duties.....although he is able to take walks for two or three miles for his own recreation, he stated he was physically unable to walk two or three miles to visit guards when requested to do so by the Adjutant.*

At this early stage of the war there were competing arrangements for new recruits. The Cheshire Territorials were recruiting, as were the 6th Manchesters, their neighbours north of the Mersey, who mainly recruited amongst the city centre's middle class employees. The Cheshire Regiment

New recruits parade at Stalybridge drill hall. Photo: Tameside MBC

was also directly recruiting for newly established "service battalions" – ones formed for the duration of the war only. Some 250 had been recruited in Stockport for the latter and, on 7 September, they paraded, ready to catch the train to Chester, only to be told that they were not immediately needed and that they should return to home and work, although they would receive army reserve pay and be sent for in due course. Another group had been drilling at Stockport's cricket ground. Most of them were members of local lacrosse clubs or the friends of players. They had been hoping to join the 6th Manchesters as a complete group as they had many colleagues or friends already serving with them. The Manchesters did take most of them at the end of August but a number of the remainder now joined the 6th Cheshires. Recruitment for the 2/6th Cheshires was slow but steady. By the end of October, about eighty five men from Stalybridge wanted to enlist. Some were rejected as being too young, others because they were not medically fit but around fifty had joined up.

The men trained in Stockport on land belonging to Woodbank Hall (now, fittingly, Woodbank Memorial Park, having been purchased by Thomas Rowbotham and gifted to the Council in 1921, *in honoured memory of the men of Stockport who fought and died for their country*). There was also training at the cricket ground at Cale Green and at Happy Valley, in Bramhall. The *Stockport Advertiser* commented: *A few weeks military training has transformed them into a smart, upstanding body of young soldiers, the pride of their friends and the envy of those who have not yet mustered or come forward.[23]*

As mentioned in Chapter 2, the early recruits went to Northampton at the beginning of November to join the main Battalion. This party was under the command of Captain Edgar Dowson. He was a prewar lieutenant with the Glossop company and had only been promoted to captain on 11 August. Born in 1869, Dowson was older than many of the officers and, in civilian life, a manager of a calico printworks. The remainder of the reserve Battalion moved to Northampton at the end of the month to take over from the 6th Battalion which had gone to France.

> *Though it was nearly midnight when the Reserve Territorials from this town entrained on Saturday, the people of Stalybridge lined the streets and besieged the station. The men did not march to the station as their predecessors of the original Sixth did when they went away. They came direct from their own home and each was given a hearty cheer and a handshake by his companions and acquaintances.*
>
> (*Stalybridge Reporter*, 28 November 1914)

When they got to Stockport, they lined up, about eighty of them, and were issued with blankets so they could try to sleep for a while. At 4am the bugle sounded for them to 'fall in' and they were given coffee and sandwiches.

It did not take too long to get to Northampton, as described by Robert Davies to the *Stalybridge Reporter*.

> *We landed at Northampton in the early morning and, when we got out into the street where we live, we saw hundreds of girls dressed up to the mark, as if they were going to church. But they were going to work. Well, they called it work. But it is play, in a sense. It is all boot making and book binding.*

Davies had arrived in a town, very different from the smoky industrial town that he called home.

As the 2/6th left Cheshire, recruitment started for another reserve battalion – the 3/6th. The intention was that the 2/6th Battalion would soon be deployed on to home defence duties, whilst the 3/6th Battalion trained new recruits for overseas service. In practice, the lines between the two appear to have become blurred over the coming months. A number of men enlisted on the first day and it was noted with interest that two of the companies would be reserved for 'pals'. Territorial units had always recruited in defined communities, so men who worked or socialised together or were neighbours would be serving together. However, although there had been a rush to join the army in the early days of the war, recruitment had started to taper off by late August 1914. It seemed to be the middle classes who were holding back and it became clear this was probably related to the strict divisions in Edwardian society where people from different social classes would not generally mix. The solution was to create new battalions for the duration of the war, which permitted men who joined together, to serve together. They quickly became known as 'pals' battalions and were an instant success. It is interesting that a concept well established in the territorials appears to have come back to them as a "new idea". With the 'pals' now in the public imagination, it aided recruitment, the Regimental History noting that the Burbage Silver Prize Band from Buxton joined as a group, even though they were from outside the Battalion's usual recruiting area. Until numbers had risen, men would start their initial army training in their own districts, no doubt using the drill halls at Glossop, Hyde and Stalybridge, as well as Stockport's Armoury.

Command of the new Battalion was given to Captain, later Lieutenant Colonel, Herbert Stott. He was another prewar officer with the Cheshires and, in private life, was a director of the family firm of cotton spinners and lived in Cheadle. In 1917 he was in command of the 14th Bn South Lancashire Regiment, another home service battalion. All of his active service during the war was in Britain, although he did make a very brief visit to France at some point during the war, although not to engage in combat. This quick trip was sufficient for him to qualify for the award of the British War Medal and the Victory Medal, the same medals

Lieutenant Colonel Herbert Stott.
Photo: Regimental museum

that would be issued to soldiers serving in the trenches for the whole period of the war. Whilst these medals were sent to other ranks after the war, officers were required to apply for them if they wished to have them. Stott made sure he applied.

The Stalybridge men of the 2/6th Battalion were soon settled into their new life at Northampton.

> We parade at 7.15 for Swedish drill, breakfast at 8, second parade 9.15, dinner 1 o'clock, third parade at 2.15, then we finish work for the day at 4 o'clock unless we have a night attack. We have got good billets and good food. All the Stalybridge boys are billeted at Victoria Park, Victoria Promenade. It is quite amusing to see us taking out tea in a bath and cheese, bacon, etc in a hand cart.[24]

They were regularly joined by newly recruited men. When war was declared, eighteen year old Sam Chandley, from Gatley, was working as a shop assistant selling stationery. On 2 September 1914 he went into Manchester to try to enlist in the Manchester Pals but was rejected for medical reasons. Presumably recovered, he tried again to join up on 29 December, this time at the Cheshires' recruiting office at the Armoury in Stockport. He was accepted and within a few weeks was posted to Northampton, where he was attached to the Battalion signalling section, then under the command of Second Lieutenant James Goodall. Goodall was also from north Cheshire and was five years older than Chandley. He trained in alkali manufacture at Manchester's Municipal School of Technology (later UMIST) and, when war broke out, joined the 7th Manchesters as a private but was commissioned shortly after.

Chandley's stay at Northampton was brief and he was soon posted to 3/6th Cheshires, then at Oswestry. He became an officer's servant (the term 'batman' did not come into general use until after the Great War). His officer was newly commissioned Geoffrey Cheshire. Born in Nantwich in 1886, Cheshire was commissioned on 8 January and promoted to lieutenant in March. In between those dates, he married Burella Barstow

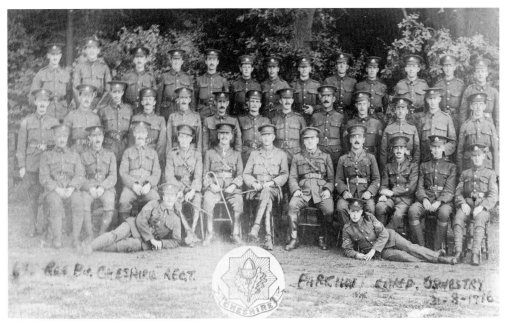

Men of the 3/6th Battalion at Oswestry in 1916. Photo: Regimental museum

in London. In 1917 the couple had a son who they named Geoffrey Leonard. He would serve during the Second World War, being awarded a Victoria Cross and, later, founded the Leonard Cheshire Foundation which provided homes for disabled ex-servicemen.

From around this time Chandley wrote an account of his service, which is held by the Imperial War Museum.

I got out of plenty of dirty work. Food was not all one could expect and weather neither. For the first six weeks, we had one continual downpour of rain and August Bank Holiday was an absolute treat, it rained all the Sunday, Monday and Monday night. Our things were in a shocking state and the camp ground was up to the ankles in mud. We stayed under canvas, the very last of the Division under canvas, till the first week of November, when we moved to hutments across the road, which were nothing like ready for us when we went in. The name of our new camp was Park Hall Camp. Hut life was much more comfy than tent life – you felt as if you had room to move about. In one hut, thirty men were supposed to live and, being signallers, we were again favoured and were kept together in one hut and had only twenty two men. Christmas Day we spent there

*and, thanks to our quartermaster, we had a jolly good time – turkey,
roast potatoes, oranges, apples and mince pies.*

Meanwhile the 2/6th Battalion had moved from Northampton to Cambridge
on 23 December 1914, where the men were billeted in private houses and
in boat houses along the River Cam. Many of the local families invited
soldiers to join them for Christmas dinner. Those in the boat houses were
reported to have made the best of things but it was still a 'rough & ready'
Christmas.

Back in Cheshire, recruitment was still slow. By early January 1915
the 3/6th Battalion was only a little over half strength, although fifty were
enlisted on 8 January for both the territorials and the Cheshire service
battalions. Stockport's mayor had organised a "smoking concert" at the
Armoury, every man in uniform who attended expected to bring a potential
new recruit with him.

At the end of the month nearly 250 men from the 2/6th Battalion went
overseas to join the first line unit (now officially known as the 1/6th
Battalion). They were badly needed to replace the soldiers who had
reported sick or been wounded. However, their departure caused some
discontent in North Cheshire as they had not been granted leave before
going overseas. Stockport's mayor had written to Major General Lindsay
and received the following reply:

*I can assure you that the authorities are fully cognisant of all the
facts mentioned in your letter. I have myself represented them more
than once but it is evident that, in their opinion, the military
exigencies of the moment require the presence with their regiments
of all men capable of bearing arms. I desire to add that I cordially
sympathise with the men in their desire to visit their friends and
relatives and I promise you that, as soon as the present rules
regarding leave are relaxed, I will do my utmost to gratify the
wishes of all the men under my command.*

*Their conduct since mobilisation has been exemplary and it will
be a pleasure for me to be able to grant them an indulgence they
have thoroughly earned and deserved.*[25]

To replace these men, two large groups left the 3/6th battalion on the 6th
and 8th of February. Before leaving Stockport they were addressed by the
mayor, who said that he, and the mayors of the other towns, took pride in
their conduct and that the 6th Cheshires had been amongst the first

New recruits from Glossop just before they left the town to join the 2/6th Battalion at Cambridge. Photo: Glossop Chronicle

territorials to go to the front. He added that he thought eligible men who had not yet joined the forces should feel very ashamed of themselves and he would not envy their position after the war. The Stockport Comforts Committee had continued its fundraising and was able to present each man in the draft with a pair of socks, handkerchief and a packet of cigarettes. As with earlier 'send offs', there was a large crowd lining the streets as they marched to the station.

There was another recruiting drive in early March 1915. The 3/6th Battalion was moving to Aberystwyth but, before doing so, held a rally in Stockport. The Stockport men met up with those from Glossop at Tiviot

Stockport's market place.

Dale Station and, led by the bugle and brass band, marched along Prince's Street to Mersey Square, where a speech was made to the crowd. Three hundred men were still needed and men aged between nineteen and thirty eight were urged to join up. Two new companies were being formed under the command of Lieutenant George Mackenzie of Marple and Lieutenant Frederick Sutcliffe of Hyde. Men could select which company they wished to join so that they could be with friends. Born in 1892, Mackenzie was a tall man for those days, standing at just under 6 feet. He had attended Manchester Grammar School and worked as a cotton buyer. His service with the Cheshires was relatively brief, joining the Brigade Machine Gun School in October 1915. The following year he transferred to the newly formed Tank Corps, with which he was awarded the Military Cross for an act of bravery in 1918. Sutcliffe is believed to have practised as an architect in Colwyn Bay before the war and was commissioned as an officer in January 1915. His service with the Cheshires was also brief; he was transferred to the Divisional Cyclist Company in May 1915 and then to the Army Cyclist Corps. All of his wartime service was at home. In February 1916 he fell off his bike and was badly concussed. It took some considerable while for him to recover fully. An army medical board held in November 1917 found only that his condition had improved and that he was sleeping better with fewer headaches.

Regimental Sergeant Major James Rowen had been a regular soldier with twenty two years' experience. When he left the army in about 1910 as a sergeant, he got a job with the 6th Cheshires as drill instructor to the Stalybridge Company, later transferring to Stockport in about 1913. He was due to retire but, when war was declared, rejoined the army and was promoted to be the senior non-commissioned officer with the 2/6th Battalion. He was with the Battalion at Cambridge when he was taken ill at his billet on Aylestone Road on 4 March, dying shortly afterwards of a cerebral haemorrhage at Cambridge Hospital. Reporting his death, the *Stockport Advertiser* wrote that he had been *a strict disciplinarian, a fine soldier and was a tower of strength in the Battalion.* He was given a military funeral and is buried in Cambridge. He left a wife and two children in Stockport.

Regimental Sergeant Major James Rowen, died at Cambridge.

A group of men from Hadfield, holders of the 'Profumo Cup', awarded at annual camp. Standing – Private John Burns (killed in action, July 1917) and Private E Fearnley. Seated – Sergeant Clifford Booth, Corporal Joseph Barber and Private John Pogson.

The senior NCOs of the 3/6th Battalion at Aberystwyth in spring 1915. Company Quartermaster Sergeant Harold Chadwick noted 'eleven of them are teetotallers and the others "moderates". That is saying a lot for "sergeants of the line".' Photo: Stockport Express

The work of recruiting new soldiers continued. In the middle of the month, 150 men left Stockport to join the 3/6th Battalion at Aberystwyth. It still left them some 200 short of a full establishment. The job of overseeing recruitment in the wider Stockport area was given to Captain Samuel Hill-Wood (see Chapter 1), who until then had only been responsible for the Glossop area. He was already a busy man, with responsibilities as a Member of Parliament and to his family firm. There was a military funeral at Aberystwyth in early April. Eighteen year old Isaac Deaville had joined up at the end of January but died of pneumonia on 9 April. It was reported that his mother, Ruth, attended the funeral. The army would pay for funerals near to where he died but the family would have had to pay the full costs of a funeral in Stockport.

The work of the various comforts committees continued to be appreciated by the men overseas. Frederick Leah, now promoted to major, had been exchanging letters with the wife of Stalybridge's Conservative Member of Parliament, John Wood. Gertrude Wood was active in the Women's Unionist Association, which had offered to send shirts and socks to the men. Leah wrote, thanking the Association and asking if it could consider sending towels and handkerchiefs as well. There had also been fund raising in Hyde, under the supervision of the mayor, Councillor Stanley Welch, which had enabled a case of assorted comforts to be sent overseas. He had received several letters of thanks:

> *It was a great treat to receive the presents as, at that time, I was without cigarettes of any kind. All the Hyde lads are in the best of condition. We are having a jolly time of it now, but we shall have a lot better when all is over.*[26]

Another request coming from the men overseas was for footballs. It was a popular sport amongst the Cheshires and, during the early months of 1915, it was regularly played as a way of improving blood circulation and general fitness amongst the men not suffering from frostbite.

Meanwhile for the 2/6th Battalion, at Cambridge, training continued. Sport formed an important part of maintaining the men's fitness and, towards the end of March, many of the Cheshires took part in what the *Cambridge Independent Press* described as the largest ever cross country race held in the town. There were thirty two teams, drawn from all the units of the Welsh Division. The 230 runners would race over a three and a half mile course from the rifle range, over Madingley Hill and back to

The 3/6th Battalion at St Mary's Court, Shropshire.

Grange Road in the city centre. The winner was a Private Whitechurch, of the 1st Monmouths, who ran the course in 32 minutes and 4 seconds. Coming in fourth, with a time of 32 minutes and 39 seconds, was Private W Ingleson of the 2/6th Cheshires. The Monmouths also took the team prize, just beating the Cheshires.

The 2/6th Battalion returned to Northampton on 22 April. A few days later the Cheshires were drilling on Cow Meadow when they heard shouts from the direction of the River Nene. Privates Hague, Noble and Smith dashed over, where they saw a man in the river, clearly in difficulty. Noble found a ladder and held it out for the man to grab, but he lost his hold. He and Smith then went into the river up to their waists and were able to drag the man out. They gave him artificial respiration and the man, Benjamin James, was then taken to hospital. James, who was partially sighted, was thought to have fallen into the river by accident. The Cheshires stayed at Northampton until 17 June when they moved to Ongar, in Essex. They appear to have been well received there. A concert was held for them on 29 July in the Congregational Church school room. Thanking the organisers, Captain Dawson spoke of the generous way in which the regiment had been treated. Perhaps by way of reciprocating for the concert, the Battalion organised a dance at the Public Hall in nearby Wickford. The local newspaper reported that *a large number of ladies attended.*

There was another move, to Bedford, in August. The weather that month was a typical mix of heavy rain and sunshine, although temperatures were unseasonably low. The relative coolness provided a good opportunity for the Cheshires to have a busy training week towards the end of the month. On the 21st, there was a long route march. Tuesday, 24 August saw them breakfasting at 6.15am. This was followed by another route march and they then undertook a 'sham fight' exercise, along with other battalions in the division. It was disappointing for many of the Cheshires as they did not get to even see the 'enemy', let alone engage them. They did, however, take the opportunity of a rare warm day to catch forty winks. They marched back to Northampton for a late dinner at 3.30. The band had been practising every morning and, on the 26th, they took part in a large military tattoo on the Victoria Promenade.

The band was in some demand and the *Bedfordshire Times* reported it would play at the Royal County Theatre on 29 August.

> *They will play selections and give some instrumental solos. The following artistes have consented to sing – Miss Doris M Clayson, Miss Lillie Lee, Mr Fred Hall, Mr Gosney and Mr Sam Heath. The choir of the 2/1st Welsh Border Brigade, Army Service Corps, will give several selections.*

They played another concert there in early November.

Hugh Burn joined the 3/6th Battalion in March 1915, as a newly promoted lieutenant. The twenty one year old was born in Northumberland in 1894 but the family had moved to Wilmslow at the time of the war, where they lived a comfortable middle class life. His father, Thomas, was Secretary of the Federation of Liberal Associations. Educated at Manchester Grammar School, Burn worked for a "grey cloth" manufacturer with offices in Manchester. As with many young middle class men working in the city centre, he joined the 7th Manchesters as a private within days of war being declared but was quickly singled out to become an officer. He was commissioned as a second lieutenant on 23 December 1914, before joining the Cheshires. On 7 August, he was enjoying a swim at Stockport Baths when he became a victim of a thief who had rifled through his clothes and stolen five ten-shilling notes. The culprit, who was quickly arrested, was eleven year old Frank Shingler. Giving evidence, the Chief Constable said there had been a considerable amount of pilfering at the Baths in recent times. The magistrates ordered Shingler to receive four strokes of the birch. Burn remained with the

Cooks of the 2/6th Battalion in September 1915. Front row – Corporals D Ryan and J Hackney. Second row – Privates S Turnbull and J H Thomas. Third row – Privates A Gray and C Blackburn. Photo: Stockport Express

Battalion until the summer of 1917, when he prepared to go overseas. In late November 1917 he went to Africa and was attached to the Nigeria Regiment. The war there was characterised by long marches to get into contact with the enemy. The Germans, based in their East African colonies, in what are now Burundi, Rwanda and Tanzania, fought a generally successful harrying campaign against the British forces.

The locals in Bedford soon became used to the Cheshires marching round their town, as noted by the *Bedfordshire Times* on 24 September 1915.

> *At frequent intervals of the day, the tramp of armed men is heard in the precincts of our offices and our staff no longer start when a stentorian voice orders a squad of men under the window to "Halt!.*

The same edition of the paper reported that 115 men from the Battalion's C Company, were departing for six days' leave.

Christmas 1915 was enjoyed by the 3/6th Battalion at Oswestry, as described in the *Stalybridge Reporter* by a corporal writing under the pseudonym of 'Roldo':

> *We never imagined what a glorious and happy time we could have. The best compliment we can say is that, with the exception of family gatherings, it was on a par with Christmas at home. A day or two before Christmas, it was announced that prizes would be given for the best decorated huts. It was soon observed that the competition would be extraordinarily keen. Eventually the first prize was awarded to the hut occupied by the band.*
>
> *After the Colonel's inspection, preparations were made for dinner, each company using the huts as dining rooms. The officers and NCOs were detailed to wait on the men. When dinner was ready, the Colonel came round each room, wished the men the compliments of the season and drank the health of all present. Three cheers were given for the Colonel and captain of each company.*
>
> *The men sat down to a hearty repast consisting of*
> *Goose, turkey and sausage*
> *Potatoes and sprouts*
> *Apple sauce*
> *Christmas pudding*
> *Mince pies*
> *Apples and oranges*
> *Beer and mineral water.*

In the evening, there was a 'Free and Easy' concert, with prizes for the best performers. 'Roldo' notes that the first prize was won by Drummer Fletcher of Stalybridge for a recitation of his own composition.

> *Second and third prizes were won by men from Glossop. After the concert, supper was served, consisting of roast beef and pickles, bread and butter, and cocoa. The men retired to rest, having spent a very enjoyable day.*

Samuel Chandley also enjoyed Christmas at Oswestry, although at the end of November he had received news that his father was seriously ill. He travelled back to Gatley but it was too late. Samuel senior died on the 26th, aged 63. Chandley notes that *We buried him on November 30th, which was my birthday.*

> *On New Year's Day, I was asked to a Scouts Tea at which there were about fifty scouts. I started a friendship which I shall never forget. The Scout Master was a real good friend. From then to the time of me leaving Oswestry, I made Mrs Jones, 1 Ash Cottage, Gobowen, a second mother. To me, she was a friend true as gold and when the time came to part we did so as if leaving my own mother. Mrs Jones also was the finest comrade I ever had.*

There was a sad incident in early January 1916. Nineteen year old Private Isaac Nelms of 2/6th Cheshires was cycling from Northampton back to his billet in Bedford when he was in collision with a bus. The bus driver said that he was driving under a bridge and he saw the cyclist coming towards him. The cyclist appeared to be riding straight and confidently but, just as they were passing, the cyclist swerved, appearing to lose control of the bike. He missed the front of the vehicle but the coroner concluded that he must then have fallen and gone under the rear wheels of the bus. Nelms was badly injured and was taken to hospital, where he died next day. His body was brought back to Stockport and was buried in the churchyard at Brunswick Methodist Church. The church was demolished in the 1950s and much of the burial ground is now enclosed by the modern roundabout at Portwood.

Private Isaac Nelms.

In March two of the Cheshires stationed at Bedford were arrested by the police on suspicion of being absentees from their unit. Privates John James and Thomas Ostler had been found on a train from London without

Frank Wheatley Jones joined the 7th Manchesters as a private, before becoming an officer of the 3/6th Cheshires in January 1915. He was badly wounded in action in November 1916 and was later discharged from the army. He became a chartered accountant and was a keen player at Withington Golf Club, where members still compete for the Frank Wheatley Jones Cup.

tickets. The two admitted they were indeed absent without leave and were held by the station until a military escort could arrive to take them back to camp. It is not recorded what punishment they received but it was usual for such offenders to be confined to barracks for a period and fined the number of days pay that they had been absent.[27]

John James Davies joined the Cheshires in November 1914, leaving his wife and his job as a candle maker in Stockport. His body was found in the River Ouse in early May 1916. There was no doubt as to what had happened. Jack Davies had been in indifferent health for some time and had been depressed as a consequence, although his friend Corporal Ashton said he had seemed more cheerful of late. A note was found on his body:

> *My dear wife*
> *Forgive me for the rash act I have done but I could not stand it any*
> *longer. I hope we shall meet again in heaven.*
>> *Your loving husband*
>> *Jack*
>> *Heartbroken*

His body was brought back to Stockport, where it is buried in the Borough Cemetery.

There are few records remaining of the 2/6th and 3/6th Battalions after this time. The National Archives holds some very scant notes about the 2/6th during 1915, but these exclusively deal with a few personnel matters – officers arriving and leaving, men being sent on courses or being discharged from the army. For example, the notes record that Second Lieutenant B Berry joined the Battalion on 18 September 1915. Bernard Berry had enlisted in the London Regiment as a private and had only just become an officer. He served with the 2/6th and 3/6th Battalions until he went overseas on 29 April 1918, when he was attached to 9th Cheshires. He was killed in action with them six weeks later. Harry Cropper joined in October 1915, also as a second lieutenant. He was from Ashton under Lyne and had worked as an analytical chemist. He did not remain long with the Cheshires and was posted to the Royal Engineers, where his skills were used in the development of chemical warfare.

In the autumn of 1916 the 2/6th Battalion moved to coastal guard duties at Lowestoft, then to Great Yarmouth in March 1917 and, finally, to Southwold in Suffolk from July 1917. It was disbanded shortly after. Whilst they were at Great Yarmouth, twenty year old John Gee had routine army vaccinations prior to going overseas, but fell ill with enteric fever (typhoid). He was admitted to an isolation hospital in Great Yarmouth, where he died about three weeks later. The family lived in Hayfield until Gee, along with his mother and siblings, emigrated to Canada in 1913. He returned to Britain to join the army in December 1914. Gee's body was brought back to Hayfield where, on 17 November, it was buried with full military honours in the parish church's cemetery.

The 3/6th Battalion ceased to be a separate unit in September 1916, when it merged with the 3/4th Battalion, along with the 3/5th and 3/7th. The new unit is known to have been at Kinmel Park, near Rhyl, in April 1918 and at Whitstable in October 1918

Samuel Chandley had reached the end of his training by the late spring of 1916.

I was storekeeper for about a month and then I was Divisional Signals Office Clerk, where I had a nice soft job of it. On Friday morning, May 5th, I was warned for draft and, on Monday night, we had supper prior to leaving England for France. Fifty hearty lads left Whittington station en route for France. We entrained at 8.50am and arrived at Southampton about 4.30pm. The train took us right up to the landing stage and we embarked on the Arundel. Left Southampton at 6.30, arriving at Le Havre, after a pleasant voyage, at 2.10am. The harbour was a very pretty sight – little twinkling lights and the coloured lights. On board, all of us had life belts.

Within weeks of the start of the Battle of the Somme, this documentary film was showing in cinemas across the country, including the Alexandra at Hyde.

It is time now for the reader also to go to France and to return in time to the beginning of 1915. There will be more of Chandley's account of his service in Chapter 6.

CHAPTER 5

Out of Harm's Way

Charles Brockbank had hoped to celebrate New Year's Eve in Bailleul but he found few places open and hardly anyone around. He went back next evening and *had a grand feed to drown my misery as they say leave is to be cancelled.* He had not had the best of starts to 1915 being *ticked off for reproving the Regimental Sergeant Major.* He had also had a wasted journey to the Field Cashier to draw pay for the company. *This was my first attempt at riding a horse and probably was amusing to the spectators, personally I could not see anything funny about it.* Meanwhile, the men were spending the day undertaking drill and physical training.

On 4 January, the Battalion moved to new billets at nearby Ravetsburg. The next few days would be spent digging trenches and helping to construct redoubts in the front line. They worked long nights, marching six miles to Wulverghem, near where they had spent Christmas, work for four hours, then marching back. Brockbank said he *stumbled along in the dark down an awful road, sometimes getting off it and into this beastly stinking mud up to our knees.* He did not think much of the new billets, either. There were no beds and he was sleeping on the tiled floor. The men also supplied carrying parties – in this case moving supplies for the Royal Engineers from the village to the front line. Much of it was barbed wire, which was placed in No Man's Land as a defence against attack. There was mud everywhere – up to the ankles in most places and, from time to time, men would go in up to their knees. The 1st Norfolks, who Brockbank knew well, were going into the front line and the trenches there were filled with muddy water, up to the waist in parts. To make matters worse, it rained all day on the 7th.

When not working the men were encouraged to play football and matches were organised between the different companies. They had recently received three balls sent by the Stockport Football Association. Brockbank played a match on the morning of the 9th, before setting off on another carrying party.

This time it was not so bad or dirty because it was not raining and we had to go by a different route. Nearly trod on three dead Frenchies. My word this district does stink of rotting turnips, dead men and cattle, and mud. It is a wonder we are not all down with illness. Nearly had my eye poked out when helping a man over a ditch. He had slung his rifle over his back and when he half jumped towards me his rifle barrel caught me just below the eyeball and blacked my eye beautifully before we got home. If it had been a wee bit higher up it would have burst the ball, so I have something to be thankful for. We got home very tired at about 2.30 A.M.

George Fowden wrote home to a friend to say that, in another match, A Company had beaten B Company 7 – 0. Both of these companies included men from his home town of Stalybridge. Aged about thirty, Fowden was a long standing member of the Battalion and had been working in a cotton mill card room before being mobilised. He had found himself in trouble on Christmas Eve, when he used threatening language to an NCO. It was a rash act that saw him fined eight days' pay. In 1916 he might have found himself in trouble with his wife, Ethel, whom he married in 1908. He may have had to explain why he was hospitalised for three months with gonorrhoea.

The Battalion's machine gunners were still in action at the front. They had two Maxim machine guns, each operated by a team of six, which could fire 500 rounds a minute – the weapons of mass destruction of the day. They were commanded by Lieutenant Francis White, from Hadfield. He gained a degree in law from Owens College (later Manchester University) but decided to follow medicine as a career. He had been an officer with the Battalion since 1910 and was killed in action, whilst serving with 1st Cheshires, on 4 September 1916. Writing home, George Birkenhead, a grocer's warehouseman from Stockport, gave a detailed account of the period after they went into the trenches on 7 January:

We went into action with the [censored] Regiment, to relieve one of their gun teams, as they have had a very strenuous time during the last few months. We joined them at their headquarters and

The Battalion machine gunners 'somewhere in France' in early January 1915.

marched on towards the firing line as far as we dared take the carriages for safety. Then carrying the gun, tripod, ammunition, etc, between us, we commenced to wade through a sea of mud to the trenches, a distance of 1½ miles, Several laughable incidents of which, however, we did not see the humour at the time, occurred on this journey. I will relate one of them. Our No. 1, carrying the tripod, was missed from the file. The sergeant, on going back, found him stuck in a shell hole up to his waist in water. He assisted him out and helped him rejoin the Section. During all this time, the German snipers were busy, bullets whistling around us all the way *up. On arriving at the gun emplacement, we relieved a team of Regulars. On enquiring the range of the German trenches, we were rather surprised to be told seventy yards. Our trench is knee deep in water and it rained torrents the whole night. But we were already soaked, so didn't mind. In our emplacement, we had a small dugout into which we could crawl; others were not so lucky. While it was still dark, we went to a deserted farm for straw to lie on in the dugout. In spite of the nearness of the Germans and the pouring rain, we were not prevented making hot tea, to say nothing of buttered toast produced on a charcoal fire made in a perforated mess tin. We take twenty four hours rations with us into the trenches – bread, butter, tea, sugar, bacon, cheese and jam. Charcoal is issued for use in the trenches. Rations are brought up every night for the following twenty four hours*

Every morning at daybreak, we get the order to 'stand to' with loaded rifles and fixed bayonets. We stand to, the guns ready for any charge of the enemy. Of course, there are lookouts every few yards along the line, awake all through the night. Each man takes his turn at lookout. We stand to for an hour at dawn; it is then we get the usual 'Good Morning', from the artillery, who generally continue the bombardment all through the day. And so it goes on – artillery fire, rifle fire and bursts of machine gun fire. The machine gun is a favourite weapon of the Germans. We were lucky on Saturday. The Germans sent four shells over at our gun. Two of them dropped short of their own trenches. One struck a few yards from our gun, turning it over on its side. This was followed by a shrapnel shell which burst right over our trench. Neither did any damage worse than cover us in mud. Two machine gunners of the [censored] Regiment were wounded by shrapnel, one seriously. There was an Indian battery on our left rear, which was doing fine work dropping shells right in the German trenches. It is an awful sight to see overcoats and trousers flying in the air when shells do burst in the trenches. We are all in good health: it's a strenuous life but we are doing our best in this campaign in which the freedom of our native land is at stake."[28]

Frank Croft, from Compton Street, Stalybridge. Mortally wounded by shrapnel in the stomach and thigh on Boxing Day, 1914. He died in hospital in Boulogne on 7 January.

George Birkenhead later transferred to the newly formed specialist Machine Gun Corps. He survived the war and emigrated to New York in 1920, where he intended to work as a photographer. He died the following year of a now unknown illness or injury connected with his war service. He is buried at the city's Evergreens Cemetery, where his grave is in the care of the Commonwealth War Graves Commission.

On 11 January fourteen men were sent home as unfit for service either at the front or on the lines of communication. Five days later the Battalion moved to new billets for a few days at St Jans Cappel, a small hamlet just north of Bailleul. This was to be a rare period of rest, without any working parties. Brockbank enjoyed the rest, if not the weather, which was mainly rain, for the whole period. He did, however, enjoy a couple of good meals at the hotel in Bailleul – the Faucon d'Or. He also enjoyed the hot baths that were available to officers at the town's lunatic asylum. Stanley Hughes, from Hyde, had received a minor shrapnel wound to his head on 23 December but had now recovered.

> *I've got a piece of shell that was pulled out and I shall keep it as a souvenir. My feet have been very bad. I don't know if it's chilblains, but it's rotten. They are all right now, but I could hardly walk at first. You should have seen us. We had a proper limping parade.* [29]

The rest was over on the 24th and the men returned to the Ravetsburg area, marching past the Divisional commander, Sir Charles Fergusson, at Bailleul. On arrival, B and D companies marched straight to the billets, whilst the other two companies went to the trenches under the command of Major Hesse. A Company and part of C went into the front line, while the remaining men from C spent their time in the support dugouts, about a hundred yards behind the front line.

For the Cheshires, this tour of duty was quite memorable and well recorded although, in itself, was fairly representative of any period in the front line when there were no major attacks underway.

> *A silly ass let the straw of his dugout catch fire during the night so we shall probably get some hell today. The only gratification we had was that he got a bullet in the leg when the fire was on, so will have something to think about.* (Charles Brockbank).

Job Wade also had something to say about the 'silly ass'.

We were in the trench where a man was cooking some bacon on a charcoal burner when a bit of fat got on the fire and it ignited the straw and wood in the dugout, which was occupied by four of us. The Germans did not know properly where we were until they saw this and then they got the range of us and shells began to come over. We extinguished the fire by means of earth which we threw upon it but we had to stop. At the same time, one or two of our men were missing but, fortunately, turned up again. Private Taylor was missing for fifteen hours but he eventually found his way back. He had been rambling around all the time and was lucky to be alive.[30]

There was some German shelling that wounded two men on the 25th. The following day, Sergeant Walter West, a hatter from Stockport and serving with A Company, was looking out across No Man's Land, using a pair of field glasses. Perhaps there was a glint of light from the lens that gave his position away, but he was killed outright by a sniper's shot through the head. It was a difficult time for James Boardman and the other stretcher bearers.

We could not move about in daylight except with great danger. Johnny Bennett and myself were commended for our work at this place, and were eventually mentioned in despatches by Sir John French. Besides carrying out the dead and wounded the stretcher bearers had the job of digging the graves and burying the dead.

Although Boardman does not mention anything in his diary, he was twice awarded the Military Medal for acts of bravery during the war and Mentioned in Despatches a second time in 1917. Private John Bennett was also honoured with the award of a Military Medal. The war diary tells the story better than the modest Boardman. At about 9am on the 25th, the two men were called to go to another trench, about sixty yards away, to aid Sergeant John Goddard, who had been hit by shrapnel while he was cooking some bacon for his breakfast. They ran across open ground to get to Goddard, dressed his wounds and returned to their own trench. An hour later, another call came. This time it was from a trench about a hundred yards away and two men had been hit. Again they ran across the open ground, under enemy fire, struggling through a barbed wire fence. They attended to the men and stayed with them until the late afternoon. Although it was still light and they could be seen by the Germans, they ran back to get their stretchers as the men were now urgent cases. It was bravery most certainly meriting the recognition of the Medal.

Unfortunately, none of the three men survived. John Goddard was taken to a dressing station at nearby Dranouter but died on the 28th. He is buried in the village churchyard and remembered on the Hadfield war memorial. Fred Stubbs, a cotton piecer from Millbrook and son of the village policeman, was evacuated to the 2nd Base Hospital at Boulogne. The Matron, Miss Ethel Denne, wrote to his parents saying that he was badly injured in both legs and his right hand. *He is a splendid patient, so good and brave. He sends his love to you.* Miss Denne said he was very ill but not in a critical condition. However, he deteriorated and died on 3 February. Alan Asquith was a month short of his seventeenth birthday when he was mortally wounded. The shrapnel had shattered his right arm and both legs. He had been with the territorials since 1913. Although he had lain in the trench for hours, he insisted that Boardman and Bennett take Stubbs first before coming back for him. Asquith was taken to 8th Casualty Clearing Station at Bailleul. One of the nursing sisters there wrote to his mother saying he died soon after arrival on the 25th. The doctors did all that they could but it was clearly a hopeless case. In his last letter home, young Asquith had concluded *Buck up, mother, we are all right. I only wish to do my duty for my King and country.*

On 27 January Brockbank had a narrow escape. He was in his dugout when a German shell landed very close by, blowing in the trench parapet and almost burying him. Later in the day, Major General Fergusson, the Divisional commander, came round the trenches on a visit – perhaps helping to nail a myth that the 'top brass' spent all their time well away from danger. He spoke to Brockbank, shaking his hand and saying he was glad that no one had been injured. The troops had

Alan Asquith, died of wounds, aged 16. He had written to his mother saying 'I only wish to do my duty for my King and country'.

Private Fred Stubbs.

been expecting significant action from the Germans by way of them giving a 'birthday present' to the Kaiser but, in the event, there was no attack and only the minor shelling. Harold Beard, from Hyde, wrote home:

> *They wished to give him a good account of themselves but they got it back from our gunners who got the right range and blew gun and ammo column up for them. One of their guns made it very uncomfortable for us. I had my shoes off and they got buried but rather the shoes than my humble self.*[31]

On the 28th, B and D Companies took over the front line and the other two companies marched back to the billets. The Battalion war diary notes that the men's health was much better than in December, no doubt due to the trenches being *comparatively dry,* although the surrounding land was very water-logged. The men could move around more freely during the night and they spent this time repairing trenches and improving the parapets. On the 29th a very welcome draft of re-inforcements arrived from Britain, numbering four officers and 243 other ranks. Amongst the officers was newly commissioned Second Lieutenant Arthur Walmsley, a self-employed mechanical and electrical engineer from the Fylde area of Lancashire. He was a keen motorist; his service records note that he had owned a Delage 15 horsepower, Vauxhall 25hp and a Talbot 25hp. He would serve with the Battalion until August 1916, when he was invalided home suffering with rheumatism. On recovery he successfully applied for a transfer to the Royal Engineers, where his technical skills could be put to good use. Walmsley joined Brockbank's company who described him as a 'decent fellow'. The group also included Private John Birkenhead, younger brother of George mentioned above. He is believed to have also been a specialist machine gunner who later joined the Machine Gun Corps. He was killed in action on 15 September 1918.

At 6′ 1″, George Howard was one of the tallest men in the Battalion. It had its benefits as well as its drawbacks.

> *I was glad, when we were going in the trenches, that I was so tall because the shorter ones sometimes fell into holes full of water but I could stride over. But when I got to the trenches, I wished I was a little one. I had to stoop down all the time.*[32]

He ended January 1915 by being invalided back to Britain with frostbite but returned to duty with the Battalion, later having attachments to the 13th Gloucesters and the 118th Trench Mortar Battery.

The Cheshires moved back to billets at St Jans Cappel on 1 February and stayed there for a week, forming part of the Division's reserve troops. There was little for them to do and it was generally regarded as a holiday of sorts. On Saturday, 6 February, in one of several football matches played around this time, the officers took on D Company. Brockbank was played at outside left and reckoned that, because he was right footed, made a mess of things. *We lost 9 – 3 but considered we had done very well.*

On the following Monday morning the whole Brigade was paraded near Bailleul for an inspection by Albert, King of the Belgians. He was accompanied by several very senior officers: Field Marshal Sir John French, commanding the whole of the British Expeditionary Force; the commander of Second Army, General Horace Smith-Dorrien, together with the divisional commander, Major General Fergusson, and the brigade commander, Brigadier General Gleichen. The Brigade war diary notes that Gleichen felt the Cheshires were much improved – 'steadier, cleaner and better'.

On the same day as Brockbank wrote in his diary about the inspection he also wrote this intriguing entry:

> *The deadly feud between the 1st and 6th Cheshires has been started by a Corporal in the 1st Bn running away from the line, being court-martialled and shot for cowardice. We were down in rest billet here when it happened, but the 1st Bn. are trying to put the blame on our shoulders because we are 'only Territorials'. I can quite see we shall never be able to discredit the tale, and there will be no end of fights between men over the matter. It is a filthy lowdown trick.*

It has not been possible to establish the exact nature of the feud or how it manifested itself in France but it was a matter that, as will be recounted later, would be the source of gossip, innuendo and potential scandal across north Cheshire.

The details of what happened to bring Corporal George Povey, 1st Cheshires, before a court martial are well documented. That battalion was in the front line near Wulverghem. During the early hours of 28 January, it seems that a solitary German had crept across No Man's Land and had grabbed a man's rifle that was poking out through a loophole. It caused a general panic and several men ran away from the trench. One of them was

Povey. He and another four men were charged with the military offence of quitting his post without orders. In military law, this is a very specific offence – you are either at your post, or you are not – there are no grey areas. And leaving your post when in front of the enemy was regarded as a very serious offence, as it left that part of the line undefended. Povey's defence was that he had been asleep in the dugout and was woken by the noise of the panic and heard someone shout 'Clear out lads, they are on us'. However, his evidence was contradicted by Sergeant Cook, who said that he did not hear anyone shout for the men to 'clear out', but he did hear someone shout 'Come on boys, let them have it', and several men started firing. All five men were convicted. The four privates were sentenced to ten years imprisonment but Povey received a death sentence. It can be assumed that the harsher sentence was due to his more senior rank – it being an established part of British civilian and military law that persons in positions of trust can expect harsher sentences for the same offence. The sentence was confirmed by each of the reviewing senior officers, right up to Field Marshal French. Povey was executed at St Jans Cappel on 11 February.

It is difficult to understand on what basis the men of the 1st Battalion might try to shift the blame for one of their own men's actions onto the Cheshire territorials. Whilst, as Brockbank notes, two of the companies were in billets at the time, the other two were in the trenches near Dranouter, some five kilometres away, and were clearly not involved in the incident. Perhaps it was just by innuendo when chatting with other troops who only knew, vaguely, that it was a Cheshire who had been executed.

On 9 February the Battalion returned to the trenches at Wulverghem and would remain there until the 18th. It was a quiet period. Frank Osbaldiston and his older brother, Albert, lived with their parents in Marple and had been territorials for some while. Frank wrote home at this time saying that they were

> quite at home in the trench. We have a fire in our shelter – four of us – and we had toast and condensed pea soup, butter, Swiss milk, salmon and we cooked out own bacon, toasted our cheese and boiled six mess tins full of tea. It was quite comfortable……We have just had four days in the trenches and we had five casualties, three having died. One out of A Company was seriously injured but he was very brave. Brother Albert was carrying him and he said to

him 'It's a wonder I hadn't my head blown off.' The poor man died the same day. I was only twenty yards from his place. One shell had blown the next shelter to our out so altogether it has been the warmest time we have had.[33]

The nights were misty and Charles Brockbank found leading patrols into No Man's Land to be very nerve-wracking, as he could not see more than twenty yards ahead and was constantly worried he might come across a German patrol.

Just about 9 o'clock I lost a man. He was hit through the neck standing next to me, messy business, but quite painless for him. Upset me a lot. We buried him in Wulverghem churchyard near our other men………Cannot sleep owing to my nerves. I have been lying down all day but only got about an hour's sleep.

The man was Harold Smith, from Hyde. A married man, he worked as a clerk at a paper mill before the war.

Around this time, Major and Quartermaster John Rawlinson reported sick. An older man, he was finding the rigours of active service simply too much. Since they had been overseas he had lost three stone, was suffering memory loss and had fallen from his horse three times. He was diagnosed with neurasthenia and was sent home. Away from the front, Rawlinson's condition improved and, in 1916, he was able to return to duty, albeit not overseas but was posted to 3/6th Cheshires as its quartermaster.

Brockbank was still in the trenches on 15 February. His company had been due to be relieved but had received orders to remain in the front line as a German attack was expected.

I was sent out on patrol tonight (a muddy job, crawling) to try and find out if the Germans were doing anything. We crawled about their wire but as far as we could make out there was nothing out of the ordinary. We could hear them talking and bailing out their trenches.

The attack did not materialise but he spent most of the next day in the trench. He enjoyed a hot breakfast even though it was just two rashers of fatty bacon, sodden bread from a sandbag and milkless tea. He played host to his friend and comrade, Bill Innes, whose own dugout had flooded. They chatted about cars and motorbikes all morning. Innes was twenty six and worked in the family pharmacy business in Stalybridge. The same day, there was an incident involving an accidental discharge of a rifle. It went off, wounding George Want in both legs. He had been at the front for less than a month. He was evacuated back to Britain, where he was admitted to hospital in Southend. Want's condition started to improve but later deteriorated and he died on 16 July. His body was brought back to Stockport and he is buried at Willow Grove Cemetery.

Private George Want. The fatal shot was an accident.

Two days later, Private Harry Winkle was a member of a patrol creeping out into No Man's Land, just as it was getting dark. The plan was to get over to the German line and see if they could capture a prisoner or two. The twenty three year old was an ironworker from Stalybridge.

It had been raining for four days and it was dark before we had gone a great way and I slipped. I put my hands out to save myself and, of course, my rifle dropped when I let go of it and I dropped upon it. I was getting up again when something caught the trigger and the end of my finger was missing.[34]

He was evacuated back to Britain for treatment but did not serve overseas again. Towards the end of the year, he married his fiancée, Ellen Turner, at St John's Church, Dukinfield. He left the army when his contracted time as a territorial came to an end in 1916. Winkle is believed to have died in 1959.

Tom Mather sent a letter to his parents at Gee Cross on the 22nd.

It is getting time they gave us a rest and a furlough, but there is no sign of any. It's all right going into the trenches for about twenty four or forty eight hours, but eight days is too much for factory lads.

He also asked them to send him an 'ambulance book'.

You like to be able to do something for a wounded lad, when you are in the trench with him and he cannot be got to hospital till dark and you have to look after him as best you can.[35]

Saturday, 27 February started with an extraordinary incident recorded in 15 Brigade's war diary. In the early hours they spotted a signal being sent in Morse code by lamp from the German trenches. It said, in English, that they were going to attack and 'take the hill' at noon.

Conceivable that, whilst probably all nonsense or a 'leg pull', there was a 50 to 1 chance of it being genuine and sent by some sympathiser to us.

Two companies of 1st Dorsets were ordered forward to offer support to the Cheshires if need be. In the event, no attack happened, but the day was not without its dangers. The men stood to for most of the day.

Arthur Wood, from Hyde, was one of the Battalion's stretcher bearers and describes what happened later in the day.

Sergeant Long was shot in the side. I ran down the trenches after him and, in pulling him in, I was hit in the shoulder. The bullet went through the equipment, through my coat but, I am glad to say, it only touched my shin. I got a shot that went through my haversack and through my tin of corned beef, taking the buckle off and out the other side, so I think I was very lucky. The trenches we were in were death traps, like a circle. We were fired up from the back by the enemy snipers. My mate, Tom Mather, was coming to help me with Sergeant Long and, in doing so, was shot in the head. He died later on.[36]

Tom Long was evacuated back to Britain, where he was treated in hospital in Brighton.

I was running about with ammunition. I only ran down the trench twice before they had me. I could not feel I was hit at first. I found out when I fell.

Long recovered but never returned to duty. He was discharged from the army in 1916. Arthur Wood was Mentioned in Despatches for his bravery and, in 1916, was awarded the Military Medal for carrying the wounded to safety. Tom Mather was taken to a dressing station near Wulverghem, where he died and is buried in the nearby military cemetery He is also remembered on the Hyde war memorial and the memorial at Holy Trinity, Gee Cross. Mather was also Mentioned in Despatches, although not until many months after his death. The King's assistant military secretary wrote to his parents:

> *I am to express to you the King's high appreciation and that His Majesty trusts that the public acknowledgement may be of some consolation in your bereavement.* [37]

Private Tom Mather, from Gee Cross. Mortally wounded while trying to help a comrade.

Later in the day the Battalion was relieved and moved back to its billets. They now received orders to move to the Expeditionary Force's GHQ to take over duties in the reserve area from the 2nd Battalion Royal Irish Regiment. As indicated earlier, Brigadier General Gleichen had concerns about the Battalion's quality when it first arrived under his command and may have originally suggested the transfer. However, a few days before, he had written to his superior officer stating that he wanted to

> *put on record that the Battalion has "come on" immensely during the past month. Both officers and men are much steadier and more experienced than they were several weeks ago; and the men (and officers) are very keen to have a go at the enemy (so the CO and Adjutant tell me). All ranks feel much disappointed at the order to go into reserve and I think they would give a good account of themselves in the firing line if called on.*

Lance Corporal George Taylor, wounded on 27 February 1915. He returned to duty, later serving with the Labour Corps, but was demoted in 1917 when he absented himself from a working party.

The divisional commander, Major General Morland, supported Gleichen's view urging that the Cheshires be retained in the forward areas, *owing to the weakness of the incoming brigades*. The recommendations by the commanders who best knew the Cheshires were not adopted.

They would not return to the front until February 1916. They were now out of harm's way but the move would soon provide the "evidence" for the rumour mongers in north Cheshire to bring up the 'feud' between the Battalion and the 1ˢᵗ Cheshires.

It would seem that a story quickly took hold that the withdrawal from front line service was directly related to the earlier incident, even though that had no factual connection with the 6ᵗʰ Battalion. The rumours were to the effect that the Battalion was being 'punished', therefore the allegations of cowardice must be true.

One 'Indignant Mother' wrote to the *Stockport Express*:

> *I have a son, my only son, in the 6ᵗʰ Cheshire Territorials. He left home ten months ago, with the first draft who went away; they were in the trenches almost three months during the worst part of the winter. Last week, I spoke to three different people. Two of them said 'The Cheshire Terriers had to be brought out of the trenches because they had lost their nerve'. The other said 'the Cheshires had to be brought out because of their terrible conduct'. Just imagine what the feelings who have given their nearest and dearest are when they hear such talk as this. Is there no way to stop these lying scandal mongers. I am quite sure there is no truth in the matter and, even if there was, Stockport people should be the last in the world to repeat it. It is a poor bird that will dirty its own nest.[38]*

The rumours spread across all the towns from where the Battalion was drawn. One Hyde soldier, presumably on sick leave, writing to the *North Cheshire Herald* as 'One who knows' responded ...

> *Allow me to say as one who had been with them and endured the privations and hardships that I can really say it is not on. The boys have been brave and taken their part with great courage. If those who are so keen at scandalising our brave local lads would go and do their share, they would have room to talk.[39]*

Joe Elliott was a married man from Hyde who worked as a cotton weaver before going on active service. He had received a letter from his concerned parents who had heard the rumours going round the town. He wrote back:

You asked me if there is any truth in the rumour going about Hyde, about the Terriers being a 'disgrace'. Well, it is the first I have heard about it and it is a scandalous lie. It would look a jolly sight better if those who set these rumours afloat if they would come and do a bit. Whoever set it out certainly knows nothing because we have only just got back from the front today, forming an escort over a few hundred German soldiers. I think people who scandalise their own town's boys, who are doing their fair share and who have gone through the hardships that we went through in the winter, ought to be treated as Germans and lynched. I don't know why such traitors are at large. It makes my blood boil.[40]

Later in the war Elliott was transferred to the South Lancashire Regiment; he was mortally wounded and died on 3 June 1918.

Eventually, Colonel Hesse wrote to Stockport's mayor, asking him to do his best stop the rumours.

I need hardly tell you there is not a word of truth in the rumours. The Battalion did its duty in the trenches and was complimented by the Brigadier on the way they did it. The boys of the 6th Cheshires set an example to older men by showing utter contempt for rifle and shellfire.[41]

The matter petered out in the local press but it was a rumour that simply would not go away and it was resurrected in the spring of the 1916. It prompted Captain Richard Kirk to write to the *Stalybridge Reporter*:

I regret to hear that a rumour which was current in Stalybridge last winter appears to have started again. I refer to one that the 6th Cheshires had run away from the trenches. I am surprised that the people of Stalybridge give credence to such a

Captain Richard Kirk. Photo: Royal Bank of Scotland

tale and I am sure if they only knew the pain it gives to the boys out here, they would take every opportunity of killing the rumour. Ever since it came out the Battalion has done its work well and has had nothing but praise and commendations from generals under which it has served at any time.[42]

Although clearly nothing to do with their actual current performance, it must be a matter of speculation as to why the 6th Cheshires were withdrawn from combat against the recommendations of its Brigade commander. With the growing size of the Expeditionary Force, there was a need for more support troops in the reserve areas. They were going to replace 2nd Battalion Royal Irish Regiment – a regular army battalion which had suffered very heavy losses during fighting at Le Bassée in November 1914 and which, presumably, was at full strength again. This exchange was in the context of negative attitudes amongst certain of the senior commanders towards the Territorial Force as a whole. The issues of poor training, marksmanship and the quality of many of the prewar officers, as discussed in Chapter 1, were well known. Lord Kitchener, the respected military hero and Secretary of State for War, is reported to have said *I prefer men who know nothing to those who have been taught a smattering of the wrong thing.* [43] It would also be reasonable to note that many of the experienced prewar Cheshires had been invalided home, to be replaced by men hurriedly trained in the 2/6th and 3/6th Battalions. Everything taken together, it may have been a relatively easy decision to take. And so it was that, on 1 March, the Battalion moved by bus to St Omer, where it would initially act as the guard for the headquarters of the Expeditionary Force.

There are few official documents recording the Battalion's activities over the following months. Even the war diary has whole weeks where there are no entries. It is, therefore, necessary to rely on the diaries and letters of the men to tell the story. Inherently, this means that the account is incomplete.

Second Lieutenant Charles Brockbank returned from leave in Britain on 4 March and travelled to Bailleul before he found out that the Battalion had moved. He managed to get lifts on several army lorries that got him to St Omer but it took about eight hours. He felt that it was strange to see everyone in clean clothes rather than covered in mud as they had been in the trenches. The same day, fifty men under the command of Captain Leah and Lieutenant Hoyle provided a guard of honour for the visiting French General de la Croix.

Although the Battalion was providing the town guards, C Company was detailed to undertake a working party on Sunday, 7 March. It was an early start, leaving the barracks at 6.30. They were taken by bus to Aire, about ninety minutes away, and spent the day under the direction of the Army Service Corps, transferring boxes from a train to a barge. There were cases of tea, army 'dog' biscuits, tinned meat, sugar, etc.

The next day, Brockbank was the designated Orderly Officer and wrote in his diary the duties that would be expected of him:

1. His tour of duty is from Reveillé to Reveillé.

2. He will attend Rouse Parade 7.0 A.M.

3. He will inspect mens' breakfast, dinners & teas.

4. He will inspect all guards dismounting.

5. He will visit Guard Room, Cells, Field Punishment Room by day and enquire if there are any complaints.

6. He will visit and inspect all Regimental & Garrison guards and Examining Posts, once by day and once by night. He will make his nightly inspection after midnight, he will satisfy himself the sentries know their orders.

7. He will visit the Cook-house and all institutes once per day.

8. He will not leave the Barracks during his tour of duty except to visit the guards etc.

9. He will collect reports at Tattoo Staff Parade at 8.45 p.m.

10. He will see "Lights Out" at 9.0 p.m.

11. He will report to the Adjutant at Guard Mounting.

12. He will inspect Regimental Picquet at mounting and dismounting.

13. He will report to the Adjutant at Office Hours on the day following completion of his tour of duties.

It was a busy day.

Around this time, Chris Jones, a postman from Dukinfield, wrote home to his wife, Nellie, telling her he had attended a concert. The show had opened with the cast singing 'Uncle Joe'.

The battlefield mimic, Lance Corporal E Bradbury, gave a good imitation of a sniper after he has fired and the bullet passing by, then he imitated a shell

Chris Jones, a Dukinfield postman before the war.

bursting in mid-air, with Private Brierley, of the band, coming in with a crash at the right moment. Privates Higginbottom and Wrigley came next with 'Floss and Fluss', a sketch which caused a lot of fun among the boys, the repartee being very good.[44]

On 10 March, the BEF launched its first major attack of the war, now known as the Battle of Neuve Chapelle, after the village, which is roughly halfway between the French towns of Béthune and Armentières. The plan was to overrun the German trenches, capture the village and press on to take tactically important higher ground on the far side of the village. There would be a heavy artillery bombardment of the German front line for thirty minutes. The infantry would then attack, while the artillery shelled the village. In the centre of the attack everything went well, with the village being captured very quickly. Things had not gone well for the troops on the two wings of the attack. To the north, the shelling had not been effective and, to the south, the infantry lost direction and plunged into a sector untouched by the artillery and heavily defended by the Germans. At this point, the attack stalled and, over the next two days, the Germans made unsuccessful attempts to counterattack. This first major attack can be regarded as a qualified success but it was a costly one. Some 40,000 British troops had taken part and, by the end of the three days, about 11,500 were dead, wounded or missing. German casualties were of a similar order, including nearly 1700 taken prisoner.

The 6th Cheshires played no part in the attack but about a hundred of them were ordered to Neuve Chapelle to act as stretcher bearers, burial parties and prisoner escorts. Private William Lees, a cotton spinner from Demesne Street, Stalybridge, was amongst the group:

We had just got nicely to bed last Friday night when word came that our company had to get dressed and go up to the firing line and bring down the wounded. Off we went about twenty miles in motor ambulances and I shall never forget it as long as I live. I tell you I could do anything after what I saw there. Besides our own wounded, we brought about twenty wounded German prisoners down on stretchers to the dressing station – and the Germans shelling us all the time. How one got through it without some of us being hit, God only knows. It was awful. One poor lad, a German, I do not think he was more than seventeen years old, told me he had been lying wounded for three days.[45]

Neuve Chapelle after the German defeat.

James Boardman was also at Neuve Chapelle. He recounted how he and the other regular stretcher bearers each took charge of a group of men.

> *My word, didn't we have a time! The dead were lying here, there, and everywhere. We were carrying wounded for about two days. We had a very narrow escape at what was appropriately named Suicide Corner. We had just put a stretcher case in one of our ambulance wagons when a shell burst right amongst us. How some of us are here to tell the tale I don't know! The horses, wagon, and all in the wagon were blown to pieces with the exception of one man — a German — who was the last case to be put in. We slept in this place one night in a church which was full of our wounded men. As one lot was taken away more would take their place. All through the night and early next morning there was one continual stream of civilians coming in to pray. Many of the wounded were Indians, mostly Ghurkas.*

Back at St Omer, Charles Brockbank undertook a job that he enjoyed on 19 March. He was in charge of Field Marshal French's personal guard.

> *It is a job I like as you see all the Brass-hats & the aristocracy. I have a good view of the Prince of Wales & Prince Arthur of*

Connaught as I have to pass their rooms and they sit at a table in the window.

The next day, he attended a lecture given by the Adjutant on Fire Control – finding targets, etc. *It was very interesting but he is a bad lecturer.* The Adjutant was Captain Marshall Clarke. He is believed to have been a professional soldier, who fought in South Africa during the Boer War. He was posted to the Battalion at the end of November 1914 but his stay was brief and, by 1916, he was serving as a major with the 1st Cheshires. In his diary, Brockbank calls Clarke 'Specky' – although presumably not to his face.

Captain Marshall Falconer Clarke, in his younger days during the Boer War.

There was bayonet practice on the 23rd, followed by a ten mile route march. In the afternoon the Battalion football team took on the 6th Welsh. It was a strong team. Privates Taylor and Fowden had both played for Stalybridge United and, in his younger days, Sergeant James Connor had played professionally for Derby County. The *Ashton Reporter* quoted a letter from Lance Corporal Jones, of Stalybridge, who said there was no score until just after half time, when the Cheshires forced two corners. D Company's commander, Captain Arthur Smith, scored from the second. They got a second goal later.

The remainder of the month followed the above pattern, with a mix of route marches, drill and bayonet practice, together with occasional football matches. The Cheshires took on a team of signallers from the Royal Engineers, beating them 3-0. Fred and Richard Wilkinson, from Bredbury, served together with the Battalion. Richard, a painter and decorator, wrote home saying that in another tournament the Cheshires had won their first three matches but then the signallers got their revenge winning 2-1. The Cheshires went on to thrash the Army Service Corps team 5–1. Richard Wilkinson was killed in action in 1916.

Brockbank did another day as commander of the Field Marshal's guard on the 30th. He notes that it should have been Bob Cooke's turn but he had been admitted to hospital. Robert Rostron Cooke was aged about twenty and had been commissioned on 30 August 1914. It is not known what he was suffering from but he was posted back to Britain where, on recovery, he spent some time with the 3/6th Battalion before returning to overseas duty in the spring of 1916.

At the end of the month orders came that the Battalion was to be split up to undertake lines of communiciation duties. This term refers to the route from the various supply bases to the forward areas. It would involve the Cheshires in a variety of tasks over the following weeks – providing guards, burial parties, moving stores, etc. The Battalion headquarters staff and B Company left for Le Havre, A Company for Rouen and C Company for Boulogne. D Company would be further divided, with half going to Dieppe and the other half to Abbeville.

In civilian life George Furness was a labourer, living with his parents in Stalybridge. He was now one of the Battalion cooks. It is not known which town he was sent to, but he took "Kitty" with him. He had been given the cat while the men were at Shrewsbury, back in August, and he had kept it ever since.

Charles Brockbank arrived at Boulogne at about 7.30pm, only to find that no-one was expecting them and no arrangements had been made for billets, etc. They were sent to St Martin's Camp, about a mile out of town. He quickly settled in and got to work:

The officers and sergeants at Rouen celebrate Meeanee Day, commemorating the Regiment's victory there in 1843. It is one of the days of the year when Cheshires proudly wear an oak leaf in their hats to commemorate action at the Battle of Dettingen in 1743. Photo: Regimental Museum

It is Easter Sunday today, it poured with rain all this morning but about lunchtime it cleared up and was quite a sunny Sunday. The camp is jolly nice, tin huts with very nice boarding inside, electric light and hot water laid on to each. The camp people have treated the men splendidly, gave them breakfast, (steak, bread, butter and coffee), which was very decent of them when you consider they were not forced to do it. We are shifting down to the town tonight to the barracks, which are really a big fishyard. It does not smell, in fact it is quite a decent place except that our quarters are a bit cramped so we officers are sleeping out at an hotel. I really begin to think Boulogne is going to agree with me.

Monday. Orderly Officer today, and as I do not know where any of the posts are it will take me some time to go round. Some of them are right along the seashore by one of the searchlights. Of course it is still raining, it has not stopped today. Two of the guards are at a Hospital made from two huge hotels, (No.11 General), they are a treat. The men are guarding prisoners and lunatics, which is quite exciting, as the lunatics are continually breaking things, some of them are men pretending to be cracked so as to get their ticket. I got back from my second round at 11p.m. feeling wet, tired and distinctly cross.

Tuesday. We are really very busy just now getting things shipshape and finding out the various stores and offices that we shall have to deal with, to say nothing of the various places of refreshment. I was Officer in charge of an officer's funeral today. It was a most pathetic scene owing to its extreme simplicity. We marched to the mortuary, presented arms when the flag draped body passed, then fell in behind the hearse with reversed arms and slow-marched up to the cemetery. The 'Last Post' is almost too touching and I got an awful lump in my throat, but everything went off all right, except it rained all the time we were there.

Company Sergeant Major Albert Higgs wrote to his parents shortly after arrival at Boulogne. He was assigned to duties at No. 2 Base Hospital. He had joined the territorials' Hyde company in 1909 and worked locally as a warehouseman.

I am exceedingly pleased to hear from you again and I am very sorry I have neglected to write to you oftener, but you will understand what a job it is here with a barrack room full of noisy soldiers. I am in perfect health and I must say I feel almost a surprise to myself to be so, after I look back at what I have tackled and done, considering I had four or five of the worst winter months in the trenches. However, I have still a good fight left in me yet and if we ever have to go up again I shall go with a good heart, but at the same time I am not asking to go. You will see a rather big change in the photo from the last I had taken. Every day puts more of the soldier into a chap and it is nine months since I left home. It does not look to me now, but it seems years doing it. If I started I should fill books and then the censor would cross it out. My final word to you both is don't worry about me; I am absolutely in the pink; never better and every day is a day nearer the end. I remain, your loving son, Albert.

Higgs's contracted time as a Territorial ended on 31 October. He returned home but, within a few weeks, had joined the Navy. In 1917 he married Gertrude Taylor and, after the war, the couple are believed to have moved to St Helens, where he embarked on a new career as a police officer.

Private William Lees did not enjoy his journey to Le Havre on Easter Sunday.

Instead of Easter eggs, we got a loaf each and tin of bully beef and then we were packed up and came down country about 250 miles in cattle trucks. It was very wearying. We are on garrison duty.[46]

Before the war William Metcalf had worked in a draper's shop and lived with his parents at Woodfield Road, Cheadle Hulme. He was now at Rouen. He was *no longer sleeping in a cushy bed, but in the regulation bell tent on boards with three blankets. I have had a good look at Rouen, a beautiful French town, quite large and I have seen a portion of partially gay France. I say partially because mingled with the crowd are English soldiers, some of whom have tasted war as I have. You see the typical high class restaurants and cafes with the verandas and tables and chairs outside, the theatres, cinemas, etc. There is also the River Seine which is busy all day with its shipping and the busy streets but, not least, the cathedral, a beautiful structure.*[47]

Also writing home from Rouen, was Captain Frederick Leah. His letter was to thank the staff at Staley Mills, Millbrook, for sending gifts of socks and handkerchiefs. The socks were particularly welcome as they *wear out remarkably quickly and there is no feminine hand to darn.*[48]

Standing – Company Quartermaster Sergeant Arthur Taylor and Acting Company Sergeant Major Albert Higgs. Seated – Sergeants Harold Taylor and Patrick Moores.

While at Rouen A Company was split up, with half being based at the barracks and the remainder at the École. James Boardman recalled they mainly undertook various guard duties – on ordnance, wood, petrol and cotton stores. Football continued to be played and he remembered a great match between England and Scotland, in which his comrade, Joe Hobson, was picked to play for England. The England team scored the only goal,

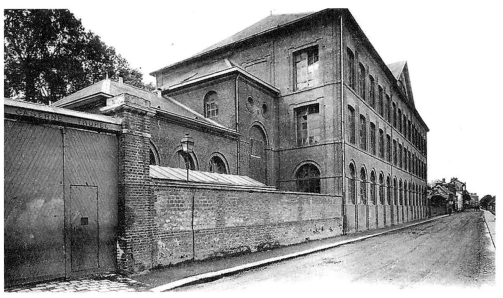

Trupel barracks, Rouen.

from a penalty. Company Quartermaster Sergeant Edmund Ward wrote to the *Stockport Advertiser* appealing for donations of sweaters and pants for the Battalion's footballers. The twenty one year old was well thought of, and had been quickly promoted since he joined the territorials in about February 1913. Educated at Stockport's Commercial School, he had worked as a clerk at the town's railway station but, latterly, before being mobilised, he was employed as a commercial traveller. He was killed in action on 13 November 1916, when he was hit by shrapnel.

Thanks to the generosity of fund-raising activities by the Stockport Lads Club, the men of A Company were enjoying regular hot baths. The Club had sent out a portable unit of five baths, each 4' 6" long and 1' 6" deep, with all the necessary equipment, including a store, water boiler, towels, soap and scrubbers. It was a very welcome addition to their equipment.

Company Quartermaster Sergeant Edmund Ward. Killed in action on 13 November 1916.

On 18 April Captain Henry Cooke was admitted to hospital at Wimereux with measles. Charles Brockbank went to visit him on the 28th and found him looking very well. Two days later Brockbank commanded a party of twenty men sent to St Martin's Camp as 'police' for 2500 recently arrived Canadians.

What a time we had. All they wanted was drink and the police were kept busy trying to prevent the men getting to the village. These Canadians have no discipline, they don't salute officers and never say 'sir' but their physique is excellent.

Around this time Colonel Hesse would have got the news that his younger brother had drowned. For some years Henry Hesse had represented Holt Brothers Ltd, of Liverpool, in West Africa and had been home on holiday for several weeks. He was returning to Africa aboard the *SS Falaba* when the ship was torpedoed by the German submarine U-28. The submarine announced its intentions and had ordered the British crew and passengers to abandon the ship immediately. A number were able to get away in life boats but about half of the passengers and crew were not able to escape. Henry Hesse was one of the 104 people who did not survive.

For much of May, Second Lieutenant Brockbank's main duty was the supervision of burial parties. The dead were men who had died in one of the several army hospitals at Boulogne. Records indicate that, in the spring of 1915, there were four major hospitals in and around the town – 11th and 13th General Hospital and 7th and 13th Stationary Hospital. The burials were in a military plot in the town's civilian cemetery – the Cimetière de L'Est. Over the course of the war nearly 6000 men were buried there. On 2 May, there were three officer funerals.

A horrible accident occurred. One of the coffins slipped out of the rope whilst being lowered into the grave and fell to the bottom, it nearly made me sick and it upset the relatives very much but the other two went off all right.

On one such occasion, on 8 May, he found that he knew the chaplain conducting the service from before the war. It was the vicar of St Wilfrid's Church in Northenden, Reverend Francis Hamilton. Hamilton had been the vicar since 1901 and had only arrived in France the previous day. There is a note of melancholy creeping into Brockbank's diary entries – he concludes his entry for the 8th hoping he has the following day off from duty: *Thank goodness there are no funerals.*

His 21st birthday was on 14 May, but there was no celebration, only the supervision of three more funerals. On the 28th, Brockbank wrote that *I buried young Lord Grenfell V.C. here today, it was a very plain funeral, but very pathetic.* In fact, the man being buried was not the Victoria Cross

The Battalion cooks. Back row (l to r) – Harry Bramhall, William Davies, Harry Cuthbert, John Marsland, Richard Wilkinson, William Bowers and Ernest Burke. Front row – Thomas Donlan, George Furness, 'Kitty' and John Wood. 'Kitty" had joined the Cheshires at Shrewsbury and had accompanied them into the trenches. Photo: Stockport Express

winner of the same surname. However, Captain the Honourable Julian Grenfell was still a brave man, having been awarded the Distinguished Service Order while serving with the 1st Dragoons. He was wounded in the head by shrapnel about two weeks before he died. The man who had been awarded the VC was his cousin, Captain Francis Grenfell, who was killed on 24 May.

On a more cheerful note, one of the Cheshires wrote to the *Stockport Advertiser* in May.

We are very much amused at the consideration that reigns in the old country in regard to the prices of intoxicating liquors. That's a matter which doesn't trouble us much here as there is very little beer drunk by the troops. They mostly go for cider, which is produced locally in huge quantities and is very cheap. Spirits, of course, are taboo to us. The rum ration has been stopped till the winter campaign commences, so you see temptation has been taken out of our way.[49]

Charles Brockbank's particular friends amongst the Battalion's officers appear to have been Cooke and Innes. Both men had caught measles in April and had returned to Britain. On recovery, they were attached to the 2/6th Battalion, at Northampton for a while, but returned on 24 June. Brockbank and Captain Bill Dodge were treated to dinner by the other two. They went to Mony's restaurant on Boulogne's pier. It was a notable restaurant that had been mentioned in 1908 in the "Gourmet Guide to Europe", by Nathaniel Newnham-Davies:

The 6th Cheshires 'somewhere in France'.

The moules to be obtained there are always of the freshest and its fish dishes – Sole Normande or Sole au vin blanc or Sole Dieppoise – are excellent. I have eaten as good a Chateaubriand there as any man could require.

On 1 July the Battalion received a reinforcing draft of ninety four men from the 2/6th Battalion, together with thirty five men returning from various hospitals. The draft arrived under the temporary command of Second Lieutenant Alan Hartley. Hartley had originally joined the Manchester Regiment as a private, leaving his job as a salesman for a cotton manufacturer. He was commissioned in November 1914 and served with the 2/6th Battalion until he went on active service in July 1915. He returned to Northampton on 6 July, Brockbank regretting his leaving as he was a 'cheery soul'. Over the coming weeks Hartley would bring further drafts from Northampton before joining the Battalion full time, transferring to the Royal Flying Corps in 1916.

Brockbank does not seem to have got on well with his company commander, Captain Dodge. He noted in his diary that he wished Dodge could have had a longer period of leave as it was 'different' without him. On 27 July, he notes,

Lieutenant Haworth and his platoon, September 1915. Photo: Stockport Express

Dodge was Orderly Officer today and when an order came through that in future the Orderly Officer had to spend the night down at the docks in a tent, he sent me to pitch it. It was late afternoon when we started off and so we got it all done by 7.30. When I reported it all finished, he calmly asked me if I had got everything down there that I should need during the night. A dirty trick.

He was also less than thrilled to learn that Lieutenant George Churchill, recently arrived from Britain, was being attached to his company.

He is a 1ˢᵗ Lieutenant and I am only a 2ⁿᵈ, although he was gazetted three or four weeks after me.

He did, however, cheer himself up by buying a new, albeit secondhand, gun – a Colt automatic, for which he designed a holster and had it made for him.

One of the main duties of the Cheshires during this period was to act as guards escorting prisoners of war. On 12 August Brockbank commanded the guard for 135 Germans who had arrived at the port of Boulogne.

We had to supply the escort to take them to the Field Punishment Barracks at 6.15 A.M. The French civilians shied stones and potatoes and hooted at them all the way. We had to march them back at 1.15 but had twice the number of escort & eight mounted gendarmes but even then got stones & spuds. An immense hostile crowd.

The weeks passed almost without event. Brockbank was orderly officer on 14 September. He was doing his rounds of the port area when he spotted a woman seemingly making notes. He arrested her as a potential spy but it turned out to be a false alarm. There was more football later in the month, with a victory over the arch-rivals from the Army Service Corps and another over a team from 14ᵗʰ General Hospital. *We won 4-2 and it was a jolly good game.*

The Battalion started the war equipped with two elderly Maxim machine guns. By the middle of 1915 the number of guns had been increased to four per battalion and the Maxims were slowly being replaced with the new Vickers gun. They were also being equipped with the Lewis light machine gun. This was much more portable, only needing one man to carry and fire it and another to carry the ammunition. The magazine held forty seven bullets that could be fired, in bursts, at a rate of 700 per minute. Frank White was the Battalion's machine gun officer and he arrived in Boulogne to give the troops their instruction in the new weapon. There were several training classes over the latter part of September before he left to continue instructing one of the groups at another base port.

Francis White, Battalion machine gun officer.

On 30 September Brockbank commanded a party of newly arrived troops who had arrived at Boulogne and were being sent on to Le Havre. It took until the next day, due to the fact that the train kept stopping. Once he had handed over the troops, he went to 'Cinder City'. This was a large rest camp on the outskirts of the town. The camp had a YMCA hut which, from time to time, was used for boxing tournaments. There was a match during October between the Battalion's James Laffey and a Private Higginbotham, the *Stockport Advertiser* reporting that there had been *some fine defence work had been seen in the first minute. Laffey administered a knockout just before the end of the first round.*[50]

King George visited France on 21 October and Brockbank was put in charge of the party moving his baggage. The king's ship was escorted from Britain by three airships and several destroyers. He was greeted by Field Marshal French.

> *When they had finished the King came off the boat and was introduced to various prominent soldiers. We got a fine view as no one could get in front of us. The King's valet groused at the little motor for the luggage so I commandeered a large lorry and got it all packed in. When we got to the station we put the luggage in the train and then had finished, so in walking back out of the station we had to pass within six feet of the King while he sat at table having his lunch.*

George Jackson, a twenty one year old cotton piecer from Hyde, enjoyed Christmas Eve. Writing to his mate, Percy Sellars, he said,

A group of NCOs at Rouen. Standing – Sergeant James Boyle, Company Quartermaster Sergeant Ted Ward, Sergeant John Hague. Seated – Sergeant Marshall, Company Sergeant Major Robert Morton, Sergeant Thomas Jessop. Photo: Jon Thornley

We have had a very enjoyable Christmas Eve, plenty to eat and plenty to wash it down with and we had a nice concert to follow on as well. Last Xmas, I was up to my knees in water and had bully beef and biscuits for breakfast, dinner and tea. Of course, when we were relieved from the trenches, about eleven o'clock at night, we were given a little pudding. Esther Long's father dished it out to us, he gave us a spoonful each. It ran twelve men to a pudding.[51]

Esther Long's father was Sergeant Tom Long, mentioned earlier. Jackson would only celebrate another two Christmases. He was dead by Christmas 1918, killed in action on 27 September 1918, then serving with 1st Cheshires, to which he had been posted on recovering from wounds he received in 1916.

Second Lieutenant Brockbank spent hours producing the programmes for the concert, which he thought was a great success *but the men's idea was to see how drunk they could manage to get and I must say they managed very well.* On 30 December, he heard rumours that the Battalion would soon be brought back together again so that it could return to the trenches. The rumour was right. The stay at the seaside was coming to an end.

CHAPTER 6

Givenchy

The opening days of 1916 were spent preparing to leave the various base depot areas. There was time for the officers at Boulogne to have something of a party on New Years Day. Charles Brockbank notes that Captain Dodge left two hours before it finished *absolutely binged*. He did not reappear until 2pm the next day, claiming he had neuralgia. *What a joke!* During this time, Brockbank had been taking some photographs of the men and, on the 7th, when Dodge asked him if he had a camera, he could hardly deny it. It was an offence, albeit one treated lightly in the reserve areas but a more serious one if in the front line where, if a man was captured, the photographs could give away information to the enemy. He was told to regard himself as being under open arrest. *I am therefore nominally in Bill Innes' charge but it makes no difference.* It was another indication of the poor relationship Brockbank had with his superior officer.

As they were preparing to leave Le Havre, Colonel R Money, commanding the base depot troops, wrote:

> *As the Headquarters Company of the 6th Cheshire Regiment are about to leave this Base I beg to report that this Company with Headquarters Staff of the Battalion arrived in Havre on the 4th April, 1915. Strength: 14 officers and 287 other ranks. The behaviour of the detachment has been quite exemplary, only one man having been tried by F.G.C.M.* [Field General Court Martial]. *I have not had a complaint as to the manner in which the numerous escort duties have been performed by the men of this detachment. Their guard duties have at all times been well and smartly performed. I have always been able to rely upon the thorough performance of any particularly important duty of the men of this*

detachment. Their behaviour and turnout in town has at all times been excellent. Taking into consideration the situation of Cinder City, and the temptations of Havre, the utmost credit reflects upon Lt.-Col. H. Hesse and the officers and men under his command.

During the afternoon and evening of 8 January the various parties entrained for the village of Pont Remy (with the exception of the men at Abbeville, who marched the eight kilometres). On arrival, the Cheshires had a nine kilometre march to billets in the village of Ailly-le-Haut-Clocher. The Battalion was formally transferred to 20 Brigade, part of the 7th Division and Brockbank was interviewed by the brigade commander. He could not recall his name, knowing him then only as "Hellfire Jack". He was, in fact, Cyril John Deverell who, postwar, was eventually promoted to the rank of field marshal and became Chief of the Imperial General Staff.

Brockbank and Innes shared a billet, which was comfortable, except they found the sheets damp. Sergeant George Dickinson, from Stockport, regarded the little cottage where he was billeted as a home from home, with a good bed.[52] The twenty year old is thought to have worked in a paint warehouse before being mobilised. His service number, 1186, suggests he joined the Territorials in 1911/12, but he had only recently come overseas.

By the end of 1915 the Battalion's original machine gun officer, Frank White, had transferred to 1st Cheshires and been promoted to captain. His place was taken by Second Lieutenant Norman Beaumont. Beaumont was educated at Sedburgh School, in Cumbria, and had been a member of the School's Officer Training Corps. Before the war he was in business as a woollen goods merchant, living in Wilmslow. On 11 January, he was in conversation with Brockbank and mentioned that the Battalion was to have a second machine gun officer and suggested he apply. Brockbank promptly did so and was accepted the next day. It meant he would be relieved of company duties and concentrate on his new role. *Swotted up the gun this evening, taking a lock to pieces & rebuilding it for practice.*

The next day, the 13th, he w*ent out with the guns to try two new ones and had a fine time with them in an old quarry. They fire jolly well except the foresights, which needed some attention. This afternoon we had gun-drill - in the "Mounting-gun". There was a live round put in a belt by mistake for a dummy, fortunately there was no-one hurt but we do not know where the bullet would land.* He also received extra instruction from Sergeant George Birkenhead, the experienced machine gunner mentioned in the previous chapter. On the 14th, Lieutenants Selwyn Hinton and Robert Chantler joined the Battalion, having previously served with the reserve units. Chantler was in his mid-thirties and was in business as an ironmonger, living in the Manchester district of Rusholme. As a young man he had served as a territorial with the Manchester Regiment but, when war was declared, enlisted in the Lancashire Fusiliers. He became an officer in August 1915. Hinton was a school teacher from Hampshire who had trained to become an officer with Cambridge University's Officer Training Corps. He had been serving with 3/6th Cheshires since March 1915. A couple of days after they joined, both men, together with three other officers and eighty three other ranks, were sent to the bomb school at Pont Remy, where they would learn about the use of grenades. Men were also sent for Lewis gun and signalling training at Pont Remy.

General training continued, with a particular emphasis on maintaining physical fitness. There was a cross country race on the 19th, in which all forty two Cheshires finished in the top 200 – there was a total of 1250 runners, so the men were quite pleased to have done so well. Football matches continued to be played including a particularly exciting encounter with a team from 2nd Gordon Highlanders. They opened the scoring and then the teams scored alternately until it was 3 – 3, Charles Brockbank noting,

> *It stayed like that to within five minutes of time and then we managed to pop another one through. They were unbeaten in their league so we feel very satisfied.*

Brockbank had technically been under arrest since the beginning of January over his possession of a camera. On 25 January he was escorted to Pont Remy by Major Leah and Lieutenant George Churchill. *The Brigadier gave me a "fatherly" and then released me from arrest.* The following day the Brigade practised an attack. They were up at 5am and marched the six miles to Pont Remy to join with the other battalions. The exercise was little more than a formation march over muddy fields and through villages and woods for about four miles. They then marched back to the billets.

Orders arrived for the Battalion to move to Picquigny, a village to the northwest of Amiens. The men were up and about at 5.30am on the 27th and moved off from the billets at 8.30. They got to the rendezvous point, only to find the move postponed until the next day, when there was another early start. The Battalion now included eighty new men who had just joined from the 3/6th Battalion.

Billy Innes, Brockbank's friend in the Battalion, had been on leave and rejoined at Picquigny. He was promoted to captain. It seemed to be a popular promotion amongst the men but Brockbank found it *strange for Billy to have his three pips up*. He was also unhappy that Bert George had been promoted over his head. *I wish I could transfer to a battalion which plays the game*. Herbert George was a merchant in civilian life and lived in Chorlton with his wife, Eleanor. He was commissioned on 4 November 1914 and, in 1917, would transfer to the Royal Flying Corps, initially as an observer, before gaining his pilot's wings.

Sometime in the past months, Charles Brockbank had bought a pet dog, which he named Tommy. He had been worrying about what would happen to him, as he would not be able to take the dog with him to the front line. The problem resolved itself on 30 January. *Tommy did a bunk with a battalion of the Manchester Pals today, so I shall not have to destroy him or give him away.*

Shortly after the Battalion arrived at Picquigny, the men were called out to help fight a fire which had broken out in a cotton mill on 1 February. They formed a chain passing buckets of water forward and broke the skylights on the roof so hoses could be brought to bear. Brockbank enjoyed himself on the roof directing the men with hoses. There was a move to Cardonette the next day and the Cheshires' march towards the front line continued on 3 February, when they spent the night at Pont Noyelles, to the northwest of Amiens. They spent the next day resting and there was an equipment inspection, including of gas masks (which they had worn when they were putting out the fire). There was also an inspection of the men's feet, designed to spot any early indications of trench foot, due to being in wet conditions. These inspections would be undertaken every few days when the men were at the front. A further move, on 5 February, took them to billets at Ville-sous-Corbie, only five miles behind the front line. On this day Second Lieutenant Cyril Marsden was officially taken on to the Battalion's strength but was immediately admitted to hospital. The twenty two year old originated from the Southport area, where he had been working for a wholesale clothier. He became an officer in September 1915 and had been serving with the 2/6th and 3/6th Battalions. He was suffering from bronchitis and was evacuated back to Britain for treatment for possible tuberculosis. He returned to duty later in the year.

On 7 February, A Company went into the front line. Whilst some of its number were 'old sweats' from the autumn and winter of 1914, for many of the men this was their first time under fire. It would be a short tour of duty, with B Company relieving them the next day. George Dickinson was with this group and reckoned they were *very lucky as Fritz exploded a mine (something new to us) just on our left*. It happened just as they were being relieved and James Boardman recalled that they had to 'stand to' for a couple of hours, just in case there was a German attack. Over the next two days, the other two companies also spent a day in the front line. There were no serious injuries in this period. However, there was a death. Frederick Axon, a twenty four year old hatter from Stockport, had fallen ill and was evacuated to the field hospital at Corbie. In a time before antibiotics, he died from pneumonia on 8 February.

Frederick Axon, died of pneumonia.

On the 12th the Battalion returned to the trenches to start a tour of duty that would last eight days. They relieved the 8th Devons opposite the German held village of Fricourt, located at the heart of what, in a few months, would become known as the Battle of the Somme. A and B Companies went into the front line, with C in close support and D a little further to the rear in reserve. As well as manning the trenches, the Cheshires took advantage of the hours of darkness to lay protective barbed wire in No Man's Land and improved the trench system. Two men were killed on this first day, no doubt bringing home the reality of war to the new recruits who had joined in the past

George Gouge. Killed in action, leaving a widow and four children in Stockport.

months. George Gouge was a married man with four children who had worked for one of Stockport's hat makers. He was a pre-war territorial and had gone overseas with the Battalion in November 1914, but was one of the many soldiers who had to return home for treatment from frostbite. He only rejoined his comrades in January. He was killed when a piece of shrapnel hit him in the head. Such injuries were all too common at this point in the war and would continue to be so until later in 1916, when troops were issued with the now familiar steel helmets. The other fatality,

Benjamin Sidebottom, joined up in Glossop in mid December 1914 and had been overseas since July 1915.

It was a miserable time, with almost continual heavy rain over the several days they were in the front line. On the 13th there was a heavy bombardment throughout the afternoon and the combination of the weather and the shelling caused the trench parapet to start to crumble. The men urgently got to work building it back up. George Dickinson recorded in his diary that he had had a *very narrow escape, three small shells bursting about fifteen yards from the action we were in.* The next day a German working party was spotted trying to work on improving their barbed wire defences. The Cheshires opened fire and the Germans quickly retreated back to their trench. Patrols were sent out into No Man's Land on the night of

George Dickinson. Photo: Peter Oxley.

15/16th February, but no enemy patrols were encountered. It was, perhaps, a welcome change in activity from the constant trench repair work which, by the 16th, was barely keeping pace with the collapses. One man wrote to the *Stockport Advertiser*:

> *In the supports, we get more shelling but the work is easier because we don't do any firing ourselves. However, I prefer the fire trenches as they are much drier. The Bosch machine guns are very busy and bullets are cracking and whistling past the door of our dug-out all the time I am writing.*

The machine guns were particularly active on the 19th but, even so, the work of repairing the barbed wire had to continue. One man wrote:

> *The worst task I have been engaged in as yet was that of going with a party of men over the parapet one night to repair the barbed wire in front of our trench. Before going out we sent word up and down the line as a warning to our men not to fire on us. Unfortunately, we could not similarly warn brother Bosche. Every time a flare was*

sent up, we fell prone on the ground as we were only a very short distance from the enemy. We stayed out two hours and put up about 120 yards of new entanglements and we were glad to be able to wriggle back into our trench.

Nineteen year old John Holmes had worked in the fur department at Christy's hatworks and had been a territorial since about February 1914. He was a member of this working party and was hit in the chest by ten machine gun bullets. His older brother, Edward, wrote to their parents telling them what had happened. *He was doing his duty and died a soldier's death. He died as you wanted him to die, without fear.*

On the 20th the Devons came back to the front line and the Cheshires withdrew to billets at Ville-sur-Ancre. Private John Cousil, an ironworker from Stalybridge, wrote

Private John Holmes, killed whilst repairing the barbed wire defences.

We have had a rotten time, raining and snowing and up to the waist in water in some of the trenches. But we have come out all right. We have had some near shaves. [53]

Eighteen year old Albert Mallon was the second youngest member of C Company. Like George Dickinson, he had a lucky escape when a shell burst near him. At the end of this tour of duty, he went home to Denton on leave. He would have been welcomed by his mother, Margaret, but his father was also serving with the army and was now in Salonika, in northern Greece, serving with a battalion of the King's Own Royal Lancasters.

The men spent the next few days undertaking fatigues in the trenches and road repairs. In the late afternoon of the 23rd they were ordered to stand to as an enemy attack was expected. In the event, they did not have to go into action, George Dickinson wrote in his diary *All attacks repulsed, our guns playing havoc with the attacking forces. Many heavy losses.* The next day, he was able to get a hot bath and a change of clothing. *Not before time.* 2nd Lieutenant Charles Brockbank returned from leave during the stand to and was later sent to the front line in charge of fifty men to undertake trench repairs.

What a sight it was too, the front trenches had been peppered with every conceivable sort of projectile and were in a pretty bad mess, but after five hours of hard work we had set things pretty well on their feet again. The Engineers were collecting a man who had been standing close to a 12 inch when it burst and were putting him in separate sandbags, but it does not upset you in the least to watch them.

On the morning of 25 February the Battalion paraded and marched to La Houssoye, where they boarded buses to take them to the railway station at Longueau. There had been a heavy fall of snow and the journey took ten hours to cover the forty kilometres. From there, they moved by train to Hazebrouck, from where they marched to billets at Wallon Cappel.

After messing about for an hour or more, we got settled down in a barn. (George Dickinson).

Over the coming days there would be instructional classes for the officers and NCOs, given by Captain Henry Cooke, another pre-war territorial officer. For the men, there would be outdoor training as far as the bad weather permitted.

I took my men out for a bit of a route march this morning and, after a time, got them into a field to give them a little exercise with the rifle like "Swedish" drill. I kept them at it for half an hour and then came home.

(Second Lieutenant Charles Brockbank)

At the end of the month the Battalion was transferred from the 7th Division to the 39th and was attached to 118 Brigade. When the 39th was formed in the summer of 1915, the brigade originally included units from county regiments based in south east England. The training of these men had lagged behind that of the other three brigades and it was therefore decided that they would remain in Britain to complete training. So, when the division arrived in France, 118 Brigade only had its headquarters staff. Its troops would be made up of battalions already in the field. Joining the Cheshires were other experienced territorial battalions, from the Black Watch, Cambridgeshire and Hertfordshire Regiments. The two Black Watch battalions, the 4th and 5th, both recruiting in the Dundee area, had suffered heavy casualties at the Battle of Loos in the previous September and, within a few days of joining the new brigade, were amalgamated and renamed the 4/5th Battalion. These new units brought some welcome practical knowledge of active service to the otherwise inexperienced division.

The weather was particularly bad in the first week of March, with heavy snow falls, alternating with hail and rain. The land was waterlogged, making most of the planned training exercises impracticable, so instruction was confined to lectures. On the 7th the Battalion moved to new billets at Les Ciseaux, about six kilometres away. The march was hampered by snow that fell heavily for the duration of the march. On the 9th, the war diary dryly comments that training continued. Second Lieutenant Brockbank more entertainingly describes the day.

> *We had a glorious snow fight today as there was a foot fall of snow during last night. It raged nearly all day from one end of the village to the other. Casualties, six black eyes and one broken nose. I got off with about five down my neck & one in the ear. Jolly good fun.*

There were a series of inspections by senior officers between the 13th and 15th:

> *Monday. We are to have an inspection today by the Brigadier at 3.0 p.m. The 'Inspection' was an absolute farce as he only rode round the companies and not up & down the ranks, then he gave us an address which was all whitewash, but of course it is always the same.*
>
> *Tuesday. We were inspected this morning by the Divisional Commander, who was very decent, asking all sorts of questions and he was pretty keen on everything. We were given a little talk too, after, which was rot, but he strikes me as being a jolly fine chap.*
>
> *Wednesday. We are to be inspected today by our Army Commander. (Lord [sic]C Munro), we were marched to the ground without a halt (it is five kilometres) formed up with the rest of the Brigade, kept there for three hours whilst we were being inspected and then marched home again without a halt. It was the most fatiguing and nonsensical I have ever seen - the marching us there and back with no halts.*
>
> (Second Lieutenant Charles Brockbank)

On 21 March Brockbank left the Cheshires. He, along with Norman Beaumont, who was the other machine gun officer, and forty four other ranks transferred to the newly formed 118th Company of the Machine Gun Corps. The Corps was formed in the autumn of 1915, recognising that the concentration of the heavy machine guns under a single command allowed the development of new tactics, both in defence and attack. The firepower could be brought against attacking troops with devastating effect. Similarly, accurate fire over the heads of attacking British troops could be brought to bear on the German defences, preventing re-inforcements getting forward to support their comrades in the front line. At this stage of the war, the Vickers machine gun was *the* weapon of mass destruction. As such, the gun pits quickly became targets for the German artillery, earning the Corps the wry nickname of the 'Suicide Club'. Each of the new companies would support an infantry brigade, so Brockbank was able to keep in touch with his old friends in the Cheshires.

On 24 March, the Cheshires moved to new billets at Caudescure, to the south east of Hazebrouck. It was a hard march, George Dickinson writing *everybody done up. Lots have dropped out on the march.* Training continued at the new location, although not with complete success. On the 27th, Second Lieutenant Charlie Norman was accidentally injured in the leg. Brockbank writes that he was teaching the men rapid loading. *It was his own fault, but he gets a 'Blighty'.* Born in 1893, Norman worked as an articled clerk to a solicitor before the war and lived with his parents in Stalybridge. When war broke out he joined the 7th Manchesters as a private but was quickly selected to become an officer, receiving his commission in December 1914. He served with the 2/6th Battalion before going overseas in July 1915. His injury would keep him in Britain until January 1917.

On the 30th, in preparation for a return to action, Colonel Hesse and thirteen other officers visited the trenches that they were going to occupy, near the village of Neuve Chapelle. The move was made the next day, with the Battalion occupying billets at Riez Bailleul, just to the south of the village of Estaires. During the early evening of 1 April they went into the trenches in a sector known as the Moated Grange, which George Dickinson noted was about half a mile to the left of the ruined village of Neuve Chapelle. There had been fighting here at various stages of the war, dating back to October 1914, and there had been fierce exchanges during the Battle of Neuve Chapelle in March 1915. The Battalion deployed with three companies, plus one platoon in the front line, with the remaining three platoons in reserve. The defences were breastworks, rather than trenches, built up as Dickinson wrote like *Blackpool – plenty of sand (bags)*. It was a well developed defensive system, supplied by a light railway that brought rations to the front line at night. On their left were the Hertfordshires and on their right the 7th South Lancashires, a battalion that was raised in Warrington in September 1914.

The Cheshires spent a quiet night and, in the very early morning of the 1st, sent out a patrol into No Man's Land that managed to get close to the German trenches and concluded that they were only weakly held. However, their snipers were active during the day and claimed the life of Ben Williams, a twenty two year old from the Edgeley area of Stockport. He was himself a sniper. The young man had been connected with the Salvation Army and was also a member of the Sunday School Brotherhood in the town. At about 6pm, there was an exchange of fire between the opposing artillery. *We had a very hot time for about an hour. We had about a dozen casualties* (George Dickinson). One of those injured was Henry Leach, also from Stockport. He was badly wounded and was evacuated to the field hospital at Merville, where he died the next day.

Henry Leach, killed in action. A cotton mill worker in civilian life.

The German sniper was hiding in nearby trees. Lance Corporal Sydney Buxton was the NCO in charge of the Cheshires' snipers and, on 4 April, was trying to identify where the German was located. But it was the German who found him. At 11.30am a shot rang out and Buxton was killed instantly. Educated at Stockport Grammar School and employed at a cotton warehouse in Manchester, he was a keen sportsman, playing cricket and football for the YMCA, where he was also an accomplished boxer. Buxton's interests were not confined to physical pursuits – he had a fine baritone voice and often performed ballads and comic songs. The Lewis gunners opened fire on the area of the trees and succeeded where Buxton had not. The Battalion was relieved by the Black Watch in the early evening.

Lance Corporal Sydney Buxton.

One man wounded just before we were relieved by the 4/5th Black Watch. We had a rough time getting him out as the communication trenches were packed with the relieving party. We had to do the last mile to the dressing station over the top, which was rather risky, as rifle and machine gun bullets were flying about.

(Sergeant James Boardman)

With his move to the Machine Gun Corps, Charles Brockbank was no longer under the command of Captain Bill Dodge, with whom his relationship had deteriorated over the months. However, as the Cheshires were back in billets, he decided to go and visit his old comrades for dinner. He took with him *a tin of pineapple, which I knew he hated. He was sick as a dog.*

There was a move to new billets at Merville, where the Cheshires remained until the 14th. The day before leaving they were inspected by Lieutenant General Richard Haking, commanding XI Corps. The latest move took them to the hamlets of Le Paradis and Lestrem, where Colonel Hesse, the Adjutant and the four company commanders went to inspect the trenches they would occupy. On the 15th the Lewis gunners went into the trenches and were followed the next day by the remainder of the Battalion. This was known as the Festubert right sub-sector; they had the Hertfordshires on their left and the 14th Hampshires on the right.

Lieutenant General Richard Haking , with two Portuguese officers.

There was no continuous front line trench system here. Because of the very wet nature of the land, it was impossible to dig trenches and all the defences were sandbag breastworks as separate posts or islands with gaps between each island. Three officers and 120 men occupied one of the posts, about 200 yards from the enemy positions. The remainder of the Battalion was in an earlier front line position, dating from June 1915, about 800 yards to the rear. There were no communication trenches to the posts, meaning movement during the day was impossible. It was difficult enough during the hours of darkness. Men had to walk along the open ground on duckboards and were open to German fire. There was also the risk that, in the darkness, men might walk past the posts and find themselves in the German lines. Similarly, a German patrol might be able simply to walk through the British defences and it required a constant state of alert by the sentries. It was a quiet tour of duty, with little artillery shelling by either side. On 18 April the defences were inspected by the brigade commander.

The Cheshires were relieved the next day and spent the remainder of April in billets first at Le Touret and then at Hingette. During this time they were a reserve battalion for the division but were not called to go into action in support of other battalions. On the 21st forty five men were transferred to the 13th Gloucesters. This battalion was the pioneer unit for the 39th Division. Although pioneer battalions were made up of trained soldiers, armed and capable of fighting, their main role was to provide semi-skilled manual labour, helping to construct and maintain defences, etc. This period in reserve offered the opportunity for more training and particular emphasis was given to musketry and bayonet fighting. Their musketry skills were displayed on 26 April, when they were inspected by General Sir Charles Monro, the commander of the British First Army.

During the night of 28/29 April George Dickinson wrote in his diary that he was up at 3.30am for a walk round the countryside. Perhaps he had been unable to sleep due to the noise from a bombardment he could hear some distance away. *On my way back, I get smells of gas shifting over. Several cases of gas poisoning in the vicinity. Bombardment more fierce than ever.* The bombardment and the gas were probably coming from the direction of Hulluch, some twenty kilometres to the south. The Germans had started an attack on the 27th, firing shells filled with chlorine and phosgene gas. During the evening of the 29th the Battalion was ordered to Stand To, as the German attack had intensified and it was feared it might be the start of a wider assault. In the event, the wind direction changed and the gas blew back on to the German positions. The Cheshires stood down at about 10.15.

On the last day of the month, Second Lieutenant Philip George reported sick. Born on 23 December 1893, he was educated at Manchester Grammar School and lived in the Manchester district of Chorlton with his widowed mother and four siblings. Within days of war being declared he joined the Royal Fusiliers, leaving his job as an articled clerk with a firm of accountants. He became an officer a few weeks later, serving with 2/6th Cheshires until he went overseas in June 1915. George had suffered difficulties breathing through his nose for several years and the condition had worsened since he had gone on active service. He was evacuated back to Britain, where he underwent a minor operation to correct a deflected septum. The surgery healed well and he was given six week's sick leave *in which to stay at the seaside.* He returned to duty in mid-August.

During the early evening of 1 May the Battalion went into the trenches just south of the hamlet of Givenchy-les-la-Bassée. They included a hundred men who, that day, had been transferred from 9th Entrenching Battalion. Seven platoons occupied the firing line, with one held in reserve at Givenchy itself. Their right flank was on the north bank of the La Bassée Canal. The platoon on that flank was some 250 yards away from the Germans, but No Man's Land gradually narrowed, so the left hand platoon was only thirty yards away – within grenade throwing range. The trenches were in a generally good state of repair, except on their left, where there had been much damage by explosions from German mines. Intelligence reports suggested that the Germans were from Saxony.

Givenchy-lès-la-Bassée. The opposing trenches ran across this field, with the distance between them narrowing to just thirty yards as they reached the village. Photo: author

The square heads were pleased to meet us and sent us whizz bangs, rifle grenades and a new projectile I have not seen before. 'Rum jar'[54]. But we soon quietened him down with a speedy return.

(George Dickinson)

James Boardman found the narrow trenches particularly difficult.

This made our work as stretcher bearers very hard, and as casualties were more frequent our hands and elbows were badly bruised in getting men away. We are only a few yards from the Germans. Only this morning one of the enemy shouted 'Chuck us a tin of jam over, Tommy!' One of our chaps looking over was shot through the eye.

The dead man was Private William Corbett, a nineteen year old from Stalybridge. He worked as a nail maker at Summers ironworks before enlisting in January 1915. The young soldier had only arrived in France on 12 March.

Two officers were injured by a rifle grenade during this tour of duty. For Lieutenant Robert Chantler it was little more than a scratch and he remained at his post. It was a more serious matter for Henry Yorke, who was evacuated to Britain for treatment. When war was declared he was studying medicine at Cambridge University but left his studies to join the Cheshire Yeomanry. No photograph of him has been found but his service file describes him as 5′ 9″ tall, with a dark complexion, grey eyes and dark brown hair. He had been overseas with the Battalion since July.

Geoffrey Whitehurst. He left the Battalion in May 1916, as his time as a Territorial had expired but re-enlisted and was back in action with the Cheshires by the end of June. He was wounded in 1917 and again in 1918. He survived the war and is believed to have died in 1965.

On 5 May the men in the front line were relieved by the Black Watch and moved back into support positions in Givenchy village. Private Charlton Harrison had only returned to duty the previous month, after recovering from an injury in December 1915. He was another man who had been at Cambridge University, studying theology, his ambition being to become a clergyman. Just before they left the front line Harrison was killed by a sniper. Whilst in support, 300 men worked as carrying

The main street of a wrecked Givenchy-lès-la-Bassée.

parties for the Royal Engineers. They relieved the Black Watch on the 9th. The war diary describes it as a *fairly quiet day*, although there was the *usual interchange of rifle grenades*. George Dickinson wrote in his diary that it went on all day but that there were no casualties.

Private Charlton Harrison, killed by a sniper's bullet.

During this tour of duty, two new second lieutenants joined the Battalion. Harold Foster and Vernon Spinks are believed to have both worked as civil servants, Spinks with the Inland Revenue. Both had joined the 15th Londons as privates. The Battalion was a territorial one, commonly known as the Civil Service Rifles. Spinks was a pre-war soldier, having joined the Rifles in April 1914.

The Germans blew two mines near the Battalion's positions. One on the right went off in the early hours of 10 May, with another just to the Battalion's left at about 5pm. *You should have seen the muck fly* (Sergeant James Boardman). The day saw the deaths of three men. John Comerford was thirty three and was a married man from Glossop, where he had worked as a cotton spinner. He had been with the territorials from about 1908. Lieutenant Herbert George wrote to his wife, Mary Ellen, telling her what had happened.

John Comerford, killed in action on 10 May 1916.

> *He and several companions were sitting near the entrance to their dugout when a rifle grenade, fired from the German trenches, dropped on the top sandbag above the door of the dugout and at once exploded, killing him and wounding four others. He was spared all pain and suffering. A week or two previously he had had the chance of being transferred to a Tunnelling Company but, although the work might, in spite of its hazardous nature, have offered certain advantages, he begged not to be sent away from the lads, saying he would prefer to stick it out with them to the end. This wish has been, unfortunately, only too quickly fulfilled.*[55]

John Halford, also from Glossop, was killed in the same incident. Sergeant Albert Reid, a married man from Dukinfield, was mortally wounded. He died before he could be evacuated to a field hospital. Harry Lawton, from Stalybridge, was badly wounded and was taken to the casualty clearing station at St Venant, where the surgeons decided to amputate his leg. His condition did not improve and the twenty seven year old died on 20 May

The next day, the brigadier and Major General Nathaniel Barnardiston, commanding 39th Division, came to inspect the positions. It was fairly quiet when they came and remained so until about 4pm, when both sides started up a considerable artillery barrage. It was

John Halford, worked for a paper manufacturer in the Glossop area.

Harry Lawton.

particularly heavy around Givenchy, with several shells falling near Battalion headquarters.

> *Here I am in charge of a sap, only being about 30 yards from the Germans. They shout over to us. Really very worrying. Fairly hot time between 6.30 and 8.30pm, we got all sorts – shrapnel, nerve gas, whizz bangs, grenades, bombs and aerial torpedoes. It was some hot.* (George Dickinson)

The increased activity was due to a successful German attack, some five kilometres to the south, near Vermelles.

There was a return to billets on 13 May, with the Cheshires spending the next few days at Gorre, where there were good billets in the chateau and neighbouring farms. They were officially the brigade's reserve unit, but the men were kept busy undertaking fatigues for the Royal Engineers, which included unearthing and recovering gas shells that had been found around the Givenchy trenches.

> *Germans shell our village, a big shell smashing into a big tree about 15 yards from us, bringing it down. About 30 of us playing house, when Fritz put three shrapnel shells right over us, strange to say, no-one was injured but to see the rush and scramble, bits of shell whizzing all around. An unusual occurrence in this part of the*

Gorre Chateau. It would be almost completely destroyed in the fighting of spring 1918.

line was to see an aeroplane. The Mad Major as he was called. This man was very daring, the most daring I have ever seen. He used to go up high until he was right over the German lines then he would come down with a swoop to within about 100 yards of the German trenches and train his machine gun on the trench and sweep right along, terrifying the troops, machine gun on. Rifle fire used to go up at him but he didn't trouble. He is said to have accounted for a great many of the enemy.

(George Dickinson).

A number of flyers appear to have earned the nickname of the "Mad Major", not all of them actually holding that rank, so it is probably impossible to identify to whom Dickinson was referring.

Further back, in divisional reserve at Le Pannerie, there was a mix of training and fatigues. It was hard work but the men found it relaxing in comparison with being at the front. Several of the men got home leave. William Wadsworth lived in Stalybridge and worked at John Hargreaves' paper mill. He told the *Stalybridge Reporter* that,

When I came away, we had just come out of the trenches and the Territorials have now gone on base duty, where they have got a very good home. I am a stretcher bearer at the present time. Things have been very bad in the firing line, but all the Stalybridge lads have done their best for Stalybridge people and have tried to uphold their honour. I am sorry to say that while we have been in the trenches, we have had one or two casualties. Corporal Ashton and Private Beswick, of Stalybridge, have both been wounded by shrapnel.[56]

The Battalion's rest was over on 25 May and they left their billets at 6pm to relieve the 12th Royal Sussex in the right sub-sector at Festubert, just a few hundred yards north of their last position at Givenchy. As the relief took place, Private John Hudson, from Stockport Road, Cheadle, was killed. The front line was still a series of disconnected islands and three officers and 147 other ranks occupied these, with the remainder of the Battalion in the old front line trench to the rear. At 10.30, the next night, Second Lieutenant Harold Foster and Sergeant Robert Walton went out into No

Robert Walton MM.

Man's Land to reconnoitre the ground in front of Island 10. They were looking for somewhere for a group of soldiers to be best located as a covering party whilst others put up barbed wire in front of the defences. When they were about fifty yards into No Man's Land several Germans rose from long grass in front of them and opened fire. Foster returned fire with his revolver and Walton with his rifle. At this, the Germans retreated to a ditch and started throwing grenades at the two men. At the same time, a machine gun opened up on them from the ditch, wounding Foster in the leg. Almost immediately after he suffered further injuries from a grenade. He managed to get himself back towards the British trench, under Walton's covering fire. Walton then ran back and helped his officer back into the trench. For this act of bravery, he was awarded the Military Medal.[57] Foster had only joined the Battalion at the beginning of April but his war was now over. His injuries were such that he was not able to return to duty and was discharged from the army in 1917. His family connection was with Romford, Essex and he is believed to have died there in 1959.

The tour of duty ended during the evening of the 28th, but not before Private Albert Hough was shot by a sniper. He was a married man who had lived at Old Road, Cheadle and had been on active service since the previous July. Captain Bill Innes later wrote to his family:

Private Albert Hough, a married man from Cheadle, killed in action on 28 May 1916.

> *On the night he was shot, I spoke a few words to him to cheer him up and he told me he would stick it and not worry about the wound. He thought, like I did, that he would get better, though I knew it was serious. The bullet entered his chest and he had very little pain.*

Hough was taken to 33rd Casualty Clearing Station at Béthune but there was nothing that could be done to save his life and he died the next day. His pal, Lance Sergeant Harry Jones, also wrote to his widow.

> *I was quite near him when he received his wound and although it was such a serious one, I can assure you that it was not causing him much pain. This afternoon, I was sergeant in charge of his funeral party and, in an English cemetery, we paid*

our last respects to one who was a good soldier, a cheery soul and a friend to all.

The Cheshires went back into billets at Gorre and, before the month ended, were joined by six new second lieutenants who had been serving with the reserve battalions. They were Theodore Allen, Cecil Ashworth, Thomas Casson, Jack Lee, William Lees and Frederick Russell. Ashworth's stay with the Battalion was less than twenty four hours, as he was transferred to serve with the brigade's trench mortar battery.

These officers were not the only ones to have just arrived in France. Private Samuel Chandley, from Gatley, had been training with the reserve battalion (see Chapter 4) and left Southampton on 9 May. After landing at Le Havre, he and the other members of the draft went to rest camp.

Second Lieutenant Theodore Allen. Photo: Regimental museum

We did nothing at all here, only go round the town for a march. Here we made ourselves acquainted with the French coinage. I had a little chat with one of the Frenchies, who are very amiable and accepted my cigarettes.

12 May – We marched through the town of Rouen about 8.30am, just as people were going to business and we arrived in camp at 11am. We marvelled at the wonderful organisation of the British army as, up to then, we had nothing but bully and biscuits[58] since we left England, so we're thankful for a good dinner and tea – cheese, honey and bread. In this camp, there are thousands of troops resting before they go up to the line and every regiment of the British army is represented. Indians also being here. What a marvellous organisation the YMCA is. We saw about four huts on our way to camp and we have one in our lines. We drew our rifles

Jack Lee. Photo: Regimental museum.

today, also we are told we must only write two letters per week but I am writing more and shall see if they go through. We sleep in tents and go to dining rooms for all our meals, where it is brought to us by orderlies.

14 May – I have had some mix up dinners in my time but nothing like today. Bully and biscuits, boiled meat, potatoes baked in jackets, Maconochies, currie [sic] stew and boiled rice. They all went down very well and I enjoyed it all with a little bread.

19 May - Again, boiling hot and what makes it more difficult is we can't get any water to wash. This morning, I went and washed in a tub which about 200 of us had washed in. They have issued us with our smoke helmets. I went to a lecture in the YMCA on Switzerland, which was very good indeed.

24 May – Today we had the heliograph explained to us but had to come off it, for it started to rain.

30 May – We left Rouen for the front. I was with the fatigue party and managed to get us a second class compartment. We left at 3.45pm and we were in the train all day and night. We arrived at Abbeville at 2am and stayed there till 7.30am, when we went off again on another long train ride.

31 May – All the time, men were getting out of the train and picking daisies, lying on top of the carriages and doing all sorts of things. The French were cheering us up all the way. We came through beautiful country but, also, desolation and destruction. We arrived at our destination about 12 o'clock and then had to march five miles with full packs and rifle – it nearly put us all out. We had a lovely billet – an old shippon patched up with plaster. Fifteen of us are in it and plenty of company with rats. We can hear the guns quite distinctly. We are two miles from the firing line and expect to be going up on Monday night.

We have all been sent to the 5th Cheshires but why, I don't know.

At about this time drafts totalling some 200 men arrived in France after training with the 2/6th or 3/6th Cheshires. Like Chandley, the others probably presumed they would be sent to the 6th Cheshires in the front line but, as the Battalion had not been involved in large scale action, suffering many casualties, there was no need for reinforcements. As a result the men were sent to a variety of different units, including the 5th Cheshires and other battalions of the Regiment. Others of this group were sent to other regiments. Eighty seven of them were posted to the 1/5th King's Own Royal Lancasters, where they became known as the 'unlucky draft' as, by the end of the year, a very high proportion of them were dead or badly wounded. Some were killed so soon after their posting that their official documentation never caught up with them and they are recorded by the War Graves Commission as still being 6th Cheshires. Within the constraints of this book it is not possible to tell the stories of all of this draft. Private Charles Platt was one of the first to die. The eighteen year old enlisted in February 1915, leaving his job at a local bleachworks and his parents at Terrace Place, Stockport. His service file records that, whilst in training, he had forfeited three days' pay for stealing something from the billet. On the evening of 1 August 1916, half the King's Own battalion was engaged in digging communication trenches. It was a quiet night and the work had gone well. However, whilst they were making their way back to billets, they came under German artillery fire, which killed three and wounded another eleven. Platt's head wound was serious and he had died by the time his comrades were able to get him to the main dressing station.[59]

As far as is known, Chandley survived the war and returned to Gatley where, in 1925, a man of this name got married at St Mary's Church in nearby Cheadle.

There was a return to the support trenches in Givenchy on 6 June. *Both lots of artillery opened fire, it was Hell let loose, we thought our last moments had come as the shells were dropping thick and fast all around. The place simply rocked,* noted Sergeant James Boardman. After that the situation quietened down for several days, although the weather deteriorated, turning the bottom of the trenches into thick mud. On the 11th they relieved the Black Watch in the front line, their place in the village being taken by the Cambridgeshires. *Everybody wet through. If it rains much more, we shall have to swim for it. Dugouts like sump pits,* James Boardman wrote. In spite of the conditions, it was necessary to continue maintaining the lines of barbed wire in No Man's Land. With there being no continuous trench system here, the wire assumed even greater importance as a defensive measure. On the night of the 14th, a group of men were working on the wire when a German trench mortar shell

Private William Matthews, died of wounds on 15 June 1916.

exploded, badly wounding Private William Matthews. His brother, James, tried to speak to him before he was evacuated to the field hospital but he was unconscious and there seemed little hope that he would survive. He died the next day. The twenty eight year old lived in Glossop with his wife Emma and their two children and had been employed at Johnson's rope works.

On 16 June the Black Watch organised a raid on the enemy trenches. It was well planned and adjacent units, including 6th Cheshires, were aware of the raid and were in a position to give support if needed. The German positions were 'softened up' by a combination of shelling from the artillery and by the trench mortar battery. Even a mine was blown to divert attention. The raid was intended to capture prisoners who could be interrogated. James Boardman wrote that *My squad was kept busy with casualties, and it was breakfast time before we got all the wounded away.* Second Lieutenant Douglas Rigby was injured by falling debris from the mine explosion. Educated at Marlborough College, he worked as a clerk for a steel merchant before the war. He joined the Battalion in July 1915 and, standing at six feet tall, towered over the men in his command. The debris fractured his left clavicle and right humerus. After treatment in the UK, he joined the 3/6th Cheshires as a bombing instructor, then at Oswestry. On 6 December he was instructing a group of men in how to clear a trench with grenades. A Corporal Johns dropped a grenade. Shouting 'Look out!', Rigby flung himself to the ground and was fortunate in only suffering shrapnel wounds to his ankle. On recovery, he was posted to 1/4th Cheshires and was serving with that Battalion when he was killed in action on 4 September 1918. He is remembered on two war memorials in the Knutsford area.

Raids were a common tactic at this point of the war and the Corps commander, Lieutenant General Richard Haking, was, reportedly, a keen proponent of raids, asserting that a division could not be regarded as a proper fighting formation until it had successfully carried one out. The size of the raiding party would depend on the objective and may have comprised little more than a handful of men up to a whole battalion. The one conducted by the Black Watch involved about eighty men. The practical objectives of any raid were to capture prisoners, kill anyone else they came across, gather intelligence by taking any documents or maps and to gain a sense of how well the enemy trench was defended. It was also felt that morale was bolstered by raids, which maintained the aggression and fighting spirit of the troops. Raids were always conducted during the hours of darkness, so the men could get across No Man's Land without being detected. This meant that the enemy morale would be weakened as defenders could never entirely relax at night, not knowing if a group of enemy troops might suddenly appear in their trench, armed to the teeth with clubs, knives, axes, knuckledusters – any weapon capable of killing or maiming without making too much of a noise.

Although there is no mention in the Cheshires' war diary, it seems as though some of the men must have been positioned in No Man's Land to act as part of the covering party for the Black Watch raiders, in front of their island defences. The night gave rise to an account that has passed through the generations. George Dickinson had been in hospital for two weeks, having his tonsils removed. He rejoined the Battalion on the 12th. The family account is that he was in No Man's Land and participating in the raid (although it is known none of the Cheshires actually did so). It is probable that he was either supporting the raiders or, later, was out looking for injured men. A flare went up and the German machine gunners opened fire. He dived into a shell hole for cover but was then wounded by a trench mortar shell, his leg bleeding badly. He became unconscious but came to a short while later. Dickinson heard whispered German voices and realised they must have left their trench to look for wounded raiders, whom they might take prisoner. He saw a figure, realising it was not another Tommy and feared for his life. The German looked around him and then hoisted Dickinson onto his shoulders. But instead of taking him back to the German lines, the soldier carried him through the British island line to a dressing station, where Dickinson's wound received attention and the German became a prisoner.

It is a remarkable account and one which might be initially dismissed as a 'good war story' to tell the children. But, at the dressing station, the two men exchanged names and addresses. The German, a man called Glandorf, and Dickinson kept in touch, exchanging letters and Christmas cards until the late 1930s, when contact was lost, probably because of the war.

During the night of 17/18 June, the Battalion was relieved to billets, where they stayed for the rest of the month. During this period two officers left the Battalion to join the Royal Flying Corps to train as pilots. Records indicate that Frank Astle was injured in a flying accident in early 1917 but recovered and, postwar, was still serving with 208 Squadron in Ismailia, Egypt. Samuel Collier is understood to have served with 43 Squadron, flying Sopwith Camels.

On 1 July the Cheshires relieved the 11th Royal Sussex in the village line at Richebourg St Vaast. This was on the northern edge of the sector they had been fighting in since the beginning of April, only some eight kilometres away from Givenchy-les-la-Bassée. Colonel Hesse was not amongst them. Several days before, the divisional commander had written to the War Office suggesting that Hesse was *lacking in energy, enterprise and powers of leadership*. He felt that he had served his country *well and gallantly* and that he should be recommended for being 'mentioned in despatches'. It was proposed that, because of his command of German, Hesse would be suitable for posting to a prisoner of war guard unit. In the event he was posted to the Welsh Reserve Brigade. It was not a happy time for Hermann Hesse and, in the autumn of 1916, he was tried by court martial for being drunk. Several witnesses gave evidence that they had seen him in Antelope Hotel, Dorchester, drunk or 'the worse for drink'. The court acquitted him – its reason is not recorded in Hesse's service file. He returned to command the Battalion briefly in the spring of 1918.

Some miles to the south, 1 July 1916 saw the opening of the infantry assault of the biggest British offensive, in conjunction with the French, thus far in the war, the Battle of the Somme. The fighting would go on for months, whilst on the first day nearly 20,000 British soldiers were killed, more than on any other single day, before or since. In due course, the Cheshires would play their part in the Battle, but that is a matter for Chapter 7.

On 2 July, James Boardman went to have a look at Richebourg.

> *There was hardly a house standing. There were also the ruins of what at one time had been a beautiful church. We visited the graveyard, where there were some terrible sights. Shells had dropped all about, and you could see the bones of people who had been buried for years.*

On the 4th, newly promoted Lieutenant Colonel William Stanway joined the Battalion as its commanding officer. Born in 1881, Stanway joined the army as a young man, serving in India as a private with the 2nd Royal Welsh Fusiliers. He married his wife, Emily, in Bombay in 1906. When war was declared, he was a company sergeant major and was commissioned as a second

Lieutenant Colonel William Stanway.

lieutenant, in the Fusiliers, in November 1914. He was promoted to captain by September 1915. Only a few weeks before joining the Cheshires he had been awarded the Distinguished Service Order for an act of 'conspicuous gallantry and ability' at Givenchy. Amongst the Cheshires' other ranks, Stanway would acquire the nickname of 'Black Jack', on account of his 'five o'clock shadow'.

The Cheshires returned to the support positions in Givenchy on 8 July for a tour of duty that lasted until the 14th, when they went into the front line. On the 13th five men were killed by shrapnel. They were in a working party when a shell exploded amongst them. Second Lieutenant Charles Brockbank was in the vicinity with his machine gun crew. *The Cheshires sent fifteen men out in front to put up barbed - wire for practice and of course they got seen - result five killed and seven wounded. What criminal folly.* James Boardman wrote that it took the stretcher bearers a good hour to get the wounded away and then they had to remove the dead. The same night Captain Alfred Smith and Captain Bill Innes led patrols into No Man's Land to reconnoitre the area for future offensive operations, such as a raid.

The next few days in the front line, saw the Battalion subjected to heavy artillery bombardment. It was intended as a way of pinning down troops in this sector, so that commanders could not know if it was the prelude to a German attack. Thus, if it had been intended, it made it more difficult to divert men from this sector further south to the Somme. On the 15th, Second Lieutenant Robert Morton reported for duty. Born in 1893, the stonemason from Stockport had been a territorial since 1910. At the beginning of the war he was a sergeant and, shortly afterwards, was promoted to become A Company's sergeant major. He was selected to train to become an officer, spending a few months with the 2/6th Battalion before going overseas again.

Robert Morton, recently commissioned. Photo: Jon Thornley.

This tour of duty saw a number of casualties, including several fatalities. Amongst the latter was William Harrison, who lived at 57 Brinksway, Stockport, with his wife, Annie, and their child. He had worked as a cotton doubler at the nearby Gorsey Bank mill. He was serving with Annie's brother, who wrote to her to say that Harrison had been buried by a shell explosion and when they had dug him out he was found to be unconscious and died almost immediately, without any suffering. In fact, he is buried several miles away, next to the location of a field hospital. It seems likely therefore that Harrison's death was anything but painless and that telling the widow otherwise was an act of kindness.

Another raid on the German positions was planned for the night of 19 July, at Red Dragon Crater at Givenchy. The crater had been caused by the blowing of a German mine under the British front line on 22 June. There was then an infantry attack, which the 2nd Royal Welch Fusiliers, who were holding this part of the line, fought desperately to repel. This was the incident for which Lieutenant Colonel Stanway was awarded his gallantry medal. The citation for the medal states,

William Harrison, died of wounds caused by the explosion of a shell.

> *When the enemy exploded a large mine which wrecked some 75 yards of our trench, and then attacked in force after bombarding the spot heavily, several officers being incapacitated, Captain Stanway, who commanded the next company, at once took charge and, after the enemy had been driven off, with great skill and coolness occupied the near lip of the crater and organised the defences.*

The crater was given its name in recognition of the Fusiliers' efforts and their heavy losses on the day.

On the opposing sides, small trenches, known as saps,usually ran out from the main trench line into No Man's Land. They helped patrols and raiders getting forward by providing some protection and were also manned as advanced posts to warn those in the trench of any enemy activity. The plan for this raid was to use two British saps to get forward and then rush a German sap to capture prisoners believed to be occupying it. A smoke barrage would cover the raiders and the explosion of a small mine under the crater lip held by the Germans would act as a diversion.

There were twenty seven raiders, all from B Company – two officers and twenty five other ranks. Captain Richard Kirk commanded one party

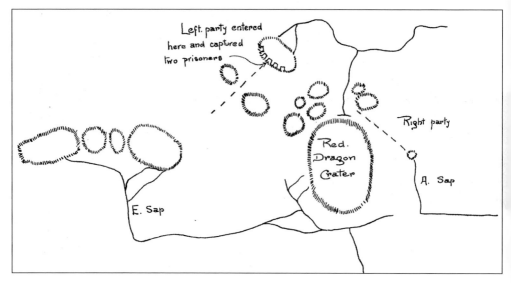

A sketch of the area to be raided on 19 July.

Lieutenant Tom Casson.

which would work round to the right of the Crater, while Second Lieutenant Tom Casson and his group moved to the left.

Under cover of the diversionary explosion, Casson and his men moved round the back of Red Dragon Crater, coming across a smaller crater, which they found to be occupied by the enemy. About fifteen Germans were manning the nearside lip of the crater. There were five dugouts excavated into the lip and two saps connected the crater to the main German trench. The Cheshires shot five men in the crater and also tossed grenades into the dugouts. Two Germans came out of the last dugout and surrendered. The Cheshires now came under fire from rifles and trench mortars, so withdrew back to the British lines with their prisoners. The two Germans were escorted to the rear and handed over to an officer from 118 Brigade headquarters.

On the right, Kirk's group pushed forward in spite of the heavy rifle and mortar fire, entering a sap at the rear of Red Dragon Crater. They found this to be badly damaged by artillery fire and unoccupied. The heavy fire made it impossible to make any further progress and, after fifteen minutes, the party withdrew.

Casson was awarded the Military Cross for this action, the citation noting that the action's success was *largely due to his fine leadership*. Born

Givenchy-lès-la-Bassée. This field is the site of Red Dragon Crater, created by the explosion of a German mine. In the copse of trees, there is a recently erected memorial to the British tunnellers who were also mining under the field. There is also an older memorial to the 55th Division. Photo: author

in 1896, he lived in Stockport and worked as an audit clerk for the Co-operative Wholesale Society in Manchester. In September 1914, he was one of a number of lacrosse players from the town who joined the 6th Manchesters as privates. He saw action at Gallipoli where, on 9 June 1915, he was wounded in the shoulder. He received medical attention in Cairo, before being evacuated back to Britain. After he had recovered, Casson applied for a commission and was posted to the Battalion in May 1916.

Casson was not the only man to receive a medal. John Titley had worked in a draper's shop in Stockport. He was one of the specialist grenade throwers on the raid. He was awarded a Military Medal, as was his chum, Fred Utley.

John Titley MM.

Lance Corporal Fred Utley was wounded early in 1917 and evacuated home, where he died at a military hospital in Southampton on 8 March. His body was brought to Stockport for burial, with full military honours. Three volleys were fired over the grave and the Last Post was sounded. One of the firing party was Thomas Casson, who had returned to Britain at the time, due to illness. Casson himself died on 17 May when, during a training exercise, a faulty grenade exploded.

Fred Utley MM.

John Jackson, from Stalybridge, was another awarded the Military Medal. Promoted to sergeant, he was killed in action in November 1916.

The Battalion was relieved from the front line on 20 July and moved back to the support positions in Givenchy. However, before that happened, there were four fatalities. During the early hours, Jimmie Robertson was out in No Man's Land searching for a man who had been wounded during the raid. He was killed by shrapnel. Sometime during the day a grenade was thrown into the British trench, mortally wounding three men. William Mellor was a

Jimmie Robertson, from Stockport. Killed in action on 20 July 1916.

John Jackson MM. A prewar Territorial. Photo: Regimental museum

twenty two year old from Glossop, who worked at a paper mill. He had two brothers serving, although one had been taken prisoner earlier in the year. Two of his mates tried to help, but he died almost immediately. Frank Heathcote's mother, Esther, got a letter from his friend, Bert Heelis.

> *I saw him receiving first aid in the trench and every care and great patience was taken in rendering it. He was quite conscious and it may be a source of relief to you to know that many times he was heard to whisper 'Mother'.*[60]

Private William Mellor, mortally wounded by a German grenade.

He died shortly after. The family lived in Dukinfield and Heathcote had worked as a cotton piecer at Queen's Mill. The third victim, John Ryder, came from the Glossop and Hadfield areas. He regularly attended the Sunday services held by the Battalion's Roman Catholic chaplain. When Father Philip Northcote heard he had been injured, he dashed to the spot.

> *I gave him Absolution, Extreme Unction and the Last Blessing and then helped carry him to the dressing*

John Ryder.

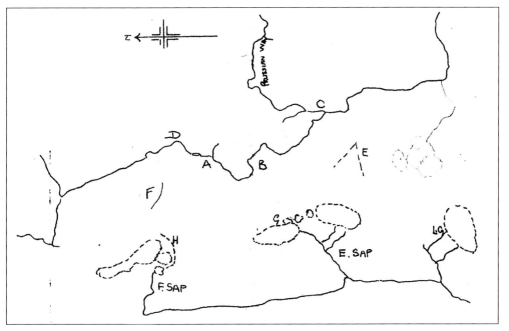

Sketch of the area to be raided on 22 July.

station. He recognised me and said "I am done, Father". We carried him along but before we reached the dressing station, he died of his wounds. My coat was soaked in blood. I said Mass for his soul this morning and buried him this afternoon.[61]

Ryder and his two comrades, are buried at the military cemetery at Gorre, a few hundred yards behind the front line.

Another raid was planned for the night of 22/23 July. It would be commanded by Captain Alfred Smith. The objectives were:-

A. To capture enemy prisoners
B. To prevent the enemy moving troops to another sector
C. To destroy the trench and a mine shaft
D. To lower the enemy morale

The raiders were split into two parties. Smith and twenty five men would be ready in one sap dug forward of the British trench, whilst another officer would command a similar sized party in another sap. Intended to be a surprise attack, only one round of artillery fire would be directed at the enemy trench. The raiders would then rush their objective. The password that the troops would need to get back into their trench at the end of the operation was, appropriately, 'Sweating'. The operation did not go according to plan.

It seems as though the Germans were expecting something to happen. As the Cheshires ran across No Man's Land, they heard whistles being blown and heavy rifle and machine gun fire opened up. Both raiding parties continued forward, finding the gaps that had been earlier cut in the German wire. However, as they got through the gaps, they could see the German parapet was lined with troops and more could be seen moving towards the front line, in answer to the signal whistle. Colonel Stanway later reported

> *Bombing and rifle fire then became intense and our men retaliated with bombs. The place eventually became too warm and it was deemed advisable to withdraw. A certain amount of damage was done to the enemy before withdrawal, the whole of the raiding party ultimately regaining our trenches with one officer and five other ranks wounded, after being out for twenty minutes. Captain Smith, although wounded, got his men out of this hot corner in a very able manner.*

William Chaisty was amongst the wounded. The twenty three year old came from Hadfield and worked as a cotton weaver at Ashton Mills in Hyde. He was taken to 1st Casualty Clearing Station at Choques but there was little hope of his survival and he died there on the 28th.

The *Glossop Chronicle*, in its edition of 28 July, reported that Captain Smith had been wounded in the heel. After that was attended to at the dressing station, he returned to the front line, where he was soon hit by shrapnel in the left arm and shoulder. He was hospitalised in Britain and, on recovering from his wounds, was posted to the staff of an officer cadet battalion, where his experience could be passed on to young men hoping to be commissioned. He remained with the cadet battalion for the remainder of his war service.

Private William Chaisty.

The Battalion was relieved to rest billets, first at Le Choquaux near Béthune and then at Le Touret for the first week of August. James Boardman recalled it being a time for relaxation and sports. On 2 August a football team from D Company played Headquarters. The match ended scoreless and a replay took place next day.

During the game a shell burst at one end of the ground. Fortunately play was at the other end and no one was hurt. You should have seen the spectators scamper. We went on with the game.

Cricket was played on the 4th. Married men played singles, the former winning 70-31. They had a rematch the following day and the married men won again, 56 – 42. There was also a football game between officers and sergeants. The officers won 4 – 1, in spite of Captain Billie Lees colliding with another player and badly dislocating his ankle. Second Lieutenant Charles Brockbank, who came to watch the match, recorded in his diary that *he had to*

Captain William Lees. Photo: Regimental museum

have a dose of morphia and then when getting it put back he had chloroform. He had to return to Britain for treatment and was admitted to a military hospital in London. It was not until November 1917 that Lees was deemed fit enough to return to duty.

There was a brief return to the trenches between 8 and 10 August. After that, the Battalion started a march south to a completely new sector. By the 13th, they had reached Villers-Brulin, where they stayed for nine days, undertaking various training exercises. The march then continued for several days, averaging about fourteen kilometres a day. The discipline on the march was very good and the stamina of the soldiers meant that few had to fall out on the long days. No doubt they kept their spirits up with the Battalion's marching song:

> We are the Cheshire b-hoys,
> We are the Cheshire b-hoys,
> We know our manners,
> We spend our tanners,
> We are respected wherever we go;
> When we're marching down Wellington Road
> Doors and windows open wide,
> We are the boys of the first 6th line,
> We don't give a fuck for the firing line.
> We are the Cheshire Boys.

On 25 August, they reached Bus-le-Artois. They had arrived on the Somme.

CHAPTER 7

Thiepval

Plans for a major Allied offensive in 1916 were first discussed at a high level Allied conference held at Chantilly on 29 December 1915. Out of that meeting came a proposal for an attack, on a sixty kilometre wide front, astride the River Somme in Picardy, where the British and French armies met. Fate intervened on 21 February, when the Germans launched a major offensive of their own, against the French town of Verdun. The town held historic significance as a protection of France's eastern border and included many forts and other defensive positions that had been strengthened after the Franco-Prussian War. The Germans believed, with some reason, that the French would not want to suffer the national humiliation of the town falling and, consequently, would divert resources to that sector. General Erich von Falkenrayn, Chief of the German General Staff, wrote to the Kaiser setting out his plan.

> *A mass break-through – which in any case is beyond our means – is unnecessary. Within our reach there are objectives for the retention of which the French General Staff would be compelled to throw in every man they have. If they do so the forces of France will bleed to death.*

By the middle of May, the French position at Verdun had become desperate and resources intended for the Somme offensive had, as anticipated, been diverted there. Even though the French contribution would be reduced, it remained vital that the offensive go ahead. Although the French would still launch an attack, mainly south of the Somme, the major contribution to the offensive would now come from the British.

General Sir Douglas Haig, now commanding the British Expeditionary Force, wrote that the objectives would be:

1. To relieve the pressure on Verdun
2. To assist our allies in the other theatres of war by stopping any
further transfer of German troops from the Western front
3. To wear down the strength of the forces opposed to us.

After several days of heavy artillery bombardment, the infantry attack went in on 1 July. As mentioned in the previous chapter, there were very heavy losses but there was also some success. The British part of the battlefield is divided by the road between the towns of Albert and Bapaume. The attack south of the road, and nearest to the French sector, was generally successful, with the Pals battalions from Liverpool and Manchester capturing and securing their objectives. To their south, the French attack was also successful. North of the Albert – Bapaume road, the attack was a disaster. In many sectors men were cut down in No Man's Land and the survivors had no option but to retreat back to their trenches. In other parts, attackers did reach the German line but were unable to hold their position against counter attacks. Over the following days and weeks there were a series of smaller offensives in the south of the battlefield which, although costly for both sides in terms of casualties, generally favoured the British attackers. In the north of the battlefield, the failures of 1 July meant there was nothing to exploit and, apart from small scale actions, there was no continuing offensive for some time.

Captain John Diggles was a pre-war officer of the Battalion. Since the beginning of the war he had commanded one of the companies and, more recently, had been the Battalion's adjutant. His administrative and planning skills were recognised when he was transferred to the staff of 118 Brigade as the Brigade Major. Diggles would be closely involved with the planning and co-ordination of the forthcoming attacks.

It was in the north of the battlefield that the 6th Cheshires went into the front line on 26 August, relieving the 2nd Durham Light Infantry near Thiepval. The village had been a prime objective for the attacking troops on 1 July and was still in German hands nearly two months later. General Haig wrote, in one of his despatches to the War Office, that the German defences in the area

may fairly be described as being as nearly impregnable as nature,
art and the unstinted labour of nearly two years could make them…
The Thiepval defences were known to be exceptionally strong, and
as immediate possession of them was not necessary to the

development of my plans after the 1st July, there had been no need to incur the heavy casualties to be expected in an attempt to rush them. The time was now approaching, although it had not yet arrived, when their capture would become necessary.

Louis Hadfield, from Glossop, was one of the men who had transferred to the Machine Gun Corps earlier in the year. Second Lieutenant Charles Brockbank recorded in his diary that Hadfield's team was in close support of the Cheshires, just fifty yards behind the front line. Within ten minutes of setting up their guns there, Hadfield was dead, killed by shrapnel. Before enlisting, twenty six year old

Private Louis Hadfield, a cotton piecer from Glossop. Killed in action.

John Smith, mortally wounded on 26 August.

John Smith lived in Denton and worked as a hat finisher for Cook, Smith & Co. He was in the front line trench, serving with the Cheshires' C Company, and was mortally wounded. His platoon sergeant wrote to his father saying that, although he had not been killed outright, there was no hope of recovery.[62] Smith is buried just behind the front line and is remembered on the war memorial at Denton.

It had been raining for several days and conditions in the trenches were bad, although James Boardman's note in his diary was, of course, not literal: *Everywhere up to the neck in slush.* There was heavy enemy shelling of the front line trench and the communication trenches, throughout this tour of duty and all available men were kept busy doing their best to repair the defences. It seemed to be an almost never ending task. As soon as repairs were made, the shelling would demolish them again or the parapet would collapse due to the wet conditions. There were injuries from the shrapnel every day and, as one of the stretcher bearers, Fred Taylor was kept busy. On the 29th, his sergeant wrote to his mother saying he had been killed in the shelling.

Stretcher bearer John Smith.

Death was instantaneous and without pain. We are all sorry to lose him for he was a very good lad. One of the best and during the time he was stretcher bearer, I have always found him ready and willing to undertake his duties regardless of personal risk.[63]

Taylor lived in Hazel Grove and worked at Hollins Mill, in Marple.

Each night officers would lead small patrols into No Man's Land to examine the extent of damage that had been done to the enemy's wire. Throughout 1 September the British artillery kept up fire on No Man's Land with the intention of destroying the wire in preparation for an attack. In response, the Germans heavily shelled the British trenches, causing considerable damage.

During that night Captain Dick Kirk led a small raiding party across No Man's Land to the German trench opposite. Kirk had commanded B Company since it was formed in the autumn of 1914 with the merger of two of the pre-war companies. Born in 1885, he lived at the family home in Stalybridge and worked as a clerk for the Manchester & County Bank (through a series of subsequent mergers, eventually part of the Royal Bank of Scotland). With him was a sergeant and five other soldiers, including Private James Eyre, who wrote to his wife in Dukinfield, telling her of his exploits.

When we got there, we entered the trenches and went up the trench. We had gone about twelve yards when we came across a dugout. Just as we were making our minds up what to do, we met a German

1 September 1916. Captain Richard Kirk led his raiding party from the front line at Thiepval Wood to attack German positions near the location of the commemorative Ulster Tower. Photo: author

sentry at the other entrance and he mistook us for one of his own. Captain Kirk shone his flashlight in the sentry's face and when he saw we were British, he took to his heels and cried for help. Whilst he was going for help, we went down the dugout and when we got to the bottom of the steps, we must have caught something, as we set an alarm going. Captain Kirk dashed the door open and we found that it was full of Germans. So we put a few of them out of the mess and then we retired. When we got to the top, we met the Germans coming from all directions. Then the fun commenced in earnest. They found out that we were only a few, so they followed us and I can tell you that we were very nearly captured. We had to fly for our lives. When I was rushing through the wire, I got entangled in it. I had to tear my clothes and my hands before I could get loose again.[64]

Within days, Eyre and Sergeant Arthur Kellie learned they had been awarded the Military Medal for their bravery during the raid. Kirk received the Military Cross, the citation in the *London Gazette* reading:

> *For conspicuous gallantry while leading a patrol in the enemy's trenches. He shot three of the enemy in a dug-out and skilfully withdrew his patrol without any casualties on finding that the alarm had been given."*

Eyre and Kellie were both discharged from the army during 1918 due to ill health; but it is not known if this was related to wounds or an illness.

Sergeant Arthur Kellie MM.

Officer patrols also went out during the night of 1/2 September. One is believed to have been led by Lieutenant Vernon Holmes. Born in 1893, he had been educated at Hulme Grammar School, Manchester and lived nearby with his parents in the then affluent suburb of Whalley Range. He was a director of the family firm of clothiers and was commissioned at the beginning of October 1914. He was awarded the Military Cross for this patrol and his action in leading a party, two days later, which brought in fifteen wounded men from No Man's Land.

The Battalion received three new second lieutenants on 1 September. They were George Cowpe, Harold White and Sydney Yorston. Cowpe was born in 1895 in the Burnley area and was educated at the local grammar school, where he was captain of the cricket team. He studied textile industries at Manchester School of Technology – his intention being to join the family cotton firm, owned by his father and uncle. He got engaged to Mabel Proctor in October 1915 and, soon after, received his commission as a Second Lieutenant and was posted to 3/6th Cheshires. Just before he left Britain to go on active service, the 3/6th Battalion played a cricket match on 22 July against Ellesmere College, in Shropshire. Cowpe was caught out for four runs – the Cheshires then declaring. The College could not match their score of 168. Once overseas George Cowpe regularly wrote home and, after the war, a book of his letters was published privately[65]. He had

Second Lieutenant George Cowpe.

arrived in France on 29 August and wrote his first letter home the next day

> *I am now in a Third Class French railway carriage, on my way to the front, but I don't suppose I shall go straight to the front line. Third Class carriages here are very poor arrangements but they have got seats… We are supplied with bully beef and dog biscuits… We have just had tea, consisting of dog biscuits and something like soft soap in appearance but called 'Green Plum Jam'. It wasn't so bad… The speed of this train is by no means excessive, but the bumping is… It is now 6.40 Thursday. We arrived at this camp forty minutes ago and were informed that we should have to get out of the train, but we have no idea what is going to happen to us. I am sat on my mac by the railway side writing this … We are going to complete our journey in a few minutes by motor coach.*

Another young officer landed at Le Havre in the early hours of 2 September. Philip Chattaway enjoyed a privileged upbringing, being educated at Eton College and the University College of Wales, where he was a member of the Officer Training Corps. He became a second lieutenant on 13 April 1916, serving with the 2/6th and 3/6th Battalions. He kept a diary of his experiences in France, which is now held by the

Philip Chattaway. Photo: Regimental museum

Regimental Archives. Chattaway records that he travelled by boat up the Seine to Rouen on 3 September and spent the following two weeks in camp there. His entry for one day notes

> *Early parade under the CO. Running about and playing leap frog down the road. Got absolutely fed up with the whole proceedings. Outpost scheme in morning and worked in syndicates. Have done this sort of thing before and know my way about. Did the thing for the syndicate in a few minutes and spent agreeable morning smoking in a cornfield.*

Meanwhile, in the front line trench on 2 September, the Cheshires were relieved back to the reserve positions and their place taken by the 11th and 12th Royal Sussex and the 14th Hampshires. These fresh battalions would take part in a large scale attack the next morning. To their immediate right, south of the River Ancre, troops would, once again, try to capture the strongpoint known as the Schwaben Redoubt, whilst others would try to wrest the village of Thiepval from German hands. Both had been objectives for the attack on 1 July. The British artillery bombardment started at 5.10am and, shortly after, the troops attacked across No Man's Land. The Cheshires moved forward to the support trenches but were not called on to go into action. Nearby, three other divisions were also attacking. For the Cheshire men, this was their first time in close proximity to a major action. Not even the 'old sweats', like James Boardman, who had been on active service since November 1914, had experienced anything like this:

> *Zero. At last the guns crash. Hell! What a row. You can't hear yourself speak. What an inferno! Wherever you look you see shells bursting. Glancing at the enemy trenches all you can see are lumps of something going up. The sky is one mass of flames. Mingled with the bursting shells you can see the colours of the different kinds of rockets which Jerry is sending up as signals. Added to all this is the whistle and rattle of the machine gun bullets. The first wave goes over. What a sight! Men being mowed down like ninepins. The second wave moves on. A third near by. Then another. The enemy is retaliating with a vengeance. We take cover and wait for news. We now get busy. The first lot of wounded arrive, those who are able to walk being first. We hear that our lads have taken the Jerry*

first line and are hanging on like grim death. In some cases we have taken two and even three lines, but by teatime are driven out of them by the heavy counter attacks of the enemy. The casualty list must be a very large one as the wounded have been pouring in since before 6 a.m. The artillery continue to blow hell out of one another throughout the night.

As on previous occasions, the German defence proved too strong and, whilst the Hampshire and Sussex men had got into the enemy front line trench, by nightfall, they had been forced out and were back at their starting point. They were then relieved by the 6th Cheshires, who now held the British front line again. Several of the Cheshires were wounded during the day.

The stream of wounded has never ceased since it started yesterday morning. The last few days on this sector have been hell on earth. About 9.30 a.m. we got a message to attend some wounded who had been collected in during the night. We took tea for them and re-dressed them. The M.O. asked me to take a message to the nearest Company Head Quarters, which was C Company. Here I got on the phone for some stretcher bearers. As I was returning I was told that a wounded man was lying in a shell hole in front of the line. I went out and got him safely in our lines. It was only just in time, as when I got in the trench the machine gun bullets began to whizz by. I thought little of it at the time, but I learnt later that I had been recommended by the C.O. We eventually got all the wounded clear, and returned to our own Aid Post for a well-earned rest, but we did not get much as the wounded were coming in all the day. The shelling is still very heavy and too close to be comfortable. At night we got the order to move up to the Advanced Aid Post. Our snipers had gone out to search for wounded. They brought in 17 and it took us all night to dress them. They were in a fearful condition. We gave them tea and food which they ate ravenously. It would be about 2-30 a.m. of the 5th when we got back to our own Aid Post again for a rest, but there is no rest for the wicked. Wounded men were still coming in at intervals all day and night. We were relieved about midnight by the Black Watch, and went back to a place called Englebelmer.

(James Boardman)

Boardman was awarded the Military Medal for his bravery in rescuing the wounded man. One of the men he attended to was Second Lieutenant Robert Chantler. Born in 1882, he served as a Territorial soldier with 6th Manchesters before the war and, in September 1914, joined the Lancashire Fusiliers as a private. He was commissioned the following year and posted to 2/6th Cheshires before going overseas. A shell had exploded near him burying him and showering him with shrapnel which caused several wounds to his arms and legs, although none were very serious. He returned to Britain for treatment, returning to duty in May 1917. He did not serve overseas again but was posted to 2/6th Cheshires and, later, to 32nd Middlesex. His army service ended, dishonourably, in January 1918, when he was court-martialled for being drunk and was dismissed from the service.

During 5 September the Germans fired gas shells at the Cheshires' positions but no injuries were caused. The Battalion was relieved in the evening and moved back to billets at Englebelmer. They had barely got settled in when they were shelled again with gas. The men put on their gas masks and took cover in the cellars of the buildings and the incident quickly passed over. Over the next few days they undertook various working parties, mainly building dugouts in the front line trench. Periodically the billets were shelled with high explosive, demolishing several houses on the 12th, about which Second Lieutenant George Cowpe commented:

> *I have just done a "bunk" into the cellar, for a good number of unwelcome visitors have just spluttered within a stone's throw of this house and a few pieces rattled round the place. A few men, about five or six, have been hit – one of our sergeants fairly badly. [He] has been carried off on a stretcher. Things like this make me feel wild with the war. If I had anything to do with it I wouldn't have another man billeted in this place.....On occasions like this, seeing a sergeant carried away, badly wounded in three places, I feel like a caged lion.*

Later that day the Cheshires moved back into the front line, opposite the village of Beaumont Hamel – another heavily defended German strongpoint. Shortly after they got there, one of D Company's specialist grenade throwers was hit by shrapnel and died within a few minutes. James Smith was twenty seven and lived with his parents at Brighton Street,

Stockport. He was a teacher at Wyclifffe School until he enlisted in November 1914.

A major phase in the continuing offensive to the south of the Somme was planned for 15 September. As diversionary tactics, troops on other parts of the battlefield would undertake small scale operations. For the Cheshires, this would mean a raid on the enemy trenches. Captain Bill Innes and Second Lieutenant William Riley each commanded a party of fifty men. Machine gunners, under the command of their old friend Charles Brockbank, would give covering fire and the artillery would lay down a barrage which would 'creep' across No Man's Land, the raiders keeping close behind the protective fire. They went over the top just after 5.30am but were held up when they found the expected breaks in the German wire had been filled by temporary barriers known as knife rests. The raiders were subjected to very heavy machine gun and rifle fire and had no choice but to withdraw back to the British trench.

There were casualties, of course, but for the men caught in No Man's Land it could have been worse. Sergeant Allan Bradshaw, a pre-war territorial from Hadfield, was dead. Born in 1892, he was a skilled engraver, working at Dinting Printworks. Captain Innes wrote to his father, telling him what had happened.

Sergeant Allan Bradshaw, killed in action on 15 September

> *His injuries were such that he must have died instantaneously. He was very close to me at the time, although I did not actually see it happen. He got out of our trench, along with me and I must tell you he had already been wounded in the arm, so that you may know how very gallant a fellow he was, to come out again more or less crippled as he was. His body was recovered and brought down to a little cemetery here and will be buried tonight."[66]*

Bradhaw's body is buried in Knightsbridge Cemetery, Mesnil –Martinsart and he is remembered on the war memorial at Hadfield.

Charles Brockbank wrote in his diary:

> *Bill Innes is all right but shaken, he was blown down by a shell. I got back to the dugout and found a parcel of kippers so we sat down and had a good breakfast, I had seven so you can see I was hungry. I tried to sleep this morning but failed.*

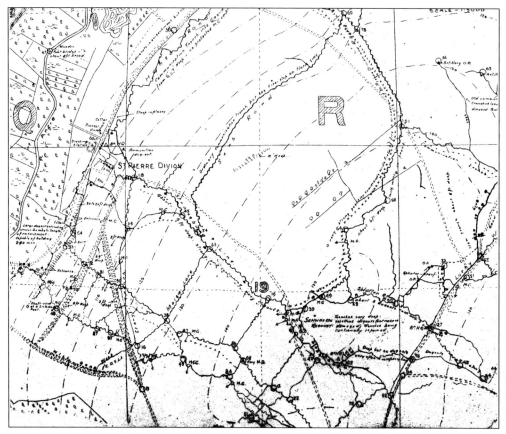

British trench map of the area of the 6th Cheshires' main contribution to the Battle of the Somme.

William Riley was not so fortunate. He had been shot in the left thigh and was evacuated back to Britain for treatment and did not return to duty until August 1917.

It was rarely safe to recover the bodies of men who had been killed in No Man's Land and, in this sector, where there was no movement of the front line, bodies lay there for weeks and often months. It was a breeding ground for rats.

> [They] *are quite a pest here. We have to hang our rations on lines. Then they are not safe as the rats can do tight-rope walking. They are a very hungry lot, as one of them bit the nose off one of our men whilst he was asleep.* (James Boardman)

The tour of duty continued to be difficult, with regular shelling from enemy artillery and trench mortars. It meant the men were again having to make repairs to blown-in trenches. Several men transferred out of the Battalion during this time. Sixty went to the Royal Engineers' 174th Tunnelling Company; Major Frederick Leah went to 2/6th Gloucesters which, in due course, he would command; Captain Thomas Gibbons and Lieutenant Herbert George both joined the Royal Flying Corps.

On the 20th, Second Lieutenant John Chorlton joined the Battalion. The young man was still only twenty and trained for his commission with the Manchester University Officer Training Corps. He was accompanied by Second Lieutenant Philip Chattaway who, as mentioned earlier, had arrived in France at the beginning of the month. Chattaway wrote in his diary:

Had dinner at HQ, with the CO and Brown, White and others and came on at about midnight to D Company. The next day, he went up to the front line and was shown round by Captain Innes. *Came back and got the fright of my life in latrines when a 5.9 landed just over.*

Another raid on the enemy trenches took place during the evening of 26 September. As for earlier raids, the primary objectives were to take prisoners and kill those they could not capture. There would be two parties. The first group would comprise two officers and forty five men and they would enter the trench. A second group, of two officers and thirty men, would remain on the parapet of the German trench, ready to give covering fire if it was needed. There would be some diversionary tactics, intended to allow the raiders to get across No Man's Land undetected. Thick smoke should have greatly reduced visibility but, at the last minute, the wind direction changed, blowing the smoke back over the British lines. At that point, dummy soldiers were lifted up by men hidden in No Man's Land. This trick worked and the German machine gunners opened fire on the dummies, allowing the raiders to get close to the enemy trench. The Battalion's Lewis gunners kept up fire on the area immediately behind the front line, preventing reinforcements getting forward; the guns of the Machine Gun Corps, in support, fired off 132,450 rounds.

Second Lieutenant Bob Morton is thought to have been one of the officers on the raid. Years later, aged ninety, he was interviewed about his wartime experiences.[67]

September 1916. Ancre British Cemetery can be made out on the rising ground on the left of the photograph. The area above and to the right of the cemetery is the area raided by the Cheshires on 15 and 26 September.

I was given the job of timekeeper. My job was to go and sit on the German parapet and blow the whistle when it was time to come out. What a daft job. No glory. No honour. No anything except to sit there and blow a whistle and keep your eye on things.

The men managed to get into the trench, as planned, but found it full of 'knife rests' and barbed wire. They had difficulty in getting themselves out again and had to rely on the covering party for assistance. Standing on top of the parapet, they were exposed to machine gun and rifle fire but kept the Germans at bay by throwing grenades. Two men were killed and several others wounded. Amongst the latter was Private Tom Slack, from Olive Terrace, Broadbottom, near Hyde. An officer wrote to his wife telling her how he had been injured. *He was amongst the leading men of his party to get into the enemy trenches. We*

Private Tom Slack. Mortally wounded during the raid on 26 September.

were subjected to a very heavy machine gun fire and your husband was hit in the back with several of these bullets. Some of his comrades carried him back to our lines, where his wounds were at once dressed by the doctor and he was then put on a stretcher and carried out of the danger area.[68] Slack was taken to a field hospital, some miles behind the front line, in the town of Doullens, but there was nothing that could be done to save his life and he died there on the 28th. He was 23.

Second Lieutenant Philip Chattaway was thankful that the situation quietened down in the days immediately after the raid. Captain Innes was in hospital, having reported sick with a high temperature, so they were *short-handed and very tired. Wet in afternoon – made trenches very sticky. Boche smashed in Long Sap in afternoon. Mended it at night.* In one of his letters home, George Cowpe recounted that night there was a German in the trenches opposite who could speak very good English. He shouted such things as 'How are the Cheshire boys?' 'When will you have enough?' 'How do you like that, Thomas?'

South of the River Ancre another attack had finally forced the enemy out of Thiepval but the defenders of the Schwaben Redoubt had another successful day. The remainder of the month was much as before, with constant efforts to repair trenches damaged by enemy fire. Private Harry Lee, from Glossop, learned he had been awarded the Military Medal for a now unknown act of bravery, probably undertaken during one of the earlier raids. Private William Evans was killed on 28 September.

He was in a dugout at the time and a shell came and went right through the roof before bursting. He was hit by a piece of this shell in both legs and one piece also pierced his heart. He became unconscious as soon as he was hit and died before recovering consciousness.
(Lieutenant George Ogden)[69]

Private William Evans, from Glossop, killed by a shell explosion.

The same day as Evans was killed, troops of 18th Division made another attack on the Schwaben Redoubt. They managed to take its southern and western edges but could not make further progress. The next twenty fours were spent hurriedly consolidating the gain, turning the edge of the Redoubt into the new British front line.

Before the war boys as young as fourteen could join the territorials and, when the Battalion went overseas in November 1914, a blind eye was turned to a number of them who were underage for overseas military service. However, since those early days the army had tightened up its procedures. One young man was found to be under eighteen and was sent back to a base camp on the Channel coast to wait for his birthday. During the afternoon of 4 October, the Cheshires were, at last, relieved from the front line and moved to billets in huts at Martinsart. It had been a long and trying tour of duty.

Martinsart, a village close to the line but far enough away to escape constant attention from German artillery.

It was supposed to be something of a rest, although the men were kept busy with fatigues, Second Lieutenant Philip Chattaway noting in his diary entry for 8 October that he had been *woken up at an ungodly hour in the morning to take trench mortar bombs up to Knightsbridge. Rained all day.*

During the morning of the 10th they returned to the front line, relieving 16th Rifle Brigade at Thiepval. As well as manning the defences, the next three days were spent digging assembly trenches, ready for an attack on the main part of the Schwaben Redoubt. Harry Garner was killed while digging. One of his mates wrote to his parents, saying he was hit by shrapnel between 4am and 5am on 13 October. The nineteen year old worked as a carriage cleaner for the London & North Western Railway at Stockport Station. He was originally buried just behind the front line but, after the war, his body was moved to a cemetery in the village of Authuille

Chattaway took the opportunity to write to his mother:

We are being relieved in a day or so and jolly glad I shall be. This place is enough to get on one's nerves. Curiously enough and quite contrary to expectations, I find my nerves are pretty well all right....

We are managing to hang here somehow. The Boche is a bit shaky after the hammering he has had and isn't very active. If he were, I don't quite know how things would go. The men are wonderful. Nobody who has not actually witnessed it can have any idea of what they go through. If after this anyone ever says anything about the working man, I shall be up in arms at once in defence of the haggard, pale-faced, eternally cheerful fellows I see each dawn. A typical example of his humour is here. These German dugouts are infested with lice. I took off my vest today and went over it with a hammer. One very small lance corporal was heard this morning explaining to his pals that he was woken up in the middle of his sleep by two of them trying to turn him over.

Construction of the Schwaben Redoubt started in early 1915 and, by the summer of 1916, was a heavily fortified area, approximately 500 metres wide by 200 metres deep. As well as a well defended outer perimeter, there was an internal system of trenches, together with strongpoints for machine gun posts. Its defenders were believed to have been of battalion strength. Its capture had been a key objective for the first day of the Battle of the Somme and, indeed, it was taken by the 36th (Ulster) Division, but they were forced out within a few hours. As mentioned earlier, the front face of the Redoubt was in British hands by mid-October. The next attack, for which the Cheshires were preparing, would take place on 14 October.

The actual assault on the Redoubt was the responsibility of the 4/5th Black Watch and the 1/1st Cambridgeshire. The Cheshires would be held in reserve but would bring their Lewis guns to bear on a trench to the immediate west of the Redoubt, known as the Strasburg Line. This connected to another strongpoint at St Pierre Divion, about 700 metres away, and their fire was intended to hamper any attempt to send reinforcements to the Redoubt. They also had orders to be prepared to support the attack by the Cambridgeshires and to exploit any opportunity to advance the line west of the Redoubt. There was meticulous planning for the attack, with each company having specific objectives and the soldiers were fully briefed, Brigade orders confirming that *Every officer, NCO and man taking part in the attack will be told what the scheme is and what his duty is.*

Zero hour for the attack was 2.45pm and the three battalions moved forward, keeping close behind the Royal Artillery's creeping barrage. Within minutes the troops attacking the left of the Redoubt reported they

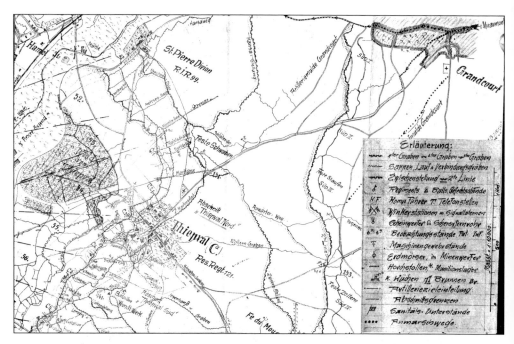

German trench map showing the Schwaben Redoubt – 'Feste Schwaben'. Map courtesy of Jack Sheldon

had captured their objective – the northern edge. To their left, the Cheshires also moved forward and, by just after 3pm, reported they had taken thirty prisoners.

The attack was supported by 118th Company, Machine Gun Corps. Their guns were to be mounted on the British trench parapet and would fire on the northern edge of the Redoubt and just behind it (to prevent reinforcements getting forward) until the attackers were nearly there. Second Lieutenant Charles Brockbank had his Vickers machine guns in position by 2pm. Then he had

Private Harold Hewitt, killed in action on 14 October. He lived in Stockport where he worked as an engine cleaner for the London & North Western Railway Company.

> *to wait until 2.46, when the barrage started and the infantry went over. I have never seen anything like it in my life. The Germans came over without coats on, boots unlaced, showing what a surprise it had been. The Bosch artillery woke up and buried my gun team without injuring any of them and then, a few minutes later, it buried me. It is an awful sensation.*

Howard Bryant left and his grave at Mill Road Cemetery, close to where he was killed on 14 October.

The Royal Flying Corps maintained observation of the attack and, at 3.50pm, one of its planes reported that all objectives appeared to have been captured. In fact a small area remained in German hands and, at 4.40pm, two platoons of Cheshires were sent to assist the Cambridgeshire men in forcing the attack forward with a grenade assault on the defenders. Howard Bryant was one of C Company's specialist grenade throwers and had gone forward alongside his platoon officer. Together they moved along the enemy trench system within the Redoubt and established a post where they could throw their grenades at the Germans. Whilst there Bryant was killed instantly when a trench mortar shell exploded on the side of the trench. The twenty year old worked as a hatter for James Robinson & Sons Ltd, in Stockport, where he lived with his parents at Christie Street. Bryant is buried almost on the spot where he died, at the War Graves Commission's Mill Road Cemetery. After the war, his family had his gravestone inscribed 'He gave his life for one and all'.

Fighting continued for several hours and it was not until 10.30pm that all of the Redoubt was securely in British hands.

Like Brockbank, many of the Machine Gun Corps men had started out with the Cheshires, transferring when the Corps was formed. Four of them were together during the attack: Ambrose Morris, a piecer from Stalybridge; Arthur Ramscar, a clerk from Stockport; Harry Gosling, also from Stockport, where he worked as a leather dresser; and Thomas Vivian, who lived in Hyde and worked as a labourer. Ramscar takes up the story.

Harry Gosling. Killed in action.

> *Ambrose, myself, the officer and three others took the first gun over. After some time, another and myself were sent back for ammunition and, after searching for half an hour, I came across one of the boys who was left with the gun. He was wounded and told me that the officer and one of the men were also wounded and that Ambrose was staying and trying to get the wounded in. Some two hours later, after dark, a party of us went out again to try and find the gun. We searched all the ground thoroughly and found nothing whatever and came to the conclusion that Ambrose and the other wounded man, Harry Gosling, had got back.*[70]

Tom Vivian said that he had seen Ambrose Morris. He had been wounded and was going back, across open country, to the dressing station. Neither Morris nor Gosling were seen alive again. Morris' body was never recovered or, at least, identified.

Ambrose Morris. His body was never found and identified.

It had been a costly day for the Cheshires. Over sixty had been wounded and twelve were dead. Amongst the fatalities were Second Lieutenant Philip Chattaway and Lieutenant Vernon Holmes. The medical officer, Lieutenant Stanley Walker, had also been killed, reportedly by a shell explosion while he was attending to the wounded. During the night the Germans kept up an artillery barrage and there was a counter attack, which was easily repulsed.

The Germans continued to shell the British positions throughout the next day and made two counter attacks, the second using flame throwers.

Much of the Cheshires' action during the Battle of the Somme took place in these few fields. Photo: chavasseferme.co.uk

Both were repulsed with relative ease. The Battalion was relieved from the front line during the afternoon of 16 October, but not before Second Lieutenant Robert Booth was wounded by shrapnel in the left buttock. The wound was sufficiently serious for him to be evacuated back to Britain, where he was admitted to hospital in London. He had recovered by March 1917 and was posted to the Army Service Corps, where he served with the 55th Divisional Train, rising to the rank of captain, until he returned to civilian life in 1919.

In the billets at Aveluy, Second Lieutenant George Cowpe took the opportunity to write home.

> *I must open with the great news that ... [censored].... will probably get the Military Cross for the way in which he persevered and finally captured a bombing post. Let's hope he is successful. From all accounts he deserves it. We shall have a lot of rewards coming to the Battalion. Everybody is shaking hands with himself..... I walked a few hundred yards from here this morning to view some Tanks, but a man ran out to tell us that we could go no further without permission from GHQ. I don't think I would trouble Sir Douglas. I think the Germans are pretty well fed up. Our adjutant[71] asked one of their captured officers how they were liking it now. He said 'Oh, it's terrible'. Our Adjutant said 'Yes, you beggars, this is what you gave us in 1914 and we are just beginning now. We have thousands of guns ready to come up.' The chap was glad to hear that he would be sent to England and when the Adjutant said 'We are not such a bad lot as you think we are,' the German said 'No, I*

A sketch of the area, taken from the regimental history.

don't think you are.' Some of the Germans went down blubbering,
absolutely demoralized… All keep your peckers up and don't worry
about me. I'm quite all right."

In the early hours of 21 October the Germans counter-attacked the
Schwaben Redoubt, entering it in two places, but their hold was tenuous
and the defenders drove them out with skilful use of grenades. Later in
the day battalions of 39th Division made small advances, capturing
positions known as Stuff Trench and the Pope's Nose. The Cheshires were
not involved in the fighting but supplied fifty men to act as stretcher
bearers. However, in the evening they were ordered forward to reinforce
the troops in the Schwaben Redoubt.

About 7 o'clock, the Battalion got the order 'Prepare to move off
immediately in fighting order'. We fell in and were moved to a place
some distance behind the firing line and settled down. As soon as

we got settled down, A Company was ordered to move up to the line at once, and was provided with a guide. This was about 8.30pm and it was a fairly dark night. We trudged on and on and the guide lost the way. We moved through mud knee-deep, which clung to your legs and you had to use nearly all your strength to draw your leg out. It was a bitterly cold night....We came across some old German dug-outs and put the men in whilst .....[censored] ....went away to try and get in communication with Battalion HQ by means of telephone. At 1pm, we got the order to return to a spot behind the lines and reaching there about 4 o'clock, we got our first food since moving off. After that we returned to our original billets. What a picnic and how jiggered we are.

(Second Lieutenant George Cowpe)

The day had claimed the lives of three men, including Jim Shaw, who was one of the Battalion's signallers. He was killed instantaneously by the explosion of a shell. The Signals Officer, Second Lieutenant Robert Morton, knew him and his brother Albert from school days. He wrote to Shaw's parents. *His death is deeply mourned by his companions in the Signal Section and I feel the loss greatly of such a good signaller, a fine soldier and schoolmate.*[72]

The next few days were spent in billets at Aveluy and Martinsart. George Cowpe quite enjoyed his time here, going to the villages in search of bread.

Jim Shaw, a hatter from Stockport. Killed by a shell explosion.

Rations were very short. We found great difficulty in buying any. We stayed in one shop about one and a half hours and had great sport in trying to make some French girls understand what we meant. We spoke very little French and they could speak a bit of English. We managed to get half a loaf from them. We bought a cauliflower and some potatoes with some other thing, rammed them in a sandbag and carried them on our backs in turn. Don't worry about me getting dumpy. I shall be cheerful to the end of the show.

The Cheshires returned to the trenches on 29 October, occupying the line near Thiepval and, from 1 November, at the Schwaben Redoubt. By comparison with earlier tours of duty, this one was relatively peaceful and casualties were very light.

Corporal George Davies, died on 5 November from wounds to his shoulder and thigh. He lived in Hadfield and worked locally as a cotton piecer. In his spare time he was assistant scoutmaster of the local troop and a keen footballer.

> *We got up into the line through mud deep enough to satisfy anybody but, after getting my platoon in position, I had still to find what mud really was. My platoon got in all right without a casualty and I set off to report "Relief complete". I found that the mud I had then to traverse was in all places up to the knees and, in several places, up to the thighs. What a terrible 200 yards! Each time I visited my platoon I had to wade through the stuff and it just about jiggered me each time. One advantage was that we had to keep low and there wasn't much of a trench. Another thing there wasn't much of was food, for the officers hadn't much time to buy in, and we just about managed to exist. We sent three of our servants out of the line to search for food. They managed very well. Yesterday afternoon, we had tea at five, consisting of porridge, three boiled eggs each and cake. At nine, we had dinner. This consisted of grand soup, meat, potatoes and peas, followed by tinned fruit and cake. This morning, we have had porridge, bacon and tomato – so things are looking up.*

(Second Lieutenant George Cowpe)

They were relieved back to billets on the 4th. Stretcher bearer James Boardman returned from home leave on the 6th.

> *Terrible weather—mud, mud, mud, once more up to the neck in it. We had just got down for the night when there was a terrible crash. We found out that an ammunition dump was in flames. It was about three-quarters of a mile away. Shells were bursting for hours, and splinters dropped in our camp, wounding several men.*

Plans were now well advanced for a major offensive which would later be given the official designation of the Battle of the Ancre. The Cheshires had been in France for exactly two years and this would be their first major

St Pierre Divion, July 1916 – still in German hands.

attack. In that regard, it can be said that they had had a lucky war up to this time. There would be seven divisions in the offensive – approximately 123,000 men – attacking both north and south of the River Ancre. The five divisions on the north bank would attack towards the villages of Beaucourt and Beaumont Hamel, whilst the two on the south bank, 39th and 19th Divisions, would have the hamlet of St Pierre Divion and the trench system south of it as their objectives.

Immediately south of the River, 16th Sherwood Foresters, part of 39th Division, would attack northwards, with all four battalions of the Division's 118 Brigade advancing on St Pierre Divion. To their right, 19th Division would advance to the east, towards Grandcourt. The attackers would be supported by the artillery, which would employ a ruse of bombarding the enemy trenches for several days, starting at thirty minutes before dawn and continuing for an hour, before falling quiet. It was hoped that the Germans would become accustomed to the shelling and, therefore, be less prepared for the actual attack when it came on 13 November.

During the night of 12/13th November, the four battalions of 118 Brigade formed up near the Schwaben Redoubt. From left to right were the 4/5th Black Watch, 6th Cheshire, 1/1 Cambridgeshire and 1/1/ Hertfordshire. Each battalion was in four waves with, approximately, fifty yards between each wave. Behind them, 14th Hampshire was in close support but remained in dugouts for protection and, held in reserve at Thiepval, was 16th Rifle Brigade. All units were in position by 3.30am. The Regimental history[73] describes the conditions the men were about to face. The ground had been churned up by shellfire for months and the mud was so deep that the rate of advance was calculated at fifteen yards a minute. Men would have to sit down to pull their legs out of the mud. All the landmarks had gone and there was nothing to act as a guide for the correct direction of the attack. The slope of the ground meant that it was not possible to dig jumping off trenches as they would be in full view of the enemy. So, before zero hour, Captain John Diggles, the Brigade Major, laid out white tapes to mark out the assembly area. It meant the men had to lie down in the mud and keep their fingers crossed that the German artillery did not spot them and open fire. Fortunately, the darkness protected them.

It was still dark at zero hour, 5.45am, and a heavy mist had come down, drastically reducing visibility. In front of the men of 118 Brigade were a number of objectives, the final one being St Pierre Divion. When fully in German hands, the Redoubt had been connected to the hamlet by a trench known as the Strasburg Line. Running north from that was Serb Road and, running south, was Maisie Lane. Both were early objectives for the attackers. On the right of the Brigade attack was the Hansa Line, with the final objectives being St Pierre Divion and Mill Road trench running north east from the hamlet.

The initial advance went well, although William Booth, a cotton spinner from Hyde, was fatally shot in the neck as the men went over the top.[74] The leading troops of the Cheshires A Company, advancing in two waves, made progress towards Serb Road; but the subsequent two waves lost contact with them due to the darkness and weather conditions. At the same time, Captain Dick Kirk led B Company forward and, twenty minutes later, sent a message saying they had taken their first objective at Maisie Lane. Men from the Black Watch had lost direction and drifted into Kirk's position. His message said he was in command of about 200 Cheshires and Black Watch. However, he was unsure of

Private William Booth, killed in action on 13 November 1916.

his exact position and would have to be certain where he was before he could go on. The message was taken back to Battalion HQ by a runner and, no doubt due to the very muddy conditions, it was not received there until some ninety minutes later.

We fixed our bayonets and were over the top as one man. I went over with the left of our first wave, my own platoon. The smoke from the bursting shells and the mist made it impossible to see many yards in front. We reached our first objective in fine style and that was the last I saw of our right. I got to the second objective with a small party and, knowing it from the map, recognised it as the right spot. Here we got lost in the mist and saw none of the later waves coming on. A party of two other battalions joined my party and here we began to get opposition. We moved on, bombing dug-outs and, seeing a party on our left, summoned them as friends. The mist made it difficult to distinguish people. The party turned out to be Germans and came on us with bombs. We fell back into a trench close behind and opened rifle fire and a Lewis gun on them. When we got back into the trench we found another party of Huns on our left, who were able to get an enfilade fire on us. There was another party behind us. We tried to coax the left to come in as prisoners but they opened fire on us and we replied.... We were pretty well surrounded and when thirty Bosche suddenly rushed out on our right without rifle and equipment to give themselves up as prisoners, things were rather interesting. I got hold of one of them and said 'Wo ist Kamarade?'. For answer, he drew a circle on his hand and represented us by a spot in the centre and I thought 'You are not far wrong.' We searched them in the trench for weapons and the wretches shook with fear and would have given us anything, but I was too annoyed with them to bother about souvenirs and merely chucked the stuff on the parapet. One Bosche was so funked that I lost my temper, biffed him one and shoved him bodily on the parapet. He was a Prussian Guardsman, I believe.

(Second Lieutenant George Cowpe)

Sergeant Robert Hall had led his section to the first objective and, although wounded, continued to lead them forward until his wound exhausted him. It was a brave act to continue and one which saw him honoured with the award of the Distinguished Conduct Medal. Just before 7am another

Captain Richard Kirk's grave at Lonsdale Cemetery, Authuille. He was originally buried at Paisley Avenue Cemetery, close to where he was killed. His body was moved to Authuille after the war. Photo: Reg Unsworth

message was despatched by Captain Bill Innes, commanding D Company. He was in Maisie Lane and found that he was the senior officer there. Dick Kirk had been killed by a sniper and Bill Dodge, commanding C Company, was badly wounded. A shell had exploded near Dodge, killing several men and burying him and some others. He had been dug out, alive but unconscious.[75] The mist was still hampering a further advance. The message reached Colonel Stanway at about 8am and, at about the same time, Sergeant Hall, reported in to HQ, saying that Captain Innes had also been killed. Hall said that the situation was very vague in the forward area, with no-one really knowing where they were. Only after making his report did he seek treatment for his wound.

As Stanway later reported, he decided that he needed to 'take the situation in hand' and sent forward the Adjutant, Lieutenant Frank Naden, with firm instructions. He was to collect every man he could, organise them into four waves and press on the attack to the final objectives, sending back reports as best he could. Naden left at 8.15 and, thirty minutes later, was able to report by a telephone link that had been established in the Strasburg Line. He had collected some 400 men, including some of the Black Watch, and organised them into three attacking waves, with two parties who would act as 'moppers up of any German dugouts or strongpoints encountered. He was ordered to deal with pockets of resistance in the main Strasburg trench, where machine gunners and snipers were still active. Naden was assisted in reorganising the men by Second Lieutenant Robert Parkhurst, who was awarded the Military Cross for his actions.

Private John Dunkerley, worked in a Hyde hatworks. Killed by a shell explosion on 13 November.

He collected every available man near him and went forward, clearing the trench and capturing many of the enemy, at the same time joining up with three waves that had been reorganised, taking command and successfully leading them to their final objective.

It was later reported that some Germans who had initially surrendered picked up their rifles again, shooting from the Strasburg Line into the backs of the Cheshires as they continued their advance. Lance Corporal John Loftus joined up on October 1914 and had been posted overseas earlier in 1916. He is thought to have been one of the 'moppers up'. He took charge of a small party, leading them down the German trench, where they cleared out the dugouts, throwing grenades in if there was no immediate surrender. It was an action for which he was awarded the Distinguished Conduct Medal, the official citation noting that he *set a splendid example throughout.* Another medal award went to Harry Butterworth. He was one of the Lewis gunners and went to support a bombing party. The citation notes that, in spite of being wounded, he held the position until reinforcements arrived, *accounting for a large number of the enemy.* The twenty

Harry Butterworth DCM.

one year old was later evacuated back to Britain, where he was admitted to Leicester Hospital for treatment for the bayonet wound to his leg.

During the attack, this area was heavily defended by German machine guns. Photo: Reg Unsworth

Private George McClellan was a Liverpudlian and originally enlisted in the Cheshires' 4th Battalion – the territorial unit based at Birkenhead – but, at some point, had transferred to the 6th Battalion. He also took charge of a bombing party, capturing twenty two men and putting a machine gun out of action after he had killed all its crew. He was another to be awarded the Distinguished Conduct Medal.

The Brigade's Machine Gun Company had set up eight guns in the Schwaben Redoubt. They would not directly support the troops advancing from there, but would provide enfilade covering fire for the 63rd (Royal Naval) Division, attacking north of the Ancre. In return, the guns of 116 Company would be positioned on the north bank to provide similar fire for the Cheshires. The day before, Second Lieutenant Charles Brockbank had gone to the Schwaben and *got a good idea of our battle positions. The Huns put down a fairly stiff barrage on our position but did no great damage.* During the action Brockbank's position again came under enemy artillery fire and he was buried twice within a five minute period. He was dug out on both occasions, without physical injury, but he was badly shell-shocked. Unable to speak for quite a while, he was brought back to Britain and hospitalised at Grantham. He left the army in January 1919 but was still receiving medical treatment. An army medical board noted that year that he still suffered from headaches, which increased on excitement and that he found difficulty concentrating. He was sleeping badly on an average of three nights a week and was sleep walking.[76]

On the right, the Hertfordshires had captured all their objectives around the Hansa Line and, by 7.20am, were consolidating east of the Line. To their left, the attack by the Cambridgeshires had also gone well.

Tanks were a new weapon and had only made their first appearance in battle on 15 September. The technology was, obviously, still in its infancy. Three tanks were assigned to assist 39th Division's attack, south of the Ancre, but they made no impact. One got stuck in the deep mud. Another had mechanical failure and did not reach its starting position. The third had orders to approach the German front line and then drive along it, crushing the barbed wire defences as it did so, before it turned north towards St Pierre Divion. This tank managed to get to the German line but quickly also became stuck. Its officer ordered the tank abandoned but, as he and four men got out, they were shot down. The remaining crew, under the orders of a Corporal Taff, managed to get the tank moving but soon became stuck again. The tank was listing heavily to one side and unable to use its guns. Taff released a carrier pigeon giving their position and saying they were under attack. They were rescued by the advancing infantry at about 9am.

Meanwhile, A Company was finally able to make contact with HQ. The creeping barrage laid down by the artillery had been excellent and casualties had been very low in consequence. Captain Hugh Sparling was able to report that he was in contact with the Cambridgeshires and that, together, they had successfully gained their final objective along Mill Lane trench, to the north of St Pierre Divion. This effectively cut off the German defenders of the hamlet from being reinforced from the north.

Captain Hugh Sparling.

Second Lieutenant Sydney Yorston was himself feeling cut off. The young man, from Worsley, left his job as a bank clerk, receiving his commission in January 1916. He had only been with the Battalion since August and now found himself in Serb Road trench. He had lost contact with his company and had only twelve men with him and was not in touch with anyone. A few minutes later, however, his party was picked up by troops advancing under Naden's command.

After some time hanging about, we made an effort to reach our third and final objective. We thought we should be the only British down there and would be wiped out, so I didn't think it worth taking my rifle to the Hun and dropped it, taking out my revolver instead. We got down to what was once St Pierre Divion and were surprised to find A Company consolidating beyond the village. They reached the village before their time. They separated from us through working too much to their right but everything turned out A1.... I had quite an exciting time but I wasn't at all nervous about the job. We just went through 'em with ease. We took the village almost before he knew there was an attack on. Sixteen of 'em were found in bed in a dugout with boots and stockings off.

(Second Lieutenant George Cowpe)

Private George Haughton, killed in action.

St Pierre Divion was a tiny hamlet on the banks of the River Ancre and, for the first half of the attack, the lie of the land meant that, being in a valley, the Cheshires would not have been able to see it. Their final assault was down a quite steep incline

Harold Beard had been in territorials since it was formed in 1908 and been overseas since November 1914. He was one of the first men into St Pierre Divion.

We got through so quickly that fighting was still going on behind us. I got to one dugout in the village with eight men in. I shouted for them to come out but whether they could not understand 'Hyde talk' or not, they did not budge. So, in went a bomb. Still they stuck it till we went in with a gas bomb and you know that gas gets round corners. Well, three of the beauties came out gasping, and surrendered to me.[77]

By 9am, the Cheshires had carried their attack forward into St Pierre Divion and were consolidating the gains. The artillery had done its job well. No buildings were left standing and there were just heaps of rubble. They had also dealt with the defenders who were in the Strasburg Line. Two machine guns and 130 prisoners had been captured. Attempts to mop up pockets of resistance were underway, but groups in the Strasburg Line were holding on doggedly. Two companies of the 14th Hampshires were ordered forward to help with the task. On the left of the Brigade attack,

Ancre British Cemetery is located on the north bank of the River Ancre, opposite St Pierre Divion. The final stage of the Cheshires attack was down the hill seen in the distance. Photo: author

The final assault on the village was down the steep slope of the valley. In the background may be seen the trees on the southern perimeter of the Newfoundland Park. Photo: Reg Unsworth

the Black Watch had also reached its final objective of the bluffs overlooking the river, just to the west of St Pierre Divion, but pockets of resistance had been left and the remaining two companies of Hampshires now went forward to clear these trenches. They completed the task by 1pm and withdrew back to billets near Thiepval.

Having joined the Battalion in July, Second Lieutenant Bob Morton had just become the Battalion's signals officer. He had assumed responsibility for the work of the signallers in addition to his normal duties as a company officer. At full establishment there would be fifteen men, including a sergeant and corporal. They were trained in Morse code and the use of semaphore flags; but their main duties were in providing and maintaining the telephone communication between Battalion headquarters and the four companies. During the periods of static trench warfare the telephone wires ran along the trench system but were subject to damage by enemy shellfire. That would mean at the periods of most danger, the signallers would have to be out of the protection of their dugouts, trying to find and repair breaks in the wire. During an attack Morton's men would have to lay wire to the newly gained positions as quickly as possible so that communication could be re-established as soon as possible. Until that was done the only way communication could be undertaken was by runners carrying handwritten messages. This was a slow process, with no guarantee that a man could successfully deliver the message and, certainly, with the sender having no knowledge that the message had reached its destination.

> *This was my first job as signals officer and I wasn't orthodox at all, because I didn't know anything about it but it worked and we'd got communication the whole of the day. I'd got telephones. From Battalion Headquarters, we took two signallers – a linesman and a telephonist. They had the first phone, went so far to the end of the lead and then the next two plugged in theirs and went along with the attack right to the final objective. We got speech on telephone all day.*
>
> *I was in a tunnel where we'd got the Headquarters and the Signal Office and I wanted to know what was going on all the time, when the Colonel wasn't on the line....When they finally got to St Pierre Divion, I'd told my Lance Corporal Signaller Collier[78] to 'pick up more wire from St Pierre Divion. The Brigade Signals will be there with more wire, so report to them.' He came on and he said*

and his language was pretty good – he had a lot of words. He said 'Sir, you told us to come to St Pierre Divion and report to Brigade and get fresh wire. The Brigade's not there, sir. And the wire's not there, sir. And ruddy St Pierre Divion isn't there either'.

And we got two different reports. One from the Adjutant, who said to the Colonel 'We've got seventy Bosch prisoners. What shall I do with them? I've sent the Battalion forward into the attack again.' So, after that, I spoke to my Lance Corporal. I said 'How many prisoners have you got there? So and so said that there were seventy'. He said 'More like seventeen – weary looking so and so's.' 'And what about this organising the Battalion to go forward into the attack?' 'Every so and so is lost in the fog.'

Frank Collier. Battalion joker and a brave man.

It was now a matter of preparing to defend the gains against counter attack and, during the early afternoon, the Cheshires were ordered to dig new trenches to the north east of St Pierre Divion. The divisional pioneer battalion, the 13th Gloucesters, were brought forward to assist with this work. The German response was fairly minimal until 3.20pm, when a heavy and systematic barrage was brought down on the captured positions. This lasted well into the evening, before the situation quietened. The men of the Hertfordshires experienced an unusual incident. Just before 7pm, they saw a party of about twenty five Germans approaching them in full marching order, seemingly unaware that the position was now in British hands. The Hertfordshires opened fire, killing ten Germans and capturing the others, together with five machine guns. Later, another German party of just twenty men tried to rush part of the trench in what was obviously a futile effort. Several were killed and the others retreated.

The wounded started coming in about 8am and from this time onwards it was one continual stream all day and night. All the objectives were taken and our Battalion was the first to enter St. Pierre Divion. Hundreds of prisoners were taken. We made them carry away our wounded.

(James Boardman)

It had been a costly day for the Cheshires. As well as Captains Innes and Kirk, Lieutenant Robert Morrison and twenty seven other ranks had been killed, with another 138 wounded or missing. Before the war Morrison was the curate at All Saints Church, Hoole, Chester. He had made the decision to join a fighting unit of the army rather than become an army chaplain. He had regularly written letters to the vicar, in one saying that, as he went about his hazardous duties, he was intensely conscious of the unseen presence of his Lord ever near him. Before Morrison left Hoole for active service the congregation had presented him with a communion set, which he took to France. Later, his family donated it back to the church, where he is remembered by a stained glass window. He is also remembered on the local war memorial.

Second Lieutenant Robert Morrison.

Also amongst the dead was Private Harry Mullins. When the Battalion went overseas in November 1914 he was its youngest member, having just turned sixteen. He had been working for the Regimental Quartermaster Sergeant and was reported to have been taking stores forward when he was killed by a shell. Allan Newton, who was

Nineteen year old Allan Newton, killed in action. The local newspaper described him as 'one of the best of lads'.

Allan Newton's grave at Mill Road Cemetery. Photo: author

employed in Stalybridge as a sheet metal worker before the war, was also killed outright by shrapnel while working as a stretcher bearer. Lance Corporal Wilfred Corscadden had known him for years as a *great chum, both at school and out here.....He suffered no pain at all.*

Sam Gould worked as a bleacher for Sykes Ltd at Edgeley and joined up in January 1915. He was acting as a servant to one of the officers and may not have been obliged to go into the attack. The day before he chatted to a mate, who later wrote to his parents.

Sam Gould, killed in action. 'He was like a brother to me.'

> *I was surprised when he said he was going over with us into the fight. He chaffed me about getting a nice 'blighty' apiece which would get us home. We shook hands and wished each other a safe return and I thought no more about it until I came down from the line on the 15th after it was all over and then I was told Sammy had been knocked out. I can tell you it nearly took what life I had left out of me, for Sam was like a brother to me and his cheery smile and cheerful talk were things one cannot forget. From what I hear, he was not obliged to go with us but he would have been the last one in the Company not to go and that did not suit Sam. He would not let anyone think he was getting out of it, so he did his bit with the rest.[79]*

Sam Gould's body was never found and identified and he is commemorated on the Thiepval Memorial to the Missing.

Company Sergeant Major Allan Corfe was not originally from the 6th Battalion's usual recruiting area of North Cheshire. The twenty five year old had spent most of his life living and working on Wirral. He served an apprenticeship as an engineer with shipbuilders Cammell, Laird & Co before moving to Stockport to work as a draughtsman for Mirrlees, Bickerton & Day Ltd. He joined the territorials in the latter part of 1913. Corfe was badly wounded in the initial stages of the attack and was taken initially to the dressing station just behind the front line. He was then further evacuated to a main hospital in Le Havre, where he died on 26 November. Thomas Cox was twenty one when he went into action and, like Corfe, was one of many of the Cheshires who were badly wounded. He had not long since returned from leave back to his home near Hyde, where he worked as a labourer for one of the railway companies and, in his spare time, was a keen footballer. The surgeons at the field hospital had to amputate his right arm below the elbow. More seriously, he had shrapnel wounds in his spine. He was brought back to Britain, where he was admitted to hospital in Coventry; but in spite of all efforts, he died on 29 November, with his mother, Jane, at his bedside.

The 14th November was an uneventful day except that, in the evening, another group of about twenty Germans, heavily armed with grenades, tried to raid the Hertfordshire trench at the same point as the previous evening. It had as little success as the previous attempt. During the evening, the men of 118 Brigade were relieved from the front line and moved back to their billets around Aveluy.

William Oldham's mother, Emily, wrote to him a few days before the attack.

> It does seem a long time since I had a line from you but I hope you are well and out of the trenches. It is two years this week that you left Stockport and only had one furlough. I do think it is a shame, for some seemed to be very lucky and get home often. How is Fred Hilton? Is he keeping well and G Meakin – are they still with you? Well, dear lad, I do not seem to have much news to send....Let me have a line as soon as you can to say the parcel was all right. Best love from all at home and your loving mother.

William Oldham, an iron founder from Stockport. Badly wounded during the attack and died the following day.

Oldham never received the letter, nor did his mother ever get a line from him. He was badly wounded in both feet during the attack and was taken to 9th Casualty Clearing Station. Mrs Oldham got a letter from Sister M Edwards at the field hospital, saying he had *passed away peacefully at 3.30pm, November 14. He did not appear to suffer a great deal of pain and spoke very little, so there is no last message which I could convey to you.* Mrs Oldham lost a second son during the war when Fred Oldham died in April 1918, of wounds received in action whilst serving with the 11th Cheshires.

Within a few weeks, Lieutenant Frank Naden learned that he had been awarded the Military Cross for his involvement in the action. The citation, published in the *London Gazette*, reads,

For conspicuous gallantry and devotion to duty. He reorganised two companies and sent them forward to the final objective, thereby clearing up the situation at a critical time. He set a splendid example of coolness and courage.

Captain Sparling was also awarded the Military Cross for his leadership of A Company in its capture of the objectives and the taking of prisoners. It had taken *great courage and ability,* according to the citation. Lance Corporal Frank Collier was awarded the Distinguished Conduct Medal for his work as a signaller:

For conspicuous gallantry in action. He successfully paid a line under fire, enabling communication to be maintained with Battalion Headquarters at a critical time. He set a fine example of courage and coolness.

Arnold Walton. Awarded the Military Medal for a now unknown act of bravery during the attack.

Collier was also promoted to sergeant. Several other men, including Ernest Dakin, William Gee, Frank Hague, Herbert McCormack, Samuel Wolstenholme and Arnold Walton, were awarded the Military Medal. Their specific acts of bravery are now unknown. Shortly after, Walton wrote to his parents in Hyde saying he was in hospital. He had not been wounded but was just 'run down'. It is, perhaps, not surprising. He joined the Territorials, aged 17, in the winter of 1912/13 and had been on active service since 1914. Before the war he worked as a hatter for Joseph Wilson & Sons at Denton. He was the third employee to be awarded the Military Medal and one of his workmates, Arthur Hill, had been awarded the Victoria Cross a few weeks before. At some point during the day, Frank Hague was promoted to Company Sergeant Major; but it is not known if this was before or after the action.

As mentioned, Lieutenant Colonel Stanway had been awarded the Distinguished Service Order for his actions at Red Dragon Crater, earlier in the year, when he was still serving with the Royal Welsh Fusiliers. He now received a bar to his DSO:

For conspicuous gallantry in action. He handled his battalion in the attack with great courage and ability. He captured the position, inflicted much loss on the enemy and took a large number of prisoners.

St Pierre Divion – clearing up. Notice the presence of French troops.

The action in which the Battalion had just taken part was the last British offensive of the Battle of the Somme. The Battle was extremely costly in terms of casualties. Around a million British, French and German men were dead, wounded or prisoner as a result of the battle. In the south of the battlefield, British and French success had pushed the Germans back several miles. In the north, around the sector where the Cheshires had fought, the gains could only be measured in yards, rather than miles. The Somme saw the development of a new style of warfare, one where technological and tactical advances, in the use of tanks, artillery and aircraft, would put increasing pressure on the Germans, as the war advanced. The main objectives for the Battle of the Somme had been met – the pressure on the French at Verdun had been relieved and the German army had been very significantly weakened. Over the coming weeks, the Germans prepared a new line of defence, miles to the rear, which would become known to the British as the Hindenberg Line. It retreated to these new defences in late February and March 1917.

The Battalion only stayed at Aveluy overnight on the 15th, leaving for billets at Walloy the next day and then to Orville, where they spent two days. During this time Harold Beard wrote to his mother at Hyde:

> *I am quite safe and well. I did not want to tell you what was coming off here until it was over. Perhaps you have seen in the papers about the big advance that has taken place out here. Our Battalion was in it. Talk about a scrap – I wouldn't have missed it for a quid.[80]*

On 18 November the Battalion marched to Doullens and, the following day, moved north by train to Belgium. Harold Beard and his mates would be in more scraps there.

St Pierre Divion – captured German stores.

CHAPTER 8

St Julien

It was an eight hour train journey before the Battalion arrived at the Belgian town of Poperinghe. Ahead of them was an eight hour march across the border to the French village of Herzeele, where they billeted for several days. It was a time for cleaning up and rest.

We are billeted in a very large farmhouse, one of the largest I have ever seen. By 'we', I mean A Company officers. We are very close to the Franco-Belgian border. I never hoped for such a billet. Now that we are so comfortable we can look back on the last three months and see what we really have been put through. The owners of this place seem well-to-do people and are always most obliging. We are billeted in a wood and it would be a very decent place in summer. It is very dark at night and, without a flashlight, one is liable to fall into several ditches. I have been in three about 4ft deep so far…….It's hard to imagine what leave will be like. I shall go half cracked.....I shall be like a mad hatter when I get home. I shall just run wild.

(Second Lieutenant George Cowpe)

During this time, the Cheshires received a few reinforcements, including Second Lieutenant Denis Crew. Born in 1895, he was educated at public school in Shrewsbury, later working for one of the silk companies in Macclesfield. Crew was commissioned in 1914 but had not gone overseas until the beginning of 1916, when he joined the 7th Cheshires in Egypt. His service with them was brief, reporting sick with rheumatism within a few days, and returned to Britain, where he was admitted to hospital in Manchester. An army medical board had recently pronounced him fully recovered and he was posted overseas again, this time to the 6th Battalion.

Three officers were invalided back to Britain during this rest period. Captain Ronald Norman would return to duty in due course; but Lieutenant Selwyn Hinton and Second Lieutenant Philip George transferred to other units on recovery. Hinton later served with the Essex Regiment whilst George served with the Royal Air Force. After the war George emigrated to South Africa, where he practised his profession as an accountant, becoming President of the Natal Society of Accountants.

On 28 November the Cheshires moved to overnight billets at Poperinghe and the following day to Elverdinghe, where they occupied farms and huts vacated by the French 79th Territorial Regiment. On the 30th they relieved French troops in the trenches at Boesinghe. Sergeant James Boardman noted in his diary that this was a very quiet sector and that the French had had only one casualty in the previous three months - and even that had been from a stray machine gun bullet. The situation continued to be quiet and the men spent their time improving the trench defences – deepening them, raising the parapets and constructing fire steps. They were relieved back to Elverdinghe on 10 December. They had not had a single casualty.

There was a move to new billets at Vlamertinghe on 12 December. A large reinforcement of 283 men had just arrived from Britain. On his way back to Britain was Second Lieutenant Robert Parkhurst. He reported sick on 19 December suffering from nephritis – inflammation of the kidneys. He did not serve overseas again and, when he had recovered, he was posted to Swansea to a position as an Assistant Embarkation Officer. It was a job where he could bring his civilian experience to bear – he had previously worked in the Marine Department of the Royal Mail Steam Packet Company. He held the post until he left the army in 1919, when it is thought he emigrated to Vancouver, Canada, where he was known to be living in 1922.

The Battalion remained there until Christmas Eve, when it moved by train to Ypres, relieving the 4/5th Black Watch in the support line. There appear to have been no Christmas celebrations and the remainder of the month passed without incident, with the Cheshires providing working parties in the front line. There were no New Year celebrations. Sergeant James Boardman recalled that the enemy raided the front line trench, held by the Black Watch, and two companies of Cheshires were rushed forward to support them. Three of the raiders were taken prisoner. During the evening of 4 January the Cheshires relieved the Black Watch and took over the front line in the left sector near Wieltje.

It is up to the knee in mud and water, and in some places up to the waist. We are walking about in gum boots. The worst job is to keep our feet warm and dry. The gum boots make your feet ache terribly. (James Boardman).

It was a long tour of duty and they were not relieved until the 13th. The enemy artillery had been particularly active, although not directly targeting the Battalion's position. In reserve, Boardman was able to have

a good look round Ypres, the first real chance to do so. It was a sight I shall never forget. Buildings of every description absolutely razed to the ground — churches, banks, cathedral, post office, police station, workshops, and houses, no matter whether large or small, hardly one brick above the other. Thousands upon thousands of tons of shells must have dropped in this place, at a cost of millions of pounds and thousands of lives.

Another tour of duty in the front line started on the evening of 18 January. On the 22nd, Second Lieutenant Reginald Pratt joined the Battalion. The young man lived with his family in New Brighton and was commissioned in the 4th Cheshires in 1915. He was not a successful officer and his commanding officer requested that he be sent back to Britain for further instruction.

He is not capable of fulfilling his duties as a platoon commander. He is 19 years of age and young for his years and seems incapable of realising his responsibilities.

The Cloth Hall and cathedral at Ypres, 1917.

There seems to have been little improvement during the further training course, his final report indicating *He does not apply his mind to the work in hand.* [He] *does not appear to appreciate the responsibility of his position.* In spite of that fairly damning remark, Pratt was deemed suitable to return to overseas service. This would be Pratt's only tour of duty. On the 25th, he was wounded by shrapnel. He had suffered twenty separate injuries, all but one of them minor. James Boardman went to attend to him.

> W*e had a warm time getting* [him] *out as the enemy shelled us all the way down the communication trench.*

The most serious wound was to Pratt's eyes and he was discharged from the army in April 1917.[81]

After a short period in reserve, another tour of duty in the Wieltje trenches started during the evening of 9 February. The next day the British and German artillery were both very active and the Cheshires came under fire from it, together with trench mortar and rifle grenade fire. It killed two men and wounded another eight. Charles McClelland and his older brother, Arthur, were both prewar territorials. Charles was married to Lizzie and they lived at Bamford Street, Stockport, with their young son, Matthew. He worked at Christy's hatworks. McClelland was one of the company runners, taking messages back to headquarters. He was taking shelter in a dugout during the bombardment when it was blown in by a German shell. His officer wrote to Lizzie saying

Arthur Arnold, killed while on sentry duty.

> *I helped to carry him to another dug-out at once, with the assistance of stretcher bearers, and attended to his wounds, which were in the back and left arm. He never regained consciousness after being hit and, unfortunately, death took place fifteen minutes afterwards.*

Arthur Arnold was a twenty two year old grocer's assistant, also from Stockport, and was on sentry duty when he was struck in the head by shrapnel and he also died within minutes. Alf Ball came from Cheadle, where he worked in one of the local bleachworks. He was also hit by shrapnel in the back. Sergeant Robert Harding wrote to his family saying

I heard him shout he was hit. So, with the help of one or two more, we got him under cover and bandaged him up as well as we could. He asked me to get him away as quick as we could, so in less than half a minute three men volunteered to carry him out across the open, which was a much quicker way than down the trench. When I left him, he had been dressed again and was being put in a motor ambulance for the hospital.[82]

Ball was taken to one of the casualty clearing stations near the village of Lijssenthoek but there was nothing to be done and he died there the next day.

The Battalion was relieved back to billets during the evening of 14 February, but not before Joe Kenworthy had been mortally wounded. The twenty year old joined the territorials at the beginning of 1914. He worked as a cotton piecer and, in his spare time, was a keen footballer. His mate, Jack Wood, wrote home, saying they had been chatting and

We warned Joe to keep under cover but as he had some of the men's rations to take, he said he would chance it and he had not been gone a minute, when word came that he had been wounded badly.[83]

Joe Kenworthy, died on 16 February from wounds received two days before.

He was also taken to the CCS but the wounds in his abdomen and chest were too severe for anything to be done and he died on the 16th.

Tragic loss of young lives was not confined to the battlefield. For Private Arthur Nield, from Boughton, Chester, news came that his twelve year old daughter, Lily, had died in an accident. She had gone for a walk with a friend and they had decided to cross the River Dee, which was then frozen over. When they were about twenty yards from the other side, the ice gave way and Lily fell in, crying out for help. A Mr Harris heard the shouts and, grabbing a ladder, the seventy year old tried to make his way to her. She managed to grab the end of the ladder but, just at that point, more of the ice gave way and Harris also fell in. Several boats set out to reach them, desperately smashing the ice with hammers to make a passage and were able to rescue Harris but it was some time before they could find Lily's body. Nield was never able to visit his daughter's grave – he was killed in action a few weeks later, on 8 July.

The remainder of the month was spent in camps, where there was an opportunity to clean up. James Boardman recalled there was time for sports, with the Battalion holding a boxing competition on the 23rd. *A good afternoon's sport. This is the best way to settle arguments, not with shot and shell.* Boardman was a good footballer but the sergeants' team was beaten 4 – 2 by the officers on the 27th. George Cowpe played at centre half for the officers. Boardman captained the Battalion side which played the Hertfordshires on 1 March, beating them 2 – 0.

The next two months were spent mainly in the reserve billets, with occasional tours of duty in the trenches. When out of the line the sporting activities continued. On 7th March Captain Sparling left the Battalion and returned to Britain, possibly wounded. Later in the year he became engaged to Grace Dawson, from Birkenhead. The couple married in June 1918 at Upton Church, near Chester, where his father was the vicar. In the latter stages of the war he commanded the 2nd Cheshires. Sparling survived the war and died in 1931, at the young age of 38.

James Boardman recalled that the trench conditions were no better than they had been earlier in the year. Starting one tour of duty at a position known as Observatory Ridge, he writes,

> *We had a bad time going in, as it hailed, rained and snowed heavens hard, and everywhere you went was up to the knees in mud.*

The British had long favoured a major attack in Flanders. Planning started as long ago as 1915 but had been delayed due to the Somme offensive. As with previous major attacks, logistics would play a vital part in the forthcoming offensive. Before any fighting could be contemplated, men, ammunition and other supplies had to be moved to the right place, in the right quantities and by the right time. Railways would play a vital part and, from 12 April, all available men from the Cheshires became navvies, building part of an expanding network of lines near Brandhoek.

> *We have been on the usual fatigue all day. I think we shall be kept on the same job for some time yet. C'est bon!* (Second Lt George Cowpe, letter home 16 April 1917.)

The railway work continued until the 28th, when they moved to Ypres, going back into the front line in the Hill Top sector, north west of Wieltje.

There was heavy artillery shelling during the first two days. It caused

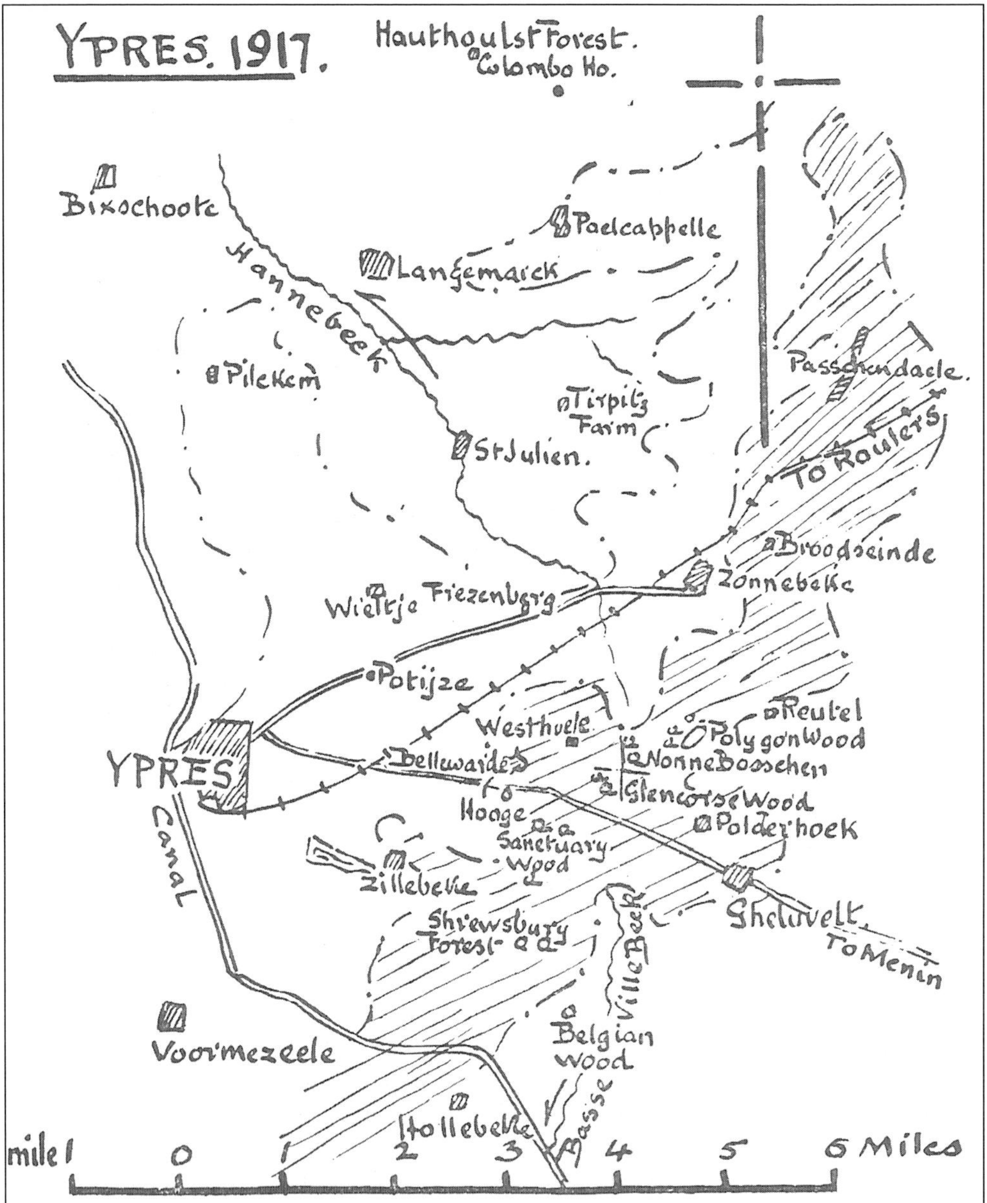

YPRES. 1917.

Hauthoulst Forest.
Colombo Ho.

Bixschoote

Hannebeek

Paelcappelle

Langemarck

Passchendaele.

Pilekem

Tirpitz Farm

To Roulers

St Julien.

Broodseinde

Wieltje Friezenberg

Zonnebeke

Potijze

Reutel

Westhoek

Polygon Wood

YPRES

Bellwaarde

Nonnebosschen

Hooge

Glencorse Wood

Sanctuary Wood

Polderhoek

Canal

Zillebeke

Shrewsbury Forest

Gheluvelt

Basse Ville Beek

To Menin

Belgian Wood

Voormezeele

Hollebeke

mile 1   0   1   2   3   4   5   6 Miles

The main ridge overlooking the Ypres
salient is shaded. The secondary
ridge - Wieltje to Pilckem - is shown by
form lines.

considerable damage to the trench defences but, surprisingly, no casualties. In the middle of No Man's Land, in front of the Cheshires, was a series of abandoned dugouts. They had been made by Canadian troops during the Second Battle of Ypres in the spring of 1915 and were known, unsurprisingly, as Canadian Dugouts and marked as such on trench maps of the time. They had a potential use as a forward listening post for the Germans or a sniper might hide there. To establish if any use was being made of them, two patrols went out to reconnoitre the area during the nights of 1 and 3 May. James Boardman noted in his diary that the patrol on 3 May was a particularly strong one, perhaps suggesting that signs of occupation had been spotted on the previous patrol. *We thought none of them was coming back, as they did not come in until 4am. They all got back with one exception.* Official records have no mention of a man killed, so the missing man must have become detached from the patrol but made his way back to the line later.

Lieutenant Charles Norman left the Battalion on the 4th, transferring to the Intelligence Corps and returning to Britain, where he married his fiancée, Marion Fletcher. In the latter months of the war he served with the Machine Gun Corps. Records suggest that, during the Second World War, Norman rejoined the army, serving as a lieutenant with the Royal Army Service Corps. He is believed to have died in 1958.

The Battalion's war diary entry for 6 May notes "1 O.R. to hospital wounded". This other rank was Private Cornelius Hayes. Older than most of his comrades, the forty year old had lived in Stockport, where he worked as a felt hat blocker. He had received very serious wounds to his abdomen, probably from shrapnel, and was taken to a CCS near Lijssenthoek where he died later in the day. That night there was a further reconnaissance of the Canadian Dugouts, which found fresh straw in one of them. It was clear evidence that they were being used by the Germans.

The next night, Second Lieutenants George Kirton and Gerald Rowley led a party of twenty men into No Man's Land to act as cover for a party of Royal Engineers who were going to blow up the dugouts. They checked the dugouts were not occupied and then took up positions on both flanks about thirty yards past them on the enemy side. The Engineers then came up to set their charges, completing the work within a few minutes. The parties moved back to the British lines, with sixteen explosions fired between 12.17am and 12.25am. There had been no casualties.

Buffs Road Cemetery, outside Ypres. The site of raids in May and July 1917. Canadian Dugouts were in the field near where the cemetery wall now is. Caliban Trench was on the rising ground to the left. Photo: Author

> *While our men were out Jerry was out mending his wire entanglements. He must have wondered what was on as the explosion was terrific.* (Sergeant James Boardman)

The Battalion was relieved during the evening of 15 May by 16th Rifle Brigade and moved to reserve positions at O Camp, near Brandhoek, where the rest of the month was spent undertaking training, fatigues and sports, including more football matches. James Boardman now regularly captained whichever team he was playing for and, after beating a team from the Hertfordshires, Colonel Stanway gave him twenty francs *to get the lads a drink. Good health, Sir!* During the evening of the 20th many of the men marched as a group to Poperinghe to watch a show by the divisional concert party. The Battalion signallers played a match against the Black Watch signallers on the 24th. Signals officer Bob Morton had offered his lads a bottle of whisky if they won. The ever sharp Lance Corporal Frank Collier said to him 'Well, one bottle won't go very far, sir. Can you make it two? Morton replied 'Alright, go on. If you beat the Black Watch, it's worth two.' The Cheshires won the match and Collier came to collect his winnings. It was only later that Morton realised he had been conned and that Collier had arranged it with the Black Watch so that they each got a bottle.

Alexander Brown joined the Battalion as a second lieutenant on 25 July 1916. He originally served with the King's Liverpool Regiment and the 15th Cheshires, before receiving his commission in 1915. He then spent some months with the 3/6th Cheshires before going overseas. Before the war Brown lived in Oxton, Birkenhead, where he practised as an accountant. On 27 May the men were training in the use of grenades when one exploded prematurely. Brown was wounded in twelve separate places, on his face, neck, abdomen and thighs. Fortunately none of the injuries were life-threatening but they were enough to see him evacuated back to Britain for treatment and recovery. He returned to duty in the summer of 1918, by which time he had been promoted to captain and was acting as adjutant.

On 29 May Major Robert Rostron left to return to Britain. He was a prewar officer of the Battalion and held the rank of captain at the outbreak of war, receiving his promotion to major in October 1914. He remained as second in command of the Battalion and would not be further promoted during his later service at home, with the Welsh Reserve Brigade.

At the beginning of June there was a move to new billets near Poperinghe. Over the following ten days the men were put to work on fatigue parties, bringing forward ammunition supplies for the Royal Artillery. This was part of the build-up for the forthcoming offensive. The plans were now well advanced and the sounds of a preliminary, smaller offensive a few miles south would have been heard by the Cheshires on 7 June. Back in 1914 the Cheshires had taken part in one of the truces at Christmas. They were then in trenches near the village of Wulverghem and were overlooked by the Germans entrenched on a ridge of high ground west of the village of Messines. The Germans still held the high ground and its heavy artillery was able to pound the British troops in the Ypres Salient with ease. Before any offensive could take place at Ypres the Germans had to be driven off the ridge. Preparations had started as long back as 1915 and by the autumn of 1916 Royal Engineers had dug twenty one tunnels from the British trenches under No Man's Land and the German line. They were packed with explosives and, at 3.10am on 7 June, they were blown to devastating effect. It has very optimistically been estimated that 10,000 German soldiers were killed by the explosion. Before the dust had even settled the British infantry was moving across No Man's Land, capturing all the planned objectives.

With the Messines Ridge now in British hands, planning for the next stage could be finalised. As with the Battle of the Somme, part of the strategy for the offensive was to relieve pressure on the French army, then in considerable difficulties not just from the Germans but from large scale mutinies of men refusing to attack in protest about the high rate of casualties. The initial attacks would drive forward from Ypres to the Paschendaele Ridge. The advance would continue to Roulers, where there was a major junction in the German railway system and whose capture would seriously disrupt the army's supply. Over the following weeks the advance was planned to reach the Channel coast, pushing the German submarines out of their bases, which were such a serious threat to British shipping.

The Battalion moved to billets in the village of Coulomby on 13 June. There was only enough accommodation for three companies and the fourth was sent to nearby Harlettes.

> *It is still very hot and we are getting brilliant sunshine. I am enjoying myself A1 here and I don't care how long it lasts. It is fine to have a bed each night and a house to live in. We haven't had a bad time since we came up north last year; but on looking back to our experiences down south we can quite see that it more than made up for the decent time we are having now....I am at present hoping for the war to be over in September and, if it isn't, I shall begin to hope for leave. You have to keep hoping for something or else live one day at a time and I can't quite manage that.*
>
> (Second Lieutenant George Cowpe. Letter, 16 June)

The Cheshires were at Coulomby to train for the forthcoming attack. As well as the expected work in musketry and bayonet fighting, there were also extensive exercises in open warfare, in anticipation that, after the initial assault broke through the German line, the advance would be across the countryside. It required different tactics and different methods of fighting from those the men were used to after so many months of what was essentially trench fighting. In particular, there would be very close co-operation between the four battalions in the brigade and, indeed, between brigades. The exercises continued after a move to Moulle on 24 June. There were a number of officer changes during this period. Second Lieutenant Harold Melling left to join the Royal Flying Corps. Before becoming an officer he had served as a private with the King's Liverpool Regiment and had been wounded in February 1916. Replacing him and bringing the Battalion up to its full strength of junior officers, Second

Lieutenants Samuel Birtles, William Clayton, John Hill, Neil (known as Nigel) Kennedy, Henry Spicer and Paul Wood all joined. On the 28th the Battalion war diary notes that one man was killed in action and another wounded. The circumstances of these injuries are not recorded and it is unusual that they should occur so far from the front line. The dead man was Corporal William Ratcliffe, from Stockport. Prior to the war, Ratcliffe worked for one of the railway companies and his records suggest that, at some point, his experience had seen him attached to the Traffic Control unit of 34th Division, so it is possible that he was still serving with them when he was killed.

The training period over, the Battalion went back into action, returning to the Hill Top sector near Wieltje on 30 June. Almost immediately plans were made for a raid on the trenches opposite, Caliban Trench and Caliban Support Trench. It was to be led by Captain John Lee – known as Jack. He was born in 1891, the youngest of four children. It was a wealthy family and his widowed mother was able to employ two live-in servants. Lee worked for a cotton manufacturer and joined the 7th Manchesters, as a private, in November 1914. As with many middle class recruits, he was

A photo showing the Wieltje area.

quickly selected to become an officer and was posted to 3/6th Cheshires. He went overseas in May 1916, having just married his fiancée, Agnes Erskine.

Jack Lee commanded a party of three officers and 133 other ranks, including several Royal Engineers. The raid was planned to take place in the very early hours of 5 July. Three days prior to this, Lee and his men were withdrawn from the front line so that they could practice the attack on a full sized mock-up of the area. It meant that every man knew what was expected of him. The objectives for the attack were detailed in the Battalion's war diary:

> *Killing or capturing as many of the enemy as possible; capturing and destroying war material; destroying dugouts, machine guns, trench mortars, dumps, tramways, etc; gaining information regarding the enemy's front line system and troops occupying same; to lower the morale of the enemy.*

During the training period the entire group were briefed by Brigadier General Edward Belllingham on the overall expectations and they were also given details by the commander of the Royal Field Artillery battery on the support his barrage would offer.

The preparatory work for the raid was carried out meticulously. Gaps were made in the outer bands of the German barbed wire defences by a combination of British artillery fire and men going out into No Man's Land with wirecutters. During the evening of 4 July gaps were cut in the inner bands of wire and, shortly before the time of the raid, a reconnaissance patrol of one officer and five men went out to check that there was still a way through. They were able to confirm that a five yard wide path had been made and that marking tapes laid out the night before were intact and the raiders only had to follow these to the gaps. There was also a ruse to distract the Germans. The units to the left of the Cheshires co-operated by arranging a feint attack. British artillery and machine gun fire would play on their part of No Man's Land and, when the time came for the raid, their soldiers would raise dummies, intended to indicate that a raid was under way there. It was hoped it would distract the Germans sufficiently to allow the Cheshires to get into the enemy trench.

Zero hour was set for 2am. Five minutes before this, the Cheshires' scouts spotted an enemy patrol of about ten men about thirty yards away in No Man's Land. The Germans opened fire on the scouts and fire was returned, at which the Germans started to retire back to their own trench. However, before they could reach it, the planned British artillery barrage opened up, cutting off their escape. Four or five of them managed to get away but the others were killed by the barrage or by the raiders when they reached them. Company Sergeant Major Arthur Shackley bayonetted several of them. Shortly after, the Cheshires were in the enemy trench, where they came across a group of about fifteen Germans who were attacked and killed, with the exception of four men, three of them wounded, who were captured and taken back to the British lines. As they advanced through the trench system, more German defenders were accounted for and another three captured.

Meanwhile the Royal Engineers sappers were placing charges but only two small dugouts were demolished, the larger ones being partially constructed from concrete and too strong for the charges available. Thirty five minutes after zero hour, Captain Lee ordered the withdrawal back to the British trench. The tapes that had been laid allowed the men easily to see their route back to safety.

The entire raid had gone to plan. A German officer had been killed and all his papers and maps were brought back and handed over to the Intelligence Department. Seven prisoners were captured. Five were wounded and the official report on the raid notes that all of these 'expired on their way to our trenches', Second Lieutenant George Cowpe describing their deaths as 'mysterious', possibly with tongue firmly in cheek. The other two men and their escort had a lucky escape as they were buried by a shell explosion. British casualties were very light, with only two men being badly wounded. However, Lieutenant Denis Crew was posted as missing, believed killed. He had been with the Battalion since the previous autumn. In fact, he was not dead. Crew was in the German trench when he was wounded. George Cowpe, who was not on the raid, heard he had been bayonetted, along with two of his men. Believing that he was dead, the raiders left him where he was. He was still alive when captured by the Germans shortly afterwards and evacuated towards one of their field hospitals; but he died soon after arrival. They buried him in the village cemetery at Westroosbeke but during the later stages of the war his grave was destroyed by shellfire. He is remembered on four war memorials in his native Macclesfield.

Jack Lee was awarded the Military Cross for his action during the raid, the citation reading:

Sergeant Harry Jones, from Heaton Norris. Awarded the Military Medal for his bravery during the July raid. Killed in action, 31 July 1917.

William Rhodes DCM.

James Sutton MM.

For conspicuous gallantry and devotion to duty when commanding a raid. His conduct throughout was of the highest order and a splendid example to the men. It was entirely due to his fine leadership that the enterprise was successfully carried out.

One of the other officers also received the Military Cross, CSM Arthur Shackley and Sergeant William Rhodes were awarded the Distinguished Conduct Medals and Military Medals were awarded to Charles Cope, Harry Jones and James Sutton. Sutton had served as a regular soldier during the Boer War. By the end of the month Lee, Rhodes, Jones and Sutton would be dead.

General Bellingham's report on the raid notes that

the hostile gun fire did not die down when we ceased fire as is customary but increased in violence and from 3.10 to 3.50 (i.e. zero plus 1hr 10 mins to zero plus 1hr 50 mins) he placed a really heavy barrage on the whole of our front line system.

The shelling killed four men and injured twelve others. The dead men were Arthur Bell from Norden near Rochdale, Thomas Brierley from Stalybridge, Leonard Cheshire from Winsford and Londoner George Griffiths. George Lomas was amongst the wounded. The twenty eight year old came from Glossop and had been a Territorial since the latter part of 1908. Fellow Glossopian Sam Garlick went to his aid.

He was the first I picked up and I did my very best to dress his wounds as best I could but I'm sorry to say it was all in vain.[84]

Private Arthur Bell, killed in action.

Lomas was taken to a dressing station far behind the front line, at Brandhoek, but he died the next day.

The next day the German artillery kept up its barrage on the British trenches with considerable success. There was also major aerial activity, in which the dominant German aircraft were able to swoop over the trenches machine-gunning the soldiers, although six of them were brought down by the Royal Flying Corps. Three men were mortally wounded and another eleven wounded. Thirty one year old James Woolley from Stockport was one of the three who would be dead within hours. He was evacuated to a CCS at Poperinghe, where he died. The hospital's chaplain wrote to his parents.

George Lomas, died of wounds on 6 July 1917.

He was seriously wounded by a bursting shell in the legs, back and neck. He was attended to by skilled surgeons and nurses and I can assure you everything possible was done for him. Before he died, he turned to me and said 'write to my mother, give her my best love. Tell her it is bad luck to be knocked out just as I should have been coming home on leave. Tell her that I will be alright.' The poor lad could not realise that he was seriously hurt. After that he became drowsy and said he would go to sleep and he did, but it was the sleep of death.

The Cheshires were relieved from the front line and moved back to positions on the canal bank just outside Ypres. Over several nights they provided working parties for the Royal Engineers, burying telephone cables in preparation for the offensive. Artillery on both sides continued to exchange almost continual salvoes for several days. Fortunately, casualties were minimal. On the 12th the Germans switched from high explosive shells to gas and intensified its use the next day. However, as James Boardman noted in his diary, many casualties came from British gas.

The enemy hit one of our dumps, and exploded some gas shells. The wind was in the wrong direction for us. Hundreds were gassed and they lay about all over the place. We had to wear gas masks as we attended to them, and it made it hard work. When the wind dropped we were still in danger as some of the victims had the gas on their clothes.

German shelling continued on the 14th. George Cowpe was *standing outside my dugout when I saw a shell burst in a nasty quarter about 150 yards away. I was afraid somebody would 'catch out'*. Second Lieutenant Roger Brierley was killed instantly. At forty four, he was much older than many of his fellow officers. He was born in the Cheshire village of Tattenhall and worked locally as an estate agent. Brierley is buried at the military cemetery at Brandhoek and is remembered on the Tattenhall war memorial. Corporal William Dunning was badly wounded in the back and thigh. Describing him as the 'Crack shot of the Sixth', the local newspaper reported[85] that he had written to his father in Bredbury, saying his wounds were nothing to get excited about but *I think I have seen the last of the war.* He would be in hospital for many months. In June 1918 he was back in England and had been admitted to a military hospital in Epsom. He must have significantly recovered as he went absent without leave between 11 – 25 June. He was discharged from the army in September and the following year married Ada Stafford. Dunning is believed to have died in 1968.

On 17 July the Battalion moved to Moulle, to finalise training for the offensive. Over several days, the men practised their attack over a full sized mock-up of the area, where tapes had been laid to represent trenches with other obstacles, such as streams, bogs and strongpoints, being similarly marked.

The plan was for fifteen British divisions, supported by French divisions on the left, to take part in the first day of the offensive. They would attack north east of Ypres, on an eighteen kilometre wide front, capturing the German front line and second line defences, pushing on to take the third line if that seemed feasible to commanders on the ground. Behind this was a further well defended trench system that would be assaulted at a yet to be determined date in the future. It was intended that,

A German postcard of St Julien, March 1917.

once through that line, the push to Channel coast would be relatively easy. In the 39th Division sector, where the Cheshires would fight, 116 and 117 Brigades would lead the attack and capture the German front line. Once that was secured, 118 Brigade, including the Cheshires, would advance, overlapping the other two Brigades and pushing on, through the village of St Julien to the second line and, possibly, beyond.

As was usual with major attacks, the British artillery would pound the German positions for days to destroy the defensive bands of barbed wire laid in No Man's Land. This barrage would involve over 3000 guns that would fire 4.25 million shells in the preparatory period from 18 July. Of course this announced to the Germans that a major offensive was imminent, so there would be no real element of surprise. The battle was later given the official title of the Third Battle of Ypres but, to many, it is simply known by the name of the village that was an objective for the first day – Passchendaele. Zero hour was set for 3.50am on 31 July.

George Cowpe was promoted to lieutenant only a couple of days before and put in command of A Company in the attack. He wrote home on 29 July.

> *You will almost certainly miss hearing from me for at least two days.*
> *Don't get excited, for I really don't think I shall. I haven't got a bad*
> *job. This is what I have been practising taking command of a*

*company for. We shall manage our job all right. Losses are much
lighter than they used to be in these affairs. I have only warned you
about the business because in seeing the paper you will assume I'm
in it. I am filled with a strange confidence.*

During the evening of 30 July the Battalion moved to assembly positions
at English Farm, near La Brique, to the north east of Ypres. There were
twenty officers and about 600 other ranks, one third understrength for an
infantry battalion. In front of them was the British front line near the
village of Wieltje. In the front line, and ready to attack the German first
defences, were the men of 116 Brigade who would attack on the right. To
their left, was 117 Brigade. They would be aided by eight tanks.

The Cheshires were first in position, by 1.30am on the 31st. They had
already suffered a number of casualties, mainly from German gas shells.
Second Lieutenant Louis Dyke was hospitalised first in France and then
in Britain, suffering from the effects of the gas, and appears to have been
discharged from the army in late 1917. He was Welsh and had represented
his country at rugby union on four occasions. Before joining the army he
worked as a cashier for a steamship company. In later life he may well
have looked back on events and thought himself lucky not to have gone
into action this day, when so many of his comrades were killed. He is
believed to have died in 1961, aged 74.

Twenty one year old Arthur Stansfield joined up on 12 September
1914, leaving his job with a tobacco company in Stockport and going
overseas in the following January. He had come through the fighting so
far unscathed.

*After many hours of waiting, the appointed time arrived which was
signalled by several hundred guns of all sizes starting to fire as
though fired by one man. It was the finest barrage I had ever seen,
even worse than those of the Somme battle in 1916. We thought the
end of the world had come at last.*[86]

As zero hour approached, the British artillery bombardment intensified
and, at 3.50am, 116 and 117 Brigades advanced across No Man's Land.
On the right, 116 Brigade, supported by two of the tanks, broke through
the German front line, securing the village of St Julien just behind it. They
took prisoner over 200 of the enemy. On the left, 117 Brigade also pushed
forward and, with use of trench mortars and rifle grenades, rushed three

St Julien in June 1917.

concrete pillboxes and other strongpoints. It had not been easy. The ground was churned up by the years of shelling by both sides and the going had been worsened by recent bad weather. There were acts of bravery in the initial assault, with Second Lieutenant Dennis Hewitt of the 14th Hampshires leading his men to capture their section of the German defences. A shell exploded, wounding him and setting fire to signal flares in his haversack. Despite the serious burns he received, he was able to extinguish the flames and led his men through heavy machine gun fire to take their second objective. At this point he was shot by a German sniper and died instantly. Hewitt was awarded a posthumous Victoria Cross.

Once the leading troops had started their advance, a hot meal was served to all ranks in 118 Brigade. They ate it under an increasing German artillery response, which was already causing casualties. With the German front line now expected to be in British hands, the Brigade started its advance at about 5.30am. The Brigade was deployed with the Cheshires on the right. To their left were the 1/1st Hertfordshires and, on the far left of the Brigade's sector, the 4/5th Black Watch. In support, and mainly behind the Black Watch, were the 1/1st Cambridgeshires. The shelling of the area by the German artillery, was ferocious and casualties started to mount. As planned, the three leading battalions stopped, at about 6.30am, when they reached the British front line and waited for news that the German front line had been taken.

The news came after an hour and the advance continued. The Cheshires' line of approach brought them to the Steenbeek by 10am. This was a stream, about ten feet wide, just in front of St Julien. Once crossed, the officers started to reorganise their men for the final advance. Company Sergeant Major Augustine Wilkinson played a major role in preparing his company to advance and led them forward with coolness and energy under heavy fire, according to the citation for the Distinguished Conduct Medal he was awarded.

An advanced battalion headquarters was set up near the village and Second Lieutenant Bob Morton brought his signallers up to establish themselves in a dugout. They had carried their equipment forward but, even though technological developments meant it was more portable than earlier in the war, they found that the weight made it a real struggle to get through the mud. When they reached the Steenbeek they crossed it on their hands and knees along a tree that had been felled. When they got to the other side, they tried to find the dugout.

A German pillbox at St Julien. It was known to the British as Hackney Villas and was captured by the 13th Royal Sussex in the initial stages of the attack on 31 July. The Steenbeek is in the foreground. Photo: Author

So we looked around and we found a German artillery position, and there was the back wall, the two sides, and the top, and gun position inside. There was no gun there, but it was a gun position. I said 'Right. Our new headquarters. Get in lads.' So I took my pack off and all the rest of it, and that was going to be our new headquarters. I got choked off afterwards because I hadn't gone to the other place. The other place wasn't there. What can you do?

Anyway we were there for some time, and then my batman - he was a good old stick - he said 'There's a chap there waving.' - there were wounded you know – 'Can I go and see what he wants?' I said 'Yes. Go on' so off he went. I didn't see him again for a time until quite later on in the day, and I didn't know until a fortnight later when he showed me a postcard from England, thanking him for what he had done, and I said 'What happened?' He said 'He was wounded' - he was wounded in the arm or the back or something like that - and he said 'So I put him on my back, and I took him into St. Julien.' - and down in a cellar there, the Medical Officer was there with his stretcher bearers, and he handed him over to him, and he said in this letter this lad had thanked him for saving his life you see. So I said 'And you carried him all that way from there?' It was not a great distance, but it was bad enough under the circumstances. I asked one or two of the others ... I said 'Did anybody see ...?' They said 'Aye. Do you know what he was doing, sir?' I said 'No' He said 'He'd got that fellow on his back, he'd got his rifle, and he'd got this other fellow's rifle, and he was carrying the lot' He was carrying the two rifles, and being a good soldier and not leaving the rifles behind.

(Second Lieutenant Robert Morton)

Morton recalled that he reported this act of bravery to Battalion headquarters as he felt the soldier[87] deserved official recognition. However, the Adjutant, Captain Naden, told him it was too late – acts of bravery should be reported when they occurred, not a fortnight later.

The men reorganised and had a brief rest so, after about thirty minutes, the advance resumed. Their objective was a position marked on their maps as the green line, 1100 yards north east of St Julien. Their advance was watched by the Cambridgeshires in support and they could see that both the Cheshires and Hertfordshires were experiencing some difficulty. Lieutenant George Cowpe was killed leading his men forward past St

Julien. His body was never recovered and identified. Lance Corporal Arthur Stansfield recalled that enemy fire had been relatively light until they reached St Julien but then they came under heavy shelling.

> *The enemy's snipers also started to be busy. Many good men we lost, but the line never wavered till we were only a mere fifty yards from the German trenches then, all of a sudden, the German machine guns opened fire on us and cut men away like a thrashing machine cutting corn. It was like hell itself let loose.*

Private Edward James, from Birkenhead. He originally joined 10th Cheshires, later transferring to the 6th Battalion. On 31 July, he was attached to the Machine Gun Company and was killed while carrying ammunition to the guns.

During the final stages of the attack, between St Julien and the final objective, several of the officers were wounded. Three of them continued to lead their men and were later awarded the Military Cross for their courage and devotion to duty. Lieutenant John Chorlton led his platoon to capture two machine guns that were holding up the advance. Captain Leo Ruddin continued to lead his company towards the objective in spite of a bullet wound to the calf, but had to retire to seek attention before they reached it. He never returned to overseas duty. Lieutenant George Kirton was also in command of a company. The forty six year old lived on the island of St Kitts in his younger days but, before the war, was working as a clerk in Manchester Council's Education Department. He also led his men to the objective, not seeking medical attention until later in the day.

To the left of the Cheshires, the Hertfordshires also had not suffered many casualties until this time, but after they passed through St Julien they came under heavy rifle and machine gun fire. One of its companies encountered a German strongpoint which they charged, killing or capturing most of its garrison. Shortly after they came across uncut German barbed wire, which held up most of the battalion, exposing them to machine gun fire from the flank. A few men, under Second Lieutenant Eric Marchington, managed to get through and continue the advance with the other units of the Brigade.

On the left of the Brigade attack, the Black Watch found the conditions very difficult. The area was boggy from the recent rains and the ground was very churned up by shellfire. However, they also managed to cross the Steenbeek with comparatively few casualties. From St Julien the Black Watch's C Company had to advance another 700 yards to reach their objective. The advance went well until they reached a position known as Triangle Farm. Here they came under heavy fire from a machine gun located on the first floor of the farm building, which had suffered little damage from the days of British shelling. They had no means to attack the gun position; even throwing grenades seemed to have little effect. A few troops were able to work their way round the farmhouse and continue towards the objective but most of the Battalion was held up. Those troops able to advance came across German infantry almost immediately and captured about fifty of them, sending them back towards the British line under escort. The handful of men moved forward with the remnants of the Brigade. The Black Watch's commanding officer, Lieutenant Colonel Sceales, later wrote in his official report on the day

> *Although everything up to this point appeared to have gone satisfactorily, beyond the fact that the advance had been hampered by machine gun and rifle fire and our own Heavies, and the fact that our covering Field Gun barrage had been considerably less than expected, ever increasing machine gun enfilade, and for the Right Companies defilade fire, from the right, not only made movement along the line very difficult and already was beginning to cause many casualties, but the fact that it was there at all made it quite evident that something had gone wrong.*

It cannot be known if he intended the irony.

The Brigade had advanced nearly two and half miles, reaching its final objective at 11.05am, exactly on schedule, but it had been at a terrible cost. When Second Lieutenant Bob Morton got the men to "count off", later in the day, there were only fifty seven men and one other officer left. The other two battalions had fared even worse, with only eleven Black Watch

Private Edward Hayward, a labourer from Pontesbury, Shropshire. He joined the King's Shropshire Light Infantry before being transferred to 6th Cheshires. Killed in action on 31 July 1917.

Thomas Hussey, from Shrewsbury. His body was never found and identified after the attack.

Corporal David Isaacs. One of the Battalion's Lewis gunners, he was killed in action on 31 July 1917. In civilian life, he was a machine joiner at the Ford Motor Company's factory in Trafford Park. In his spare time he played cricket and football for his church teams.

being counted and eight Hertfordshires. They had set out with a total of sixty officers and eighteen hundred men. The rest were dead, wounded or, simply, missing, although many of the latter were pinned down unable to continue the advance. In spite of the small numbers, the troops started to consolidate their gains. Sergeant Frank Brockbank had helped encourage his company forward through the enemy artillery barrage, later getting his men to dig in and consolidate the position. His actions were recognised by the award of the Distinguished Conduct Medal.

A patrol provided by the men of 15 Platoon, D Company under the command of Second Lieutenant Sydney King, was pushed out to Von Tirpitz Farm, some three hundred yards further on. King was the son of a Congregational minister and lived in the Wallasey area for most of his life. He worked as a bank clerk until he enlisted, as a private, in the King's Liverpool Regiment. Recently commissioned as an officer, he joined the Battalion on 3 May.

My orders were then to proceed with my platoon down the opposite slope to Von Tirpitz Farm, there to establish an outpost and

The modern building on the site of Von Tirpitz Farm. Photo: author

Second Lieutenant Sydney King's sketch of the area around the 'Green Line'.

entrench same. But on counter attack developing to retire to the Battalion on the line of resistance. This I did – leaving Langemarck Line, with remaining eleven men, we took Von Tirpitz Farm, with two casualties, after clearing dugouts and gun pits on our way. The enemy had an observation post in a tree beside the Farm, from which he could see over the crest....Whilst proceeding with entrenchment, a counter attack developed on the left, of some 150 enemy at 50 yards. After firing a magazine on the Lewis gun, I retired with my platoon in good order, but losing four men, over Langemarck trench into a large shell hole, about the line of resistance. Only wounded men of other companies were in sight.[88]

(Second Lieutenant Sydney King)

Captain Frank Naden had been awarded a Military Cross for his bravery in 1916 and would be awarded a bar to it for his actions at St Julien, which were described as being

> *For conspicuous gallantry and devotion to duty. On several occasions during the operations , he went among the men, cheering them up, assisted the wounded, organised and took forward parties under heavy fire, regardless of danger to himself and at all times was ready to render assistance in any way. He afterwards took over command of the battalion and brought them out. His conduct was magnificent throughout.*

He took command when Lieutenant Colonel Stanway was wounded in the leg earlier in the day.

> *The stretcher bearers moved forward as best they could. We had a lot of stuff to carry; dressings, stretchers, rations, and water. As we glance around we see our fellows being blown up on all sides. We eventually establish our Aid Post in what was called the Black Line. There are dead and wounded all over the place. The din is terrific. We are kept busy all the morning. Prisoners are arriving in hundreds, and we make them carry away our wounded.* (Sergeant James Boardman)

BROTHERS SPILSBURY.

Lce.-Corpl. WM. SPILSBURY,
missing from July 31, 1917.

Pte. SAML. SPILSBURY,
killed July 31, 1917.

Very shortly afterwards the Cheshires came under a strong counterattack from their right flank, caused by the units of 55th Division having been held up in their advance, leaving a gap for the Germans to exploit. In front of them, Germans who had been about to surrender now took heart and picked up their rifles again and there was fierce hand-to-hand fighting. There was a danger that the small party of Cheshires might be cut off and they were forced back a little way.

Back near St Julien, Second Lieutenant Bob Morton spotted the Germans forming up for the counter attack

I said 'What are those chaps over there?' They said 'They're Bosch'. I said 'They're coming our way.' They said 'We know. I said 'Right. Pack up.' I had no one in front of me. There was just our gang there. Supposed to be Battalion Headquarters. So I tell you, when we went back to that same tree over the Steenbeek, we didn't go on our hands and knees!

Private William Sunderland, from Hyde. He worked for a firm of cloth dyers. Killed in action on 31 July 1917.

Blondin never walked any quicker on his tightrope, and we got across - all of us - and then ploughed through all the mud, and went back to the old German line, but we were using it as Battalion Headquarters. It was facing the wrong way - that is - nice entrances to dugouts, but facing the Bosch shelling. So the Gloucester Pioneers - who were our Divisional pioneers - had been, and they'd dug a trench just over the top, and they'd done a good job, but it was all clay, and it rained, rained, rained all day, and it flooded. They dug a fire step, and I said to Lieutenant Solly - he was the only other officer - he'd been to the final objective - the green line as they called it - and he'd come back. I said 'Did you manage to get there?' and he said 'Yes, but there was no one there but me, so I thought I'd better come back'. So he'd come back and joined us. Then we got together, and I said 'Let's put our water bottles on this fire step', you know on this clay fire step, and then both of us went to sleep together, leaning against each other, and when we wakened up we found that the bottles were nowhere in evidence. They'd sunk, and we were wet through.'

Jocelyn Solly was born in Knaresborough in 1898 and was commissioned

A peaceful rural scene in the summer of 2016. On 31 July 1917, this was the 'Green Line', looking towards Ypres over the line of the advance.

in November 1916, joining the Battalion two months later. In the latter stages of the war, he served with the Scots Guards.

Second Lieutenant George Marsden took command of the few men remaining from his company when the senior officers were killed or wounded. Under his leadership, they established a strongpoint. He was awarded the Military Cross, *by his courage and determination* [he] *enabled the position to be held until the line had been re-established.* According to a letter from his officer to his wife, Company Sergeant Major Frank Phillips, from Stockport, was killed near the Green Line, leading his men on and encouraging them forward. He was, however, posted as being missing and, with his body still not recovered and identified, the War Office made an official presumption of death in May 1918. Unlike many of his comrades killed on 31 July, Phillips' body was discovered when the battlefields were searched and cleared postwar, as the land was being returned to civilian use. His remains are buried in Tyne Cot Cemetery.

Company Sergeant Major Frank Philips, killed near the 'Green Line'.

At 12.15pm it was decided that the Cheshires, along with the handful of Black Watch and Hertfordshires, should withdraw some 500 yards to link up with the King's Liverpool men of 55th Division. This was facilitated by the arrival of a company from 1/1st Cambridgeshires, who attacked the Germans, giving the other troops time to fall back. Meanwhile, the remainder of the Cambridgeshires were themselves coming under a strong attack which they managed to beat off with rifle and machine gun fire. However, the Germans were now only fifty yards from the British positions. The Cambridgeshires called for Stokes mortars to be brought forward and, indeed, they were, but no ammunition came with them.

The Brigade held this new position, under shellfire, for the remainder of the day. The withdrawal meant that some men who had been wounded or were pinned down in shell holes had to be left to fend for themselves as best they could. Lieutenant Francis of the Hertfordshires later wrote that he was in a shell hole with another officer and four or five of his men, together with one of the Cheshires. At about 1.30, the Germans seemed to be all around his position and were already putting captured Cheshires to work, searching the area for wounded men. By 4pm only he and one other were still alive in the shell hole, when they were discovered and taken prisoner.

> *I found myself in a shell hole with a wound in the thigh, which I bandaged up myself as best I could under the circumstances. I cried out for help, thinking some of our men would hear me, but it was all in vain. By this time, I had become weak through loss of blood and no food or drink. At last, God answered my prayers and I went unconscious.*

(Lance Corporal Arthur Stansfield)

Lieutenant William Rogers had been with the Battalion since the summer of 1916, having enlisted in the Lincolnshires as a private in 1914. He worked as a salesman for the Manchester cotton spinning firm of Barlow & Jones. He had withdrawn his men to a new position. Lance Corporal Thomas Potts later wrote *Lieutenant Rogers was hit by a bullet in the face and shoulder, only wounding him. A few minutes later, he was hit in the stomach by another bullet and died without speaking. I was then wounded myself and cannot vouch for anything that occurred afterwards.* Rogers left a widow, Florence, in his native Boston, Lincolnshire, where he is remembered on the town's war memorial.

An advertisement for the company where Rogers worked.

Second Lieutenant Sydney King was still pinned down in a shell hole near the green line. It was only much later that he learned the Battalion had been forced to withdraw under pressure from the counterattack that he had observed.

> *"Seeing we were being surrounded from the left, I ordered my remaining four men to leave the shell hole, one by one, towards our lines and followed with my sergeant. Shortly afterwards, in the neighbourhood of Winnipeg, N.E. of St Julien, I was shot through the right thigh, femoral artery, and was unable to proceed. During the following night, I crawled by my compass towards our lines, by daybreak reaching Schuler Farm, east of St Julien, and then just behind the enemy new front line. Here I was taken prisoner.*[89]

There continued to be numerous casualties to be dealt with.

> *In the afternoon we moved further ahead to a place called Corner Cot. It was hard work getting the wounded away as we had neither bearers nor stretchers and dusk was beginning to fall; Later in the day our lads had to retire and we also were told to retire. But what could we do? We had about thirty badly wounded men, both British and German. We decided to stay on and to try to get the wounded away. To make matters worse it began to rain.*
>
> (Sergeant James Boardman)

Boardman had been awarded the Military Medal in 1916 and was awarded a bar to it for his bravery on 31 July.

Bob Morton recalled there was a wounded soldier just in front of his position.

> *He was calling for his mother and some of the lads got fed up with him. 'Shut your ruddy mouth' and things like that, but you couldn't do anything about it. Then it went quiet – he'd gone.*

WAR NURSE'S HUSBAND KILLED.

Lance-Corpl. A. E. SEVERN.

Nurse "EDITH." V.A.D.

Albert Severn, a postman from Birkenhead, was serving with D Company when he was killed on 31 July. He had married Edith Peabody in 1910.

Another German counter attack was delivered at about 5pm. It was against the Cambridgeshires' positions near Border House. It was driven off by rifle and Lewis gun fire, with the British troops also firing captured German machine guns. The German shelling again intensified and a further withdrawal of all the Brigade's troops was ordered by Lieutenant Colonel Riddell, of the Cambridgeshires, who was the senior officer in the forward zone. Riddell made this decision not just because of the German shelling but also because the British artillery was firing short and their shells were falling on his positions.

Lance Corporal Collier was the signallers' resident comedian. Bob Morton described him as a 'regular wag'.

> *We'd got our rubber groundsheets with us, and you put them over your shoulder - they weren't much use. You were wet through to the knees - as a matter of fact we found it was better to keep your legs in the water - it was warmer with the legs in the water than out - with the wind, with the air. So Collier he came round to my left, and he'd got a couple of German rifles. He was better with that, and he put them over the top of the trench, then he got his groundsheet, and he put that over - he had to have his bivvy - he put that over the top, and he sat there quite proud. The trouble was that it was raining all day. We saw this groundsheet bending more and more and more, and all at once it went - phoosh - the lot of it, all over him. And do you know, he was sat there looking to the back - not to the front - he was sat on the firestep, and he never moved. It just came all over him. The Signals Sergeant called out, he said 'What's up Col? What are you thinking about?' He just looked as if he was in a daze. He said 'I was just wondering what ruddy sunstroke feels like!'*
>
> (Second Lieutenant Robert Morton)

At 10pm the Brigade was ordered to withdraw to the original British and German front lines, leaving the units of 116 and 117 Brigades in the advanced positions. The order was passed on to Bob Morton, now the Cheshires' senior officer in the forward area:

> *I got instructions not to come out in a blob, to come out in ones and twos, which I did. I detailed men to go this way, you go that way, and you go that way, and you two go that way, and intervals between, 'cause time didn't matter, so long as we got out, and then until finally there was Company Sergeant Major Parkin - he was a good Company Sergeant Major, from down Adswood here, and myself left you see. So I said 'Right Len, you now.' So Len went off on his own, and I - out of the whole 600 - I was the only one left at St. Julien, and so when I thought it was safe enough, I walked out with a pair of very, very stiff legs - walking like I do now! Stiff legged!*

Len Parkin joined the Territorials in 1909 and had been in the forefront of the day's fighting. He had received a Military Medal in 1916 and for his actions at St Julien was awarded the Military Cross.

> *His dash and determination during the advance was responsible for putting several machine-guns out of action, thus clearing the way for the attacking waves. When all the officers of his company became casualties, he led the company in the most spirited manner and continued in command till they came out of action.*

Glossop Lads in the Fierce Fighting of July 31st.

Lance-Cpl. Albert Booth Reported Missing.

Albert Booth was never heard of again.

Morton continued.

> *I walked, and I walked, and I walked, and I think we'd advanced about 2 miles, and so I walked, and then when I got to Brigade Headquarters near the canal bank, I went in and reported to Brigade, and the Brigadier said 'How are you feeling Morton?' He said to 'Duff'" - that was the Signals Officer at the Brigade – 'Give Morton some of that ham.' He said 'It'll do him more good than anything' - and he'd got a big doings of boiled ham, so he cut some slices off.*
>
> *The Brigadier General - Sir Edward Bellingham - came back later. 'Feeling better now, Morton?' So I said 'Yes. Thanks very much.' He said, 'I suppose you could do with a sleep now couldn't you?' I said 'I could, sir.' He said 'Well look. Go along here and*

ask my batman where my dugout is, and go and have a sleep on my bed' - and that was very nice for a Brigadier to say to a Second Lieutenant - and he said 'Or would you sooner go to your transport line to get a change of clothing' - because everything was wet. So I said 'Yes sir.' So I did that. I walked quite a distance to a little hole in the ground, and they shelled us even there.

The next day the Cheshires struggled to consolidate the gains and build strongpoints. It had started to rain again during the previous afternoon and the whole area was a quagmire. Movement was difficult, with men getting stuck in the mud, making it very difficult to bring up supplies and rations.

About 3.30 a.m. on August 1st Captain Naden gave us a call and explained the position. Eventually we got some prisoners and improvised stretchers out of overcoats and rifles, getting all the wounded safely back to our own lines. The German wounded all the time we had them with us said we were best comrades. The remainder of the day was very busy, as there was one continual stream of wounded coming in. Just outside the place we had made into an Aid Post was a battery of German guns. The wounded as they came in were in a pitiable plight, being wet through and covered with mud. It was evening before we got clear of the wounded. We had to send for our bandsmen to act as stretcher bearers, and some of these were killed and one or two captured by the enemy. Shelling was very heavy, all the day and night. The enemy got a direct hit on our Aid Post, but it stood the test.

(Sergeant James Boardman)

During the evening the Battalion was relieved and moved back to near its starting position at La Brique. They had a few hours rest but, the next day, went forward again to garrison the captured German trenches. Several stragglers had caught up with the Battalion and it now had 124 officers and men. These extra men were soldiers who had taken part in the attack and received minor wounds or had got stuck in the mud.

August 2.—With the first streak of dawn casualties again began to roll up. We were able to keep clear as we had a better service of bearers. The rain was still coming down in torrents. This put a stop to the operations.

August 4.—Odd casualties still coming in—teeth chattering and nearly famished.

(Sergeant James Boardman)

As mentioned, Arthur Stansfield had been wounded in the leg. He was in the shell hole for three days, spending much of the time unconscious.

I could see Germans walking about on a search for wounded and loot. I knew I was to become a prisoner because I was on high ground and could not see a single one of our men. So, I called the first German stretcher bearer when they came. I tried to explain and motioned to them that my leg was broken. Whether they understood or not, I do not know, but they put me on an oil-sheet suspended from a pole and carried me to a dugout. While I was being carried, I could see several other British soldiers who were in the same plight as myself. The Germans treated me fairly well, giving me food and water in the shape of black bread and bully beef, which was the best they had. After a few hours of waiting, I was carried to a dressing station and dressed for the first time since being wounded. My leg had got in a bad state with lying out for three days unconscious.

William Bennett was another taken prisoner. The twenty five year old lived in Stockport with his parents and worked as piecer at Palmer's Mill. He had been a territorial from about 1911. He was badly wounded and it was necessary for the German surgeons to amputate his leg; but he died on 28 August.

The Cheshires remained in the forward zone until relieved on 5 August, when they moved back to bivouacs at Reigersburg Chateau, near Ypres.

During the operations the Battalion had lost five officers and 193 other ranks killed or missing and twelve officers and 259 other ranks wounded. Many of those posted as being missing were never heard of again. Harold Beard had captured three prisoners at St Pierre Divion the previous year. His mother made enquiries to see if anyone had definite knowledge about his fate on 31 July. She received a letter from a sergeant saying he had seen him wounded near Schuler Farm but it was not until July 1918 that the

Private Harold Beard.

War Office confirmed that, as nothing had been heard from him, then he must have been killed. His body was never found and identified. The body of nineteen year old Tim Cronin, from Egremont, near Wallasey, was also never identified. He received a minor wound in the hand and was about to make his way to the dressing station when a piece of shrapnel caught him in the neck and he died within two minutes. George Lambert's parents put two notices in the Stockport newspapers appealing for information about him. There was a rumour that he had been taken prisoner but this proved to be false and Mr and Mrs Lambert never heard more about their son.

As well as the Military Crosses and Distinguished Conduct Medals mentioned previously, sixteen Military Medals were awarded for now unknown acts of bravery at St Julien. Amongst the recipients were Robert Adkinson, Harry Hayes, Samuel Holland, John Melia, J Mottershead, Cecil Nunn, Harry Peake, Cyril Pickup, John Timlin and William Wright. Holland was taken prisoner on 20 April 1918 and spent the remainder of the war in a camp in Limburg, Germany.

Private George Lambert. Rumoured to have been taken prisoner on 31 July but he had been killed.

The Battalion remained at Reigersburg Chateau for two days, then moved westwards to billets at Flêtre, where they remained until the 15th, before moving to tented billets at Ridge Wood. During this rest period they received a number of reinforcements. By now, new drafts of soldiers would include men from all over the country, as conscription had broken the geographical ties a territorial battalion had with its original recruiting area. On 19 August the Cheshires went into the line again, spending the rest of the month alternating between the front and support lines near Klein Zillebeke. When they moved into the sector they found no formal front line trench system, only a series of posts established in shell holes. Much of their time was spent in digging a trench to connect the holes up into a good defensive system. It was a comparatively uneventful time and there were few casualties during this tour of duty.

William Davies, killed in action on 3 September.

It was not until 3 September that they suffered their first fatalities since St Julien. William Davies from Acton Bridge and William Dutton from Stockport were killed by artillery fire. There was considerable aircraft activity on the 5 September, with British machine gunners driving off enemy planes, but one British plane was shot down just in front of the Cheshires' position. During the night a party went out and recovered the pilot's body. The Battalion returned to front line action on 19 September, in preparation for an attack the next day.

The engagement was the third major set piece attack in the continuing offensive around Ypres and was later given the official title of the Battle of the Menin Road. Eleven divisions were committed on the first of several days fighting. The Cheshires moved into their assembly positions at Shrewsbury Forest and were in position by 2am on the 20th. Their orders were to act as reserves for the battalions of 117 Brigade. Zero hour was set for 5.40am and 117 Brigade went forward, capturing its objectives. At 7.40am one company of Cheshires was ordered forward to support the attack and a second followed shortly afterwards. Captain Harry Yorke and his servant, Private Joseph Thornton from Stalybridge, went forward side by side and were still together when Thornton was shot dead by a German sniper. Yorke's company carried on to strengthen the left flank of the attack. He was awarded the Military Cross, the citation recording that *advancing all the time, under extremely heavy fire, he showed great skill in selecting his final position.*

20 September 1917. The Cheshires advanced from Shrewsbury Forest, in the far distance, taking up positions near here. Photo: author

Private Isaac Evans, wounded on 20 September, died in the ambulance on the way to hospital. His brother, George, is understood to have been killed in 1916, serving in the Manchester Regiment.

Private William Fairclough, a married man from Higher Bebington, Wirral. Photo supplied by Dave Horne, author Higher Bebington Heroes.

Private John Loftus. Killed in action on 20 September. He previously served with 13ᵗʰ Cheshire and was wounded in 1916. He joined the 6ᵗʰ Battalion on recovering from the injuries only two weeks before he was killed.

Also shot in the advance was Lance Corporal Albert Norbury, one of the Lewis gunners. His officer wrote to his wife, Matilda, saying that: *We bandaged him up and everything that could be done for him was done but unfortunately without success. The one redeeming feature was that he had very little pain.* Norbury lived in the Portwood area of Stockport with Matilda and their five children. In civilian life he worked as a mangler at Sykes' bleachworks in Edgeley. At about the same time Colonel Stanway went forward to a position known as The Ravine to reconnoitre the possibility of his remaining two companies delivering a counter attack; but he concluded that the situation did not warrant an attack.

There were several enemy counterattacks during the late afternoon and early evening and Private James

Lance Corporal Albert Norbury.

Bredbury may have died the most senseless death of the day during one of them. Living in Stockport with his wife, Annie, and their two children, he worked at Beehive Mills. He was one of the Battalion's Lewis gunners and a comrade wrote to Annie saying that he had continued firing from a shellhole until the Germans were close to him and then put a grenade under his gun, blowing it and himself up. There would have been every opportunity to retreat or surrender. William Clayton may have had the luckiest escape of the day. The young second lieutenant, from Liverpool, had only joined the Battalion in June. He was struck in the chest by a rifle bullet. Fortunately for him, he was wearing a metal body shield which the bullet could not penetrate. His only injury was some very bad bruising to the chest; but it was sufficiently serious to keep him away from duty until June 1918.

Private James Bredbury, killed by his own grenade.

Much later in the day, at 6.30pm, another company, under the command of Second Lieutenant William Riley, was ordered forward in support of the adjacent 41st Division. They advanced under heavy machine gun fire, capturing their objective, near the Bassvillebeek stream, by 7.10pm. Riley's soldiers held the position all night but were obliged to withdraw the next morning so as to keep in touch with the troops of the 41st Division. Although they remained in the forward zone, the next two days were relatively quiet. Corporal Ernest Secker, a twenty year old iron moulder from Dukinfield, was in a charge of a Lewis gun post in one of the advanced positions. He and another man continued to fire, even though their position was twice blown up and the other gunners became casualties. His bravery was recognised by the award of the Distinguished Conduct Medal.

On the 26th the Cheshires moved to support an attack by 4/5th Black Watch. All the objectives were achieved, in spite of the difficulties of advancing across very boggy ground. Corporal William Andrews of the Black Watch later recounted meeting one of the Cheshires.[90]

We had orders to dump our rations at a map reference. We found this to be a strong German built dugout. The 1/6th Cheshires dumped rations at the same point and, my carriers having started back, I went with a Company Quartermaster Sergeant of theirs into the dugout to have a rest before moving again. He was a Free

Church minister's son and had spent part of his life as an Atlantic steward. We began to swap yarns. In the middle of the conversation, the Germans interrupted by rapping the top of the dugout with a big shell. My Cheshire friend, who was very calm, said we had better beat it. We waited for the next hit and then dashed to a little trench about fifteen yards away. This was safer because the Germans, having made that dugout, knew precisely where it was and a few more direct hits would smash it in. Moreover the doorway faced the German way and there was a chance of their putting a shell through it.

I regretted that I had not hurried off back with the others the moment we had dumped our rations but the Cheshire was not a bit perturbed. 'A direct hit would blot us out' he said 'but otherwise we'll be alright. It takes hundreds of shells to kill a man.' We crouched in that little trench in the very centre of shellfire for ninety minutes during which time one missile followed another so fast that it was hopeless to attempt to make a dash for it. Our trench was ringed with shell pits at the finish, two of the explosions were near enough to bury us, but we were not hit.

Private John Leigh. Died of wounds at 41st Casualty Clearing Station. Sister Reid wrote to his family, saying everything that could be done for him was done and 'he had every care and attention but all was to no avail. He died very peacefully this morning at 4am.'

The Battalion was relieved during the evening of the 27th. Casualties during the period in action had been heavy. Sixty two men were known to be dead. Another fifty one were missing and more than three times that number were wounded. A number of men received the Military Medal for their actions during the previous days. They included Private George Foley, who was one of the Battalion's runners and had carried messages throughout the period under heavy fire. The twenty two year old cotton worker from Hyde also received a letter from the Divisional commander, Major General Edward Feetham. Foley survived the war, returning to Hyde, where he is believed to have died in 1960. Feetham had only several months left to live and was killed in action on 29 March 1918.

Private George Foley. Awarded the Military Medal

Private Arthur Brough, sitting on the floor, was wounded on 27 September. He died two days later at 37th Casualty Clearing Station. In civilian life the nineteen year old worked at Crewe railway station.

Lance Corporal Wilfred Roberts, a Glossop weaver by trade. Killed in action on 19 October while serving with the brigade's trench mortar battery. He had previously been mentioned in despatches. His captain wrote to his parents – 'Your son was always a most cheery and brave soldier; his place in the battery will be very hard to fill.'

Hellfire Corner, 1917. Photo: Australian War Memorial.

Most of October was spent in reserve billets at Westoutre, Little Kemmel and La Clytte, except for a few days in the middle of the month, when they provided working parties for II ANZAC (Australian and New Zealand Army Corps) at Hellfire Corner, just outside Ypres. On the 28th they moved by bus to Shrapnel Corner, to the south of the town, and then marched to positions near Gheluvelt. They spent several days, digging to link up isolated posts to form a defensive trench line. It was a dangerous time, as the German artillery was particularly active, resulting in the deaths of six men and several more wounded.

They withdrew to reserve positions during the evening of 31 October and to billets at Chippewa Camp on 4 November. This was not before Private Arthur Woodcock was fatally shot through the head. He was buried behind the lines but, in later fighting, his grave was lost and the twenty seven year old painter and decorator is now commemorated on the Tyne Cot Memorial to the Missing. He is remembered on the village memorial at Great Barrow, near Chester.

James Corfe, from Higher Bebington, worked as a warehouseman in Liverpool. He had only joined the Battalion twelve days before he was killed on 29 October. Photo: Dave Horne, author Higher Bebington Heroes.

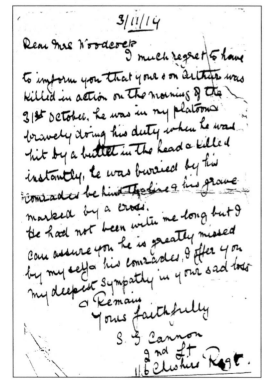

Private Arthur Woodcock and the officer's letter to his mother telling her of his death on 31 October. Photo and letter: Regimental Museum.

The Cheshires were still within range of the German heavy artillery, which was mainly firing gas shells. Several men were affected and had to go to hospital. This included Lieutenant Colonel Stanway on the 5th. The next day Captain Geoffrey Whitfield was posted to the Battalion from the Hertfordshires to take temporary command. The Cheshires returned to the front line on 11 November, taking over positions at Polderhoek. Private Vincent Brett was not with his comrades. When the orders came to go up to the line, he deserted and was not caught until 27 November. It was a most serious offence, long incorporated into military law as a capital crime. He was tried by court martial and would have thought himself very fortunate to escape the ultimate penalty. During the course of the war over 3000 men were sentenced to death, of whom just over 300 were executed. Brett received a ten year prison sentence and will have thought himself even luckier when the sentence was suspended. He later served with a battalion of the Worcestershire Regiment and was wounded in September 1918 before returning home to Stalybridge.

Private Cyril Downs, killed in action on 13 November. He lived in Glossop and was employed at a local ironworks..

On the 12th, there was considerable enemy artillery fire; however it was necessary for the men to be out in the open, linking up isolated posts in shellholes. Ben Millward, from Stockport, was fatally shot by a sniper. His comrade, Arthur Morris, also from the town, went to help him and was also promptly shot and killed.

The following days were spent alternating between periods in camp and tours of duty in the support lines, providing working parties and then returning to front line duty on 21 November. Second Lieutenant William Davidson had only joined the Battalion on 4 November. Originally from Sale, he is thought to have been working as a bank cashier in Halifax until he joined the army at the end of 1915. He was wounded on the first day of the tour of duty and never returned to active service. He was still receiving medical treatment at the end of 1918.

Private Fred Marshall, from Stalybridge, where he was employed as a colour mixer at Carrbrook printworks. Killed in action on 29 October.

My helmet was smashed on my head by a machine gun bullet which damaged my skull on the left temple and tore down my left ear, also a slight wound to my neck. I have been in hospital eleven months and as recently as seven or eight weeks ago my head was open again, for the fifth time.

Second Lieutenant Lambert Brewer joined the same day as Davidson. His service was also short, being gassed on 24 November. He returned to the UK for treatment and did not serve overseas again. Other than his wartime service, he is understood to have lived all his life in Lostwithial, Cornwall, where he married in 1923 and died in 1984. Both of these men were more fortunate than their fellow officer, Second Lieutenant Percy Brookes. He was killed on 22 November, having only joined on the 9th.

Private Ben Millward, killed in action on 12 November 1917.

Working parties continued to be supplied in the first days of December, with the Cheshires now based in Poperinghe, The work was mainly carrying forward ammunition for VIII Corps artillery and improving their battery positions. On 9 December, they moved to rest billets at Le Waast where, for the remainder of the month, they undertook training exercises, listened to lectures and played sports.

Christmas was celebrated here, as recounted to the *Stockport Advertiser* by one of the sergeants:

The commanding officer and his officers set themselves out to give the boys a great time and they had it. As a preliminary, they managed to purchase the biggest pig in the village and this was marched down in state to the village green and despatched with all the necessary rites and ceremonies in the presence of a vast mouth-watering multitude. Companies tossed up for choice of cuts and then set out among themselves to purchase the village turkeys and poultry. The people lent us their rooms and pots and pans and also the bakehouses, where the meat and poultry were cooked and prepared in an admirable manner. We even had stuffing – what it was made of goodness knows, but it was real good – and apple sauce too. Breakfast was bacon and tomato sauce, and tea, bully, cold meat and cakes from home. We have been very generously treated by the good people at home, who supply comforts for the troops and have had a good supply sent to us. In fact, for the first time for a long time, one could see bread and cake left over from tea for supper - which, considering the enormous appetites of the lads, is really a sight for the gods. Christmas pudding was also very good and plentiful, and much appreciated, and it was really astonishing the amount that was put away.

As is usual on these occasions, the warrant officers and sergeants waited on the boys for dinner and tea; and then we had our meal at a little estaminet, which we have been using as a mess. We had turkey and a nice piece of pork, and a goodly supply of pudding and cakes. The band which is now second to none played Christmas hymns all the previous night at the different billets, and the Battalion paraded on Christmas morning for a further half-hour's service and more hymns, which went ripping. At eleven o'clock the band played for dancing on the village green and, as the snow had settled firmly it was good as being on the Armoury floor.

With Christmas over, the Battalion marched to new billets at Quesques on the 29th, but had to return the next day to collect the blankets which their lorries had been unable to bring as the roads were impassable due to snow – although seemingly not impassable for marching men. It was a miserable end to a miserable year.

CHAPTER 9

The Final Year

New Year's Day was spent moving by march and train to new billets near Irish Farm, outside Ypres. Until the 7th the men undertook working parties for a Royal Engineers Tunnelling Company. That day they moved to billets in the Hill Top sector – unlike their previous encounters with this area it was now firmly in the reserve. Working parties continued to be provided for the Royal Engineers but the work was mainly digging small trenches to accommodate telephone cables. The first fatality of 1918 came on 10 January when Sergeant Stanley Clough was killed. The twenty five year old single man from Stockport had joined the territorials in the spring of 1914.

Sergeant Stanley Clough, killed in action on 10 January.

On 11 January the Battalion went into the front line again, relieving the 4/5th Black Watch near Poelcapelle. There was heavy enemy shelling, which seems to have caught a patrol of their own in No Man's Land. The Cheshires captured a wounded man there, identifying him as serving with the 237th Regiment. Conditions in the trenches were very wet and the problem of trench foot returned to incapacitate nearly a hundred men during the tour of duty. The relief, on the 15th, was considerably hampered and delayed by the depth of water in the trenches and the general flooding in the area. It meant that the incoming men from the Royal Sussex Regiment had lost their way, as landmarks had disappeared under the water. One of those falling victim to trench foot was Second Lieutenant John Hill. The nineteen year old, from the Withington area of Manchester, had been studying law at Manchester University before he was commissioned on 26 April 1917. He had been with the Battalion since June of that year. When he came out of the trenches he had felt a tingling sensation in his feet and ankles and was having difficulty standing. The condition got worse and, by the 17th, he had lost all feeling in his feet. He was evacuated back to Britain a couple of days later and did not return to overseas duty, serving with the 4th Reserve Battalion when he had recovered. He was promoted to lieutenant in October 1918, a somewhat surprising promotion, as the previous month he had been admitted to hospital having contracted gonorrhoea in Whitstable. The army regarded becoming infected with venereal disease as a serious matter, along the lines of a self-inflicted injury. Hill was probably obliged to forfeit his pay for the duration of his time away from duty.

The Cheshires left the Ypres sector on 25 January 1918, marching to Proven and travelling by train to Ribemont-sur-Ancre, on the Somme front. It was a fifteen hour journey, arriving at 8am. They marched from there to billets in houses in the village of Bray. There was another march on the 29th to Haut Aillaines, where they stayed overnight. James Boardman recalled that:

> *after being paid many of our men went to the Divisional Canteen. An enemy bombing plane got two direct hits on the Canteen. There were about one hundred casualties, and about twenty of our men were missing.*

The Battalion war diary makes no mention of this and, if men were originally missing, they turned up in due course and no fatalities are registered for the day. The journey continued next morning and they reached Sorel le Grand later in the day. On the last day of the month they relieved the 4th South African Battalion in the support trenches at Gouzeaucourt. The next few days were spent providing carrying parties as well as working on trench digging and generally improving the defences.

By the beginning of 1918 the number of available replacement troops had become a major issue. There were insufficient men to maintain the structure of the army as it had been. Field Marshal Haig had a dilemma. He would either have to disband whole divisions or reduce the number of battalions in each division. He chose the latter, reducing each infantry brigade from four to three battalions. It meant the breakup of battalions and the loss of many relationships – those between the men and their officers and those between the officers and their command structure. There was an inevitable resentment at the break up of units. The 16th Cheshires were one such battalion. They were formed in Birkenhead in December 1914, initially as a Bantam unit. The Bantams were set up to allow men to join up although they were not tall enough to meet the army's previous minimum height of 5 feet 3 inches. By late 1916, with the introduction of conscription, men of all heights were posted to these units. At the beginning of February 1918 the battalion was at about half strength and was disbanded. Most of the men were sent to the 15th Battalion – originally also a Bantam unit – but five officers and 101 men were sent to the 6th Cheshires, arriving on 2 February.

Joseph Brown.

On the night of 6 February the Battalion took over the front line trench from the Black Watch. That night, German working parties were spotted in No Man's Land. The Battalion Lewis gunners opened fire on them, scattering the troops and forcing them back to their own line. The Germans returned the next night and with exactly the same lack of success. The men spent the days improving the defences until, at 6pm on the 10th, they came under heavy attack from German trench mortars. It was covering fire for a raid on a Cheshires' advanced sap – a small trench leading out into No Man's Land from the main trench system. Three men were later posted as missing, presumably captured. The Battalion was relieved and moved to Dessart Camp on the 14th. Two days later the camp came under heavy attack from German aircraft, with bombs landing between 6.30pm and 11pm. The attack killed nine men and wounded another four, two of whom died in the coming days. John Sheard was a skilled man, working as a watchmaker in Halifax. He married Florence Mann before he went overseas. He had been awarded the Distinguished Conduct Medal, for several acts of bravery as indicated in the official citation.

Private Samuel Wilson, from New Brighton, had previously served with 13th Cheshires. Killed in action on 16 February.

> *As a runner he performed his duties in a gallant and fearless manner, on more than one occasion acting as a guide to reinforcements, guiding them to their positions during most critical periods. He went about*

Alfred Hindson, a tram conductor from Wallasey. Died of wounds on 15 February.

continually under the heaviest bombardment, setting a splendid example. On one occasion he brought in a wounded comrade from an exposed position.

Joseph Brown was another Yorkshireman: he had been transferred to the Cheshires from the Army Service Corps in September 1917. He had married Mary Brown only a few weeks before. He was badly wounded in the abdomen during the air raid. Brown was taken to a CCS at Tincourt but died there on the 18th. Sam Williams was also killed in the air raid. The twenty one year old, from Wallasey, had been wounded in August 1917 and had only returned to duty on 23 January.

During the early hours of 28 February men from the Battalion formed up in the front line trench at Gouzeaucourt, ready to raid German positions across No Man's Land in front of the village of Gonnelieu. In command was Captain Ronald Norman, one of the Battalion's prewar officers and now the senior officer in C Company. There were three other officers and 110 other ranks, together with three sappers, who would lay demolition charges. So as not to draw attention to themselves, the officers dressed as privates but took their revolvers with them. The raiders would attack different parts of the German line, in three separate groups. Zero hour was

Gouzeaucourt. At the time of this photograph, early in the war, it was in German hands.

Gouzeaucourt, severely damaged and in British hands.

set for 5.15am and, on schedule, a covering artillery barrage opened up. The right hand group got into the trench, engaging ten Germans, nine of whom they killed or wounded, taking the tenth prisoner. They found the trench to be a new one and still incomplete. Dugouts had not yet been made and the Germans had made shelters using ground sheets and, in two of these, braziers were burning. From the number of bodies lying around who had been killed by the British shelling, it was concluded that it was strongly held.

The raiding group to their left, commanded by Captain Norman, also shot and bayonetted several Germans. They then moved along the Gonnelieu – Gouzeaucourt road, finding it obstructed by well constructed barbed wire defences, but they were able to get through with relative ease. They found the tunnel that was their objective. At this point they came under attack from German grenades, which wounded two men, who were able to get back to the British line. The Germans then came on them over the ground and fire and grenades were exchanged. The Cheshires were now twenty minutes into the raid and the sappers were instructed to get on with placing their charges, firing them successfully. Sergeant Claude

Gillam had accounted for several of the Germans and, as they were withdrawing, he spotted a machine gun and blew it up with a grenade. His actions were recognised by the award of a Distinguished Conduct Medal. Lieutenant Sydney Astle was in command of the third group. He came from Stockport, where his father was editor of the local newspaper, and had only been with the Battalion since January. Only a few of his group got into the enemy trench, the remainder being held up by the barbed wire and pinned down by machine gun fire. However, they were still able to blow up a German dugout. While the sappers were setting the charges the Cheshires moved down the trench system, throwing grenades into another dugout and making their way to engage a machine gun post. However, when they reached the site, they found that the Germans had withdrawn to their rear, taking the gun with them.

Lieutenant Sydney Astle.

Five Cheshires were killed in the operation but it was estimated that the Germans had lost seventy to ninety men. Four men were awarded the Military Medal for their actions during the raid. Sergeant Robert Bates was awarded the French Croix de Guerre for rushing a machine gun post. Both Norman and Astle were awarded the Military Cross. The Battalion remained in the front line or support trenches until it was relieved on 11 March, moving to billets at York Camp, Moislains, where several days were spent in training, including musketry.

Towards the end of 1917, German military planners had to consider two major developments. The first was the declaration of war by the United States on 6 April. The second was the situation on the Eastern Front, the war with Russia. Throughout the year, the Bolsheviks gained in political strength and proposed, in their revolutionary literature, a negotiated peace with Germany. They came to power in October, almost immediately opening negotiations that led to an armistice being agreed in the middle of December. In November the German high command had already decided on a major attack against the British positions. Believing, with some justification, that the British army had been considerably weakened by the fighting throughout the year, it was intended that the attack would be decisive in winning the war. It was vital that the offensive be launched and the war brought to an end before the Americans built up their forces on the Western Front, which they expected not to be possible until the end of 1918. Peace with the Russians now allowed Germany to transfer divisions from the east, giving them numerical superiority against the British.

British military planners had also concluded that the attack was likely and that both sides planned to deal with the expected situation. On the German side, there would be an extremely heavy artillery bombardment, not just on the front line, but also the rear areas, intended to break up any attempts to reinforce the front line troops. The attacking infantry would then employ stormtroopers – units whose task was to press forward the assault, leaving pockets of resistance to be dealt with by following troops. On the British side, there was a new style of defence. In place of the traditional front line continuous trench system, the attacking enemy would first encounter lightly held outposts, two companies strong, supported to their immediate rear by the remainder of the battalion in a well defended redoubt. The intent was that these forward units would delay and break up any attack, allowing time for

Private Frederick Davies, killed in action on 15 February. He lived in Birkenhead, where he worked for a local estate agent.

the troops behind them, in what was now labelled as the battle zone, to prepare. The battle zone was a more traditional trench system a mile or so to the rear. Behind them, would be reserve troops, ready to go forward to support the main defenders.

By the early spring of 1918 the British were certain that a German offensive was imminent and men were desperately digging trenches and building other defences. The only questions remaining were where and when the attack would take place. The answer to both questions was answered on the Fifth Army front at 4.40am on 21 March 1918.

The German artillery opened fire, shelling an area of 150 square miles, around the town of St Quentin. Over the next five hours, the Germans fired 1,100,100 shells, easily the largest barrage of the war. The 16th (Irish) Division was deployed near the village of Ronssoy, to the east of the town of Peronne. The war diary of its 49 Brigade notes: *Intense hostile bombardment opened on main battle positions, support lines, St Emilie, Villers Faucon and as far back as Marquaix. Mainly gas shell on forward lines and Brigade HQ. All* [telephone] *wires cut. Communication by visual and pigeon impossible owing to dense mist.* Shortly after, the German infantry came on and, by around 10am, the 2nd Royal Irish Regiment was under attack from both flanks and from Germans who had got round to their rear. The war diary records they held out until 1.30pm, when their ammunition ran out. Those who could do so managed to retreat to a recently dug position known as Irish Trench. Even here they found that the Germans had already set up a machine gun post in the trench, but the Irish were in superior numbers and were able to clear them out. However, by 2.30pm, they were forced to retire still further, coming under machine gun fire from only 300 yards away. When they got to the relative safety of St Emilie there were, at first, only three officers and fifteen other soldiers.

Still in camp at Moislains, the Cheshires heard the German artillery fire open up only nine miles away to their east. In less than an hour they were ready to move off with the other units of the Brigade, but no orders were received until much later. At 6pm they marched to Longavesnes, where they dug a trench overnight, which was intended to provide a defensive flank. The Battalion's war diary records that shelling was light but records show that eight men were killed during the day. They included three men who had been previously wounded. Robert Callister had worked on a farm on the Isle of Man and been posted in January after recovering from wounds sustained with 15th Cheshires. Londoner Walter Cayless originally served with the Army Service Corps but had been transferred in September 1917 and was wounded in the arm a month later. Benjamin Curtis, from Bedfordshire, was injured in the back while serving with his local regiment and had been posted to the Cheshires when he recovered. He is remembered on the war memorial in the village of Southill, where he had lived and worked as a labourer.

The next morning, enemy shelling increased and the troops occupied the trench they had dug. They could see British units retiring past them, including the men from Irish regiments of 16th Division who had managed to escape the German onslaught on the forward positions. In the early afternoon they were followed by advancing German troops and, by 2pm, they were close enough for the Cheshires to open fire on the advanced parties who were assembling for an attack in the valley in front of the Battalion's position. The fire was returned and the Germans started to advance up the hill but were turned back by fire from the Lewis gunners. Above them the Cheshires could see intense air battles under way and, at 5pm, thirty to forty German planes appeared, spotting the British positions and opening fire on them. Luckily, the Cheshires suffered no fatalities. Two hours later orders came to withdraw immediately and this was done successfully but under very heavy machine gun fire.

The situation was quiet overnight but, in the early morning of 23 March, the German attack was renewed, with their troops advancing

Mont St Quentin in 1918. The view is as the advancing Germans would have seen it.

quickly on both flanks of the Cheshires' position. At 9am an order came to withdraw about four miles and take up a position on Mont St Quentin, just to the north of the town of Péronne. It was necessary to pull back immediately to avoid being cut off. There was no panic amongst the men, even though the roads were heavily congested with troops, vehicles and field artillery and the Germans were heavily shelling the withdrawal. The whole Brigade, now somewhat depleted, occupied a trench on the hill, facing south east. At about 1.30pm the enemy could be seen advancing from the south and south east, in large numbers, rapidly assembling for an attack on the positions on the hill. At 4pm a machine gun barrage was fired on the Cheshires positions with *remarkable accuracy*, as the war diary records, together with shelling. Soon afterwards the Germans overcame resistance from the units to the right of the Cheshires. Once again, the Battalion just got away in time to avoid capture. *There was no chance of getting any of the wounded away and a certain number of our men must have fallen into his hands.* (War Diary)

The men withdrew approximately two miles to the west, crossing the River Somme and taking up positions on its banks, facing Péronne. It had been a desperate race, with the bridges across the river being blown up by the Royal Engineers shortly after they crossed. By the time they had reached the new position the Germans had already occupied Péronne. They held the western bank of the Somme for most of the next day, where they

Péronne. Occupied by the Germans until 1917, when they abandoned the town. Recaptured by them in March 1918. It was finally liberated by Australian troops in September 1918.

The Cheshires took up defensive positions near this destroyed wood close to the village of Herbécourt.

93. LA GRANDE GUERRE 1914-16. — *Offensive franco-anglaise de la Somme.*
*Un bois aux environs d'*HERBECOURT
A wood about Herbecourt.

Visé Paris 1093

" Phot. Express

watched the Germans assemble large forces, bringing up artillery and transport vehicles. They attempted to screen their movements by setting fire to dry grass, which did create clouds of smoke but the British field artillery and Machine Gun Corps troops did as much damage as they could. When darkness fell a further withdrawal was made to the village of Herbécourt, about two miles to the west. The men took up the defence in an old trench just outside the village.

During the following morning, the Battalion went forward to Flaucourt to assist in fighting a rearguard action that allowed the 66th Division to withdraw behind them. They then returned to Herbécourt, occupying a trench in front of the village and preparing for the attack by what was still a rapidly advancing enemy. The attack started at 9am on the 26th, with heavy shelling from field guns of all calibres, supported by machine gun fire. The war diary notes that *This was the first morning that our aeroplanes had been active and six of them circled over enemy lines, firing into his men as they advanced to the attack.* However, the German infantry attack was in considerable strength and, as well as the frontal assault, they advanced on both flanks, forcing another Cheshire withdrawal to avoid being cut off.

The new position was to the south west, at Dompierre, and this was held with considerable difficulty until 11am. By this time the division on the right had been forced back, exposing the Cheshires' flank and forcing another withdrawal, of about four miles, to high ground near Proyart. This was carried out under heavy enemy machine gun fire and the war diary notes it caused several casualties, although records suggest that none were fatal. As before, the night passed quickly, but the attack was resumed at 9am, with heavy machine gun and artillery fire. The German infantry was soon in the village and started to send up signal flares to indicate their location to their aeroplanes. It was not long before the Cheshires came under direct attack and, after a determined resistance, pulled back along the road to Amiens, between Morcourt and Harbonnières. Here they came under machine gun fire, suffering several

Private Edward Evans, an assistant librarian at the National Library of Wales. Killed in action on 26 March. He is remembered on the war memorial at Llanbararn Fawr, near Aberystwth.

casualties. In the late afternoon the Battalion was heavily shelled for two hours. Seven men were killed during the day. They included Private Harry

Peake, a married man from Spalding, Lincolnshire. He had been awarded a Military Medal for an act of bravery on 31 July 1917 at St Julien.

By now there was little sense of units fighting as distinct entities. Everything was confused and whole divisions were mixed up and men had become scattered, with no information about where they might be or if they were dead, wounded or captured. In the evening an attempt was made to collect together all the Battalion's men in the area. It numbered just three officers and thirty five other ranks. One man who had had to seek medical attention was another Lincolnshire man, Second Lieutenant Horace Ludgate. In civilian life he had been a manager at a bottling plant in Lincoln. He enlisted in the local regiment in 1916, later receiving a commission and joining the Battalion on 4 November 1917. During the shelling in the afternoon a shell had exploded only a few yards away, knocking him down and killing a number of men. Ludgate needed treatment for shellshock and was evacuated home where, in January 1919, an army medical board found that *He suffers from general nervousness. He has fine tremors of hands and frequent twitching of facial muscles. He is now almost edentulous and consequently unable to take ordinary diet.* He left the army in June 1919, returning to live in Lincoln with his wife, Agnes, who he had married before going overseas. He is believed to have died in 1971.

Frederick Williams, killed in action on 27 March, while acting as a stretcher bearer. He lived in Birkenhead with his wife Martha, and worked as a porter at the local goods depot of the Great Western Railway.

At dawn on 28 March the neighbouring troops of 61st Division launched a counterattack but it had little success and, once again, the Cheshires were in danger of being surrounded. Orders came at 9am, effectively, that it was "every man for himself", and that small groups should make their way independently to Ignaucourt, about five miles away. The Battalion's war diary notes that the enemy soon spotted what was happening and opened up with artillery on the whole area. When they reached Ignaucourt, units had become so depleted that whole brigades were amalgamated into single composite battalions. The Cheshires had lost another five men and their contribution to the temporary battalion was only the three officers and thirty men. Once they were organised, the battalion was ordered into a counterattack that successfully drove the

Germans off a nearby hill and then held them off all night. The French army was in action to their immediate right and, the next morning, the British withdrew to allow the French to take over their position.

Early on 29 March the composite battalion was sent to a position in a sunken road near Aubercourt. A German attack was expected and, soon, the enemy infantry was seen advancing in large numbers, keeping in cover of the various woods that were about the area. In the late morning they took Ignaucourt and continued to advance. The Cheshires came under some intermittent shelling during the day but there was no infantry attack. One of the enduring myths of the Great War is that of senior officers remaining in safety well behind the lines. In fact, they would regularly visit the front line and, on this day, Brigadier General Bellingham, was taken prisoner and Major General Edward Feetham, commanding the division, was killed by shrapnel that hit him in the neck.

The 30th also passed relatively quietly, with both sides exchanging machine gun and artillery fire. The German offensive had at last run out of steam. The infantry was exhausted. Supply routes were over-extended and there were few German reinforcements available. Over a quarter of a million men on each side had become casualties – dead, wounded, missing or taken prisoner. The Allied forces could draw on replacements, particularly as American troops started to arrive in Europe in greater numbers but for the Germans there were few reserves to draw on.

The official record shows that nine Cheshires were killed on 30 March, although it is most probable that their deaths were in the previous two or three days. In the chaos of the retreat record keeping was very much a secondary task. Harold Genders, from Macclesfield, was first wounded with a shot over the heart and, just afterwards, was hit again and died instantly. They were withdrawing at the time and his mates had no opportunity to bury him. No doubt the Germans gave him a decent burial but they would have had little interest in making identifications and Genders has no known grave. George Hilton, from Stalybridge, was popular amongst his comrades. He was a born comedian, according to the local newspaper, with a good ear for music, like his father, also called George, who ran the Commercial Hotel in the town. The twenty year old had performed with the *Cheerios*, one of the various concert parties that entertained the troops. The circumstances of Hilton's mortal wounding are not known but he was evacuated to a CCS at the village of Namps-au-Val, where he died and is buried.

On 31 March the temporary battalion, designated as the 118th

Composite Battalion, was relieved and moved by bus and march to Guignemicourt, where they stayed overnight in billets.

Ten days before the 6th Cheshires had numbered thirty six officers and 830 other ranks. Their losses since then were recorded as:

	Officers	Other ranks
Killed	2	17
Died of wounds	-	3
Wounded	-	139
Wounded and missing	-	11
Missing	-	162

From when they had first gone into action at Longavesnes they had retreated thirty three miles. Theirs was a typical experience and the British Army had lost all of its gains in the Somme sector made from 1916 onwards.

After a night's rest at Guignemicourt, the Battalion marched off again, spending several days moving to Bouvaincourt, arriving on 9 April. Many of the men who had become detached from the Cheshires during the retreat had now caught up with their comrades and the Battalion numbered twenty officers and 572 other ranks. From here they moved by train, leaving at 8pm, for Arques, in northern France, near the town of St Omer. They arrived at 7am the next day, marching to billets. Another ten men caught up and rejoined that day.

On 9 April, the Germans opened the second phase of their offensive in what was to become known as the Battle of the Lys, after the river that ran through the Flemish battlefield. The attacks were on a forty mile wide front, defended mainly by British troops, but including two Portuguese divisions. The Belgian Army held the northern sector. As for the previous month, the German attack was meticulously planned. The artillery bombardment was again devastating and the infantry attack overwhelming. Again, the British were in retreat.

During the early morning of 11 April every man in Arques was pushed forward to reinforce the front line troops now being pushed back. A new composite battalion was formed from troops from 118 Brigade, including some Cheshires. It was known as 4th Composite Battalion. Together with other composite battalions, it formed part of a scratch brigade under the command of Brigadier General Hubback.

In the afternoon the remaining troops marched to billets in a farm near

Holques, but their stay was brief. At 5pm on the 12th more reinforcements were needed and a further Composite Battalion, No. 5, was formed for the defence of the town of Hazebrouck. Two officers and sixty one other ranks left in the evening to join this group.

Those remaining marched to new billets at Ganspette, where they remained for the rest of the month. Whilst there, they were reinforced by a draft of two officers and eighty five other ranks, together with forty men returned from hospital. They undertook training exercises and drill, although two officers and fourteen other ranks left to join the American 77th Division as specialist instructors.

The men joining No. 5 Composite Battalion were under the command of Captain Sydney Yorston. They moved by bus and march to Borre, near Hazebrouck, where they spent the remainder of the month digging trenches on a line running from Borre to the Forest of Mormal. A few men reported sick during this time but only one was wounded.

The larger group of Cheshires was part of Brigadier General Hubback's command. They were under the direct command of Major Frederick Gregory. He was a prewar officer with the 4th Cheshires and was wounded whilst serving with them at Gallipoli in 1915. After recovering from the injuries, he was posted to the 6th Battalion, joining them in March 1917. He had with him 361 men and they marched to St Omer, before moving by train to Vlamertinghe, between the Belgian towns of Poperinghe and Ypres. The next day they moved to Lankhof Farm, just to the south of Ypres, where they stayed for three days.

On 15 April there was a move to old trenches near Voormezeele, which the Composite Battalion was ordered to bring into readiness; the men spent several days improving the defences. Meanwhile, the German advance had been steadily continuing and it reached Voormezeele on the 26th. Major Gregory's report records that there were three periods of heavy German shelling but the German infantry did not enter the village but

> *contented themselves with reaching The Mound, outside the village defences, where he established machine guns and kept up a harassing fire on the village. The same night, we sent out a patrol to reconnoitre The Mound, who reported that the enemy was not holding this position but was digging in and wiring on his side of it.*

It was amongst the first real signs that, as with the attack in March, the German offensive was petering out.

The morning of 27 April started quietly but, at about 1pm, the German artillery opened a barrage which grew in intensity until 5pm. The infantry then made a determined attack on Voormezeele, succeeding in getting into part of the village, but being driven off elsewhere. During the evening most of the Composite Battalion was relieved from the forward zone and moved back to Dominion Camp. Part of D Company could not be relieved as it was pinned down by the German attack. During the early hours of the 29th the Germans shelled the camp and the men had to evacuate the area, taking what shelter they could find in nearby trenches and ditches. There were several wounded, including Major Frank Naden. At about 7am the men were moved back to the safety of Vancouver Camp. These days had resulted in heavy casualties, with nearly a hundred being wounded, but only three were fatalities. Joseph Hartley was one of the three. Before the war, he worked on the railways and lived with his brother in Rochdale. He was one of the Battalion's Lewis gunners. Private Frederick Carter had received

Private Joseph Hartley, a single man from Rochdale, where he worked as a platelayer for the Lancashire and Yorkshire Railway Company. Died of wounds on 29 April.

the Distinguished Conduct Medal for an act of bravery during the German attack in March. He took over a Vickers machine gun when the team had become casualties, firing it so effectively that it caused the enemy to fall back, albeit temporarily. He was badly wounded in the shelling and was evacuated to a CCS hospital; but nothing could be done for him and he died on 30 April.

By 6 May the three groups of Cheshires had reformed as a single unit and were now in billets at Estmont, where, on the 10th, they were inspected by 39th Division's commander, Major General Cyril Blacklock. The Battalion was much depleted and, at less than half strength, numbered fourteen officers and 448 other ranks. Training exercises were held over the following days until the 17th, when the Battalion marched to Volkerinckhove, a village just north of St Omer. For the next two days, they participated in a tactical exercise, taking the part of the enemy against the American 77th Division. The Americans had landed in France in April. It was the first division of conscripted men to arrive and mainly comprised men from New York State. A history of the 77th records the exercise:

The Division attacked an imaginary enemy; was driven back and counterattacked; patrols were sent out which encountered nothing more hostile than a frightened calf; reliefs were posted and "stand to" observed; kitchens were lost but there were eggs in abundance; altogether it was a "bon war" while it lasted.

Towards the end of the month the Battalion received orders to transfer from the 39th Division to the 25th Division. Like the Cheshires, the new division's units suffered heavy casualties during the German offensives of the previous two months. A total of four divisions were being sent south to a quiet sector around the French city of Soissons. It would give them time to rest and refit and, in return, four French divisions moved north. The four British divisions gathered in their new sector by 11th May. The history of the 25th Division records that *very little artillery activity was displayed by either side and the troops on the British and the neighbouring French front appeared to have settled down to a period of peaceful trench warfare.*

The Cheshires left their billets on 25 May, marching to Watten and then moving by train to Étaples, on the Channel coast, where they spent the night. Captain Ellis Spence and forty two other ranks remained with 39th Division to be reallocated to other duties. Spence had been the Battalion's transport officer throughout the war and his contribution had been recognised by the award of a Military Cross, the citation recording that he had carried out his duties *with great determination under most difficult conditions and heavy shell fire. On two occasions when several of his animals became casualties, his coolness and example were the means of saving the convoy and his conduct was at all times a splendid example to his men.* Four officers and four other ranks transferred to the American 77th Division, presumably to continue with its training.

The next day the remainder of the Battalion boarded another train at 3pm and prepared for a long journey. Everything was fine until about 7pm on 27 May when the train reached the vicinity of Fismes, about halfway between Soissons and Rheims. Here they came under attack from German aeroplanes, which bombed and machine-gunned them. A German machine gun post also opened fire. Without realising, they had ridden into the middle of the third phase of the German offensive. They were fortunate to only lose one man killed. Twenty year old Joseph Lovegrove was a steel turner from Birmingham. He had originally joined the Worcestershire Regiment in 1916. Lovegrove had only been posted overseas on 7 March and was transferred to the Cheshires on arrival in France. He had been wounded in the leg at the end of March but had, unfortunately for him, quickly returned to duty.

As with the earlier attacks, the start of the offensive was signalled by a very heavy artillery bombardment, followed by a gas shelling and then the follow-up by the German stormtroopers. It came as a complete surprise to the defenders.

> *There is no doubt that these few British Divisions, in their exhausted, untrained and unwelded state, both out-numbered, out-gunned and practically unprovided with aeroplanes, were totally unable to withstand the shock of the German assaults and successfully defend the sector of the line assigned to them.*[91]

The Germans had smashed through the British and French lines on a twenty five mile wide front and, by the time the Cheshires blundered into them, they had advanced nine miles since morning. A party of Cheshires left the train and overwhelmed the German soldiers in the machine gun post, taking prisoners. The train then reversed quickly out of danger, reaching what was now the French outpost line at Fère en Tardenoise, where they disembarked at about midnight and rested until morning. At 8am they reboarded and moved to La Ferté Milon, where they waited for several hours before moving to Dormans, some fifteen miles to the rear of Fismes.

They arrived at 2am on 29 May and immediately marched to Romigny, reporting their arrival to Corps Headquarters. They went into action at 3pm the same afternoon, taking up a defensive position at the Bois de la Vente, north of Augny and coming under the orders of 74 Brigade. They held this position until the early evening, when the troops on their left flank withdrew after coming under heavy artillery fire and infantry attack. It exposed the Cheshires' position and they were also forced to withdraw to a position at the Bois de Bouval, south east of

Private William Marsland went overseas in November 1914, twice returning to the UK to recover from medical complaints and served with 9th and 11th Cheshires, before returning to serve with the 6th Battalion in early 1918. He was taken prisoner in late May or early June. Photo: Regimental Museum

Romigny. There was a further withdrawal during the morning of 30 May.

There was another withdrawal in the early hours of 1 June, to hastily prepared positions near the Bois d' Eclisse. The Cheshires held 300 yards of this new defensive line, with 8th Border Regiment on their left and 22nd Durham Light Infantry on their right. Their losses over the three days amounted to thirty wounded and seventy unaccounted for. Most of those initially unaccounted for turned up later; or news came that they had been wounded or taken prisoner.

Frank Scholes. Photo: V Danby

George Scholes. Photo: V Danby

However, five men were killed. They included Sergeant Frank Scholes, from Romiley. The thirty one year old joined 10th Cheshires in about September 1914. He served overseas with 16th Cheshires before being transferred to the 6th Battalion in February 1918. His brother, George, joined the 6th Battalion in February 1915 and had also served with the Machine Gun Corps for a short while. Before the men went overseas on active service they exchanged watches, so that each would have something of the other. In the spring of 1917 George was transferred to the 8th Cheshires, leaving France to join them in Mesopotamia (modern day Iraq). He was on the troopship *Cameronia* when it was torpedoed and sunk on 15 April. Most were rescued but 210 drowned. He later said he only survived because he had learnt to swim in the canal at Romiley. George's watch was lost when Frank was killed. However, George had wrapped

Frank's watch in oilskin and it was undamaged by the water. It is still with the family. And it still works.

The Cheshires were briefly relieved from the Bois d' Eclisse but returned during the evening of 3 June, taking over from a French battalion. They numbered thirteen officers and 246 other ranks.

The Battalion remained in the area for several days. On the 4th, Lieutenant Colonel Hesse, who had returned to take command in March, now returned to Britain. Major Frederick Gregory took temporary command. He had been heavily involved in all the Battalion's defensive actions in the past weeks and, in recognition, was awarded the Distinguished Service Order, the citation reading:

> *By the skilful handling of the Battalion under his command he kept the line intact throughout the whole action and successfully supported the line on his left. On two occasions, he organised counterattacks and drove off the enemy with severe loss. Throughout the action he displayed leadership of a high order.*

His skills were again tested on 6 June when the Germans opened a heavy bombardment of high explosive and gas shells. This was followed by an infantry attack, which was driven off.

On 10 June the Battalion's headquarters staff withdrew to billets at St Loup, the troops remaining in the line under the command of Captain Ronald Norman until 19 June. Whilst they were away the Battalion had been significantly reinforced. The 11th Cheshires was in the process of being disbanded and sixteen officers and 492 other ranks now merged into the 6th Battalion. There was also a new commanding officer, Lieutenant Colonel Arthur Newth. Aged just twenty one, he was possibly the youngest man to command a battalion during the war. Born in Bristol in 1897, the son of a furniture dealer, he was commissioned in the 4th Gloucestershires in August 1914.

Lieutenant Colonel Arthur Newth in later life.

Newth kept a diary during his war service. The day after the arrival of Norman's troops, he wrote: *Day spent reorganising the Battalion; it ought to become a good show. There seems to be lots of good material.*[92] The Battalion remained at St Loup, undertaking training, until 1 July, when it marched to overnight billets at Euvy. On the 3rd the troops moved by train to Pont Remy, some 250 kilometres to the northwest, near the Channel coast. It was a journey that took twenty four hours. They marched to a tented camp just outside the town. The camp was shared with American troops and they were visited, on 6 July, by the British Prime Minister, David Lloyd George. He was accompanied by the Secretary of State for War, Lord Milner, the Australian Prime Minister, William Hughes and General Sir Henry Rawlinson, commanding Fourth Army. Afterwards the visiting party passed through the Cheshires' part of the camp, speaking to several of the men.

The next day there was a move to Clairmarais Forest. Colonel Newth had a row with the farmer who owned the land. *A wretched fellow.* Another move, on 10 July, brought them to St Marie Cappel, where they became part of 21 Brigade, 30th Division. Training continued here until the 15th, when they moved by bus and lorry to billets in the forward area near the French village of Godewaresvelde. Near to the border with Belgium, it was known to the Tommies as 'Gertie Wears Velvet' or, sometimes, 'God Wears Velvet'. They were quickly put to work digging trenches for the Royal Engineers so that telephone cable could be buried. *Went round the working parties at 4am. At 4.30, it rained and thundered like blazes. Got a bit wet.* (Lieutenant Colonel Arthur Newth) They left on 23 July, taking up overnight billets at Steenvoorde, before marching to Eecke, near Hazebrouck, the next morning.

The men paraded at 8.30am on the 27th, ready to be inspected by Major General W Williams, commanding 30th Division. *It pelted with rain. We turned out and got wet. The General came round at 11.30am.* (Lieutenant Colonel Arthur Newth) Training continued daily, including after a return to St Marie Cappel on 2 August. During the evening of the 8th the Cheshires returned to the front line, relieving a battalion of the North Staffordshire Regiment, at Mont Rouge, near the village of Locre. They deployed with B and C Companies in the front line, with A and D in support.

The German Army had been irretrievably weakened by the losses during the spring offensive and, although they had pushed back the British, they had not broken the line. With troops replaced from Britain and from the Middle East, the British were again in a strong position, even if many troops were inexperienced. It was time to plan for an offensive of their own. It would be delivered from the positions in front of Amiens, where the British had managed to halt the German advance in April. For the first

Mont Rouge, a photograph illustrating its dominant position.

The sad remnants of Locre immediately after the war.

time, there would be complete integration of infantry, tanks, artillery and aircraft, supporting each other in the advance. As the Cheshires came into the front line in Belgium, the attack was launched with devastating effect, the Germans losing more ground on the day than in any previous Allied attack. It was the start of an offensive that would end the war. The Cheshires would soon play their part.

It was a quiet tour of duty in the trenches and the Battalion's war diary has little to report. On the 12th a patrol into No Man's Land spotted Germans moving about near some abandoned huts and the Lewis gunners were ordered to fire on them. They were relieved on the 14th and moved to bivouac billets at Boeschepe.

During the evening of 19 August A and D Companies moved forward to the support trenches at Canada Corner, near Locre. They were to attack German positions holding a spur into No Man's Land, south of the village. Its capture would facilitate a further advance, in the near future. They took up assembly positions in the front line the next night. A Company was under the command of Captain Richard Le Brun Nicholson and D under Captain Gordon Ideson, a chartered accountant in civilian life.

Captain Richard Le Brun Nicholson. Photo: Dave Horne, author Higher Bebington Heroes.

At 2.05am the British artillery opened a barrage on the German trenches and, four minutes later, the Cheshires advanced behind a creeping barrage. They were spotted as soon as they moved forward and the Germans fired their S.O.S. flares, hoping to bring down their own artillery fire on to No Man's Land. However, due to a heavy mist, it seems as though the flare was not spotted and the Cheshires were into the German advanced posts before the shelling started.

The Germans were issuing rations at the time of the attack and the defences were weak. It meant that the Cheshires captured all the objectives without too much difficulty, although two men were killed and twenty six wounded. Twenty eight Germans were taken prisoner and three machine guns captured. Sergeant Frank Riding, from the Northwich area, had

21 August 1918. The Cheshires captured German positions in this field, south of the village of Locre. Photo: author

transferred from the 11th Cheshires in June. He captured six Germans single-handed and later took command of his platoon when the officer was wounded. He was awarded the Military Medal for his actions. Other Military Medals were awarded to Sergeants Duncan Cowan and George Gray and to Lance Corporal Thomas Smith. Gray was instrumental in capturing one of the machine guns, killing two of the crew and taking eight prisoners. Cowan, a carpenter from Crosby Street in Stockport, went back to the old front line under the heavy barrage and brought up a reserve section of men to help with the consolidation. Smith was another man who had previously served with 11th Cheshires and was now one of the Lewis gunners. He and three others had captured some twelve prisoners and another of the German machine guns.

At 6am Germans were spotted advancing under cover of the mist for a counterattack. The Cheshires sent up their own SOS flares and the British artillery, together with machine gun fire, dispersed them. The day was quiet but, towards evening, another weak counterattack was attempted but was driven off, as recorded in the war diary: *our intense machine gun barrage and Lewis gun fire creating havoc with the enemy.* Lieutenant Hugh Tooker had displayed excellent leadership in the attack and, later in the day, took command of the line, organising the troops against the counterattacks. He was awarded the Military Cross.

The next day was spent in consolidating the gains, often under considerable high explosive and gas shelling, together with almost incessant machine gun fire. The fire killed five men and wounded another fourteen. During the night of 21/22 August, Captain Nicholson led a party out into No Man's Land to set up new barbed wire defences. At least one of the five men killed were in the group. Corporal William Swann was a married man from Glossop, where he worked as a cotton spinner until he enlisted in December 1914. Nicholson wrote to his widow, Maria:

> *During the night a machine gun opened fire and he was shot in the throat. He fell right beside me and I did all I could to make his last moments comfortable for him. It was all over in a minute or so. He could say nothing. He was a splendid fellow. His section were devoted to him.* [93]

The bravery of two men was significant in breaking up further attempts at a counterattack. Thomas Grimes, from Ellesmere Port, was a Lewis gunner, regularly firing at groups of Germans as they tried to form up for an attack. Lance Corporal William Walker, from Birkenhead, went back to the old front line with an urgent message when the telephone lines failed, calling for artillery support. Both men received the Military Medal.

The Cheshires withdrew from the front line on 23 August, rejoining the other two companies in the support lines at Locre, where they stayed until the 27th, when they returned to the front line. The Battalion's war diary notes that 28 August was a quiet day, although one man was killed and another seven wounded. The dead man was Second Lieutenant John Pickersgill. Colonel Newth recorded his death in his diary.

> *One of the tragedies of war occurred early this morning. Poor Pickersgill was shot dead by the Battalion on our right, when coming in from patrol. Poor fellow, it was very hard lines. He was one of my best officers.*

He joined the Rifle Brigade, as a private, in 1914, serving in action with its 1st Battalion, before becoming an officer in August 1916, when he was posted to the Cheshires. He served for a time as Brigade Intelligence Officer. Before the war he worked as a clerk in Petrograd when, in June

1914, he secretly married. It is not known why the couple kept this from his family but, after his death, it caused some discontent when it was realised that she, and not other family members, would be entitled to an army pension.

James and Harry Murphy were brothers from Stockport. Harry had been awarded the Military Medal at some point, the general commanding the division writing to him expressing his *appreciation of your gallantry and devotion to duty when you performed admirable work as a Battalion runner under the most difficult and dangerous conditions.* Both of them were wounded by a shell explosion. James's injuries were to his chest and Harry's to his leg. Both are believed to have been evacuated to the CCS at nearby Arneke. Surgeons had to amputate Harry's foot but it was not enough to save his life and he died on 31 August. James survived and was later discharged from the army.

Private Harry Murphy MM. Died of wounds on 31 August.

During the afternoon of 30 August intelligence was received that the Germans were withdrawing and abandoning their trench line. At about 4.30pm many large fires could be seen and explosions heard as, presumably, the Germans were destroying anything that might be useful to the British. There was almost no artillery fire, only the occasional long range shell. Colonel Newth immediately ordered patrols out into No Man's Land.

C Company on the left were to send out two and B, on the right, one. Information is very slow in coming through, but long after dark we heard that the enemy was still in position on our left but the right was clear. Meanwhile, a general advance had been ordered. C Company were to send one Platoon to establish itself in Tinkle Farm and another to Septic Farm. D Company moved up in support on the left. A Company sent two Platoons through B on the right to seize Locrehof Farm and the hedges N.E. of it. The other two Platoons were pushed through and ordered to advance to Rumbold Farm. A Company Headquarters moved up to Locrehof Farm and Battalion Headquarters to Alma Farm at 11 p.m. I received information that the Brigade on our left was not moving forward at all. This meant that my left flank was exposed to Kemmel Hill, a rather unenviable position, as it seemed unlikely that the enemy would retire from Kemmel without a fight. Consequently I was obliged to form a Defensive Flank on the left flank by echeleoning D Company down it. They were ordered to occupy Neame House, Rooner Farm and Swindon. The operation presented enormous difficulties in the dark and as a matter of fact was never completely carried out.

There had been no significant opposition to the Cheshires' advance, except for an occasional machine gun post that fired on them but retreated before the Cheshires came close. The advance continued through the night. The conditions were difficult as it was very dark and pouring with rain. By 8am on the 31st they had passed through Dranoutre. They reached a point about 1400 yards north east of Neuve Église when they came under heavy machine gun and artillery fire from Germans entrenched on a ridge. One company attempted to press forward but had to withdraw under the weight of fire. In the evening they were pulled out from the advance and returned to Canada Corner. Casualties had been relatively light, with five men dead and sixteen wounded. Amongst the dead was Private David Jones, who had previously served with another battalion of the Cheshires and had received a Military Medal serving with it. Captain Richard Le Brun Nicholson was twenty three when he was killed by a shell. He lived at Bebington on Wirral and worked for a shipping business, possibly owned by his father, who is known to have owned ships. He served with the 11th Cheshires until they were disbanded, was twice wounded and had twice been awarded the Military Cross.

Henry Mealor, killed in action of 31 August. He lived in Childer Thornton, Wirral, where he worked as a gardener. He is remembered on the village war memorial.

Robert Witherspoon was a few months past his eighteenth birthday and had only been overseas about six weeks, having left his home in Douglas, Isle of Man. He was badly wounded during the advance and was evacuated to 62nd Casualty Clearing Station at Arneke. Sister Lilian Clieve wrote to his parents telling them that he:

was admitted to this hospital last night with wounds to his shoulder and abdomen and he died at 8.30 this morning. Everything possible was done for him but his condition was serious from the first. Death

Manxman Robert Witherspoon is buried at Arneke British Cemetery.

was quite peaceful and he did not leave any message. I am sorry you have this great sorrow.

Fifteen men were noted in the Battalion's history, published in the 1930s, as being honoured with the award of the Military Medal for their actions during the advance. Several of them were recognised for their contributions to what today might be called support services. Company Quartermaster Sergeants Isaac Hammond and William Pullin both ensured their companies received supplies and hot food. Sergeant Walter Robinson, a pre-war member of the Battalion from Glossop, had led parties forward with ammunition and rations. Lance Corporal Sydney Spicer was in charge of a party with pack animals when they came under artillery attack. He prevented a stampede of the animals, reconnoitred another route and continued to lead the party forward. He would not see the end of the war and is understood to have died from natural causes on 6 November. Four men showed great bravery as runners, taking messages under heavy fire. They were Lance Corporals Harry Adams and Harold Clayton and Privates William King and George Ollerenshaw. With the exception of Robinson, it has not been possible to confirm these awards from the *London Gazette*, which publishes the official lists of such matters, and it may be reasonable to assume the men were nominated for the medal but it was not actually awarded.

The Battalion moved to new billets on 1 September, first near Locre Chateau, south west of Dranoutre, then to Mont Vidaigne, where the divisional commander presented medal ribbons and, finally, to bivouacs on Kemmel Hill. In all three locations, the men's first job was to construct the camps. Overnight on 14/15 September the Cheshires moved back into the front line at Daylight Corner, near Wulverghem. Casualties were fairly heavy, with four men killed, another four wounded and thirty four men needing attention after being gassed. The next day was quiet but, at 9.30pm, a German patrol crept close to one of the Cheshires' outposts, attempting a grenade attack, but it was driven off. It was possibly during this incident that Captain William Kenyon was mortally wounded. Before the war he lived in Alderley Edge and worked as a commercial traveller. In his spare time he was an officer with the 7th Cheshires and was posted to the 6th Battalion in October 1917 after he had recovered from wounds he received at Gallipoli. He was evacuated to a CCS at Hazebrouck, where he died.

Captain William Kenyon, died of wounds. Remembered on the war memorial at St Mary's Church, Nether Alderley, Cheshire.

The war diary entry for 19 September records '2 O.R. gassed'. One of those 'other ranks' was Private George Lofthouse. Before the war the twenty year old lived at the family home in Liscard, Wirral and had worked as a clerk for the Pearl Assurance Company in Liverpool. He was gassed earlier in 1918 but this had only kept him away from duty for a month. His injuries this time were much more severe and he had extensive burns, which were treated at first in France. On 2 October, he was evacuated back to Britain, where he was admitted to Bethnal Green Hospital. The young man's condition did not improve and, by 9 October, his pulse had weakened significantly. Two days later pneumonia set in and, on the 19th, there was gangrene in his leg.

Private George Lofthouse, died from the effects of poison gas.

He died at 7.10pm on 24 October. In a further family tragedy, Lofthouse's' mother, Annie, died two days later of a heart attack. She was buried at

Toxteth Park Cemetery in Liverpool on 31 October. Her son joined her two days later. John Lofthouse, the husband and father, lived until 1962 and was also buried in the family grave.

At midnight on 20 September Captain Henry Cooke led C Company into No Man's Land. Their objective was a German strongpoint north east of Wulverghem, which formed a small salient into the British line. Cooke had put some considerable effort into the planning and equipping of the attack. Two platoons would undertake the attack, with a third in support and the fourth held in reserve. They quickly crossed the 400 yards, supported by artillery fire, smoke shells and machine gun fire. They captured fourteen prisoners, including a sergeant major, and a machine gun. Lance Sergeant George Hobson captured eight of the prisoners while mopping up a dugout and also took the machine gun. Lance Corporal William Kane also took two prisoners while mopping up. Corporal Sydney Archer captured two Germans, holding the objective under heavy fire while the gains were consolidated. Lance Corporal John Joseph Dixon[94] kept his section very close to the artillery barrage as they crossed No Man's Land. It meant he was in to the strongpoint before the Germans came out of their dugouts and was able to capture three of them and killed others. Just seventeen minutes after zero hour the prisoners were at Battalion headquarters, where they were identified as serving with 5 Company, 16th Bavarian Reserve Regiment. Several were wearing gas masks, thinking that the smoke barrage was gas. By forty minutes after zero Cooke and his men had established a new front line at the tip of the strongpoint. The men mentioned were all awarded gallantry medals: Captain Cooke received the Military Cross while the others, and Private James Burgess, were reported to have received Military Medals.[95]

During the evening of 23 September the Battalion was withdrawn to billets at Mont Rouge, where it remained until the end of the month. During the evening of the 27th the Battalion was ordered to stand to as it was suspected that the Germans had again retired. On 1 October they moved to support positions near Tenbrielen, south east of Ypres, near the Franco-Belgian border. They were heavily shelled as they came into the trenches. Private William James was killed. He enlisted in Birkenhead but his family connection was with Barrow in Furness, where he is remembered on the town's war memorial.

During the hours of darkness on 3 October a patrol went out and captured four prisoners. The next night men from B Company went out and captured a machine gun from a German outpost. The Battalion was

21 September 1918. The photograph is taken from Pond Farm Cemetery and shows the area attacked by the Cheshires. The German positions were about two hundred yards away. On the horizon to the right is the church at Messines. Photo: author.

relieved on 7 October, going into reserve positions in concrete pill boxes near Houthem. Whilst here, the three battalions of 21 Brigade practised for an expected attack on the Germans. There was a fatal accident on the 14th. Captain Gerald Rowley lived in Southport and worked for a firm of cotton brokers. He joined the Battalion in March 1917 and was awarded the Military Cross on two occasions. On this day he was standing outside company headquarters when he was accidentally shot from behind by Private David Florry, a bleachworker from New Mills. Rowley's wound was very serious and he was taken to a CCS, where he died the next day.

During the 14th other battalions advanced and captured their objectives in the early morning. The Cheshires, having been held in reserve, were now ordered to send patrols forward to the bridges over the River Lys. Heavy fire prevented them reaching the river and, by around midday, the patrols were supported by B and C Companies. Crossing commenced at about 3.15pm. It was undertaken with a number of acts of bravery being recorded, for which Military Medals were awarded. Corporals Harry Bird and James Fish were involved in supervising the men under fire hurriedly throwing temporary bridges across the river. Private William Pascoe, from the Bideford area, was one of the runners. He had taken several messages under heavy machine gun fire and was then badly gassed. He managed to reach Battalion headquarters with an important message, arriving there in a state of complete collapse.

The Battalion continued the advance throughout the next day, reaching a position known as Paul Bucq Hill, where they were relieved to billets at

Kruisek the following day, occupying an abandoned German camp.

> *Got back to a tented camp at about 8.15 a.m. this morning, had*
> *breakfast and then turned in until 5 p.m. It has been a rotten day,*
> *raining most of the time and the camp is a dismal picture of leaking*
> *tents, shell holes full of water, damp bivouacs, and paths a foot deep*
> *in mud, with three dead horses just to make a suitable background.*
> *The men have no greatcoats and no blankets, only their waterproof*
> *sheets and leather jerkins; they are living in the acme of discomfort.*
> *Yet such a truly marvellous fellow is Thomas Atkins that there are*
> *sounds of melody, or discord, proceeding, as I write, from nearly*
> *every tent. Our lads are great. What a thing it was to have been*
> *born an Englishman.*
>
> (Lieutenant Colonel Arthur Newth, diary entry 16 October 1918)

During 19 October the Battalion moved forward again, taking up billets at Aelbeke. The Germans had been in retreat over recent days and the village was some twenty kilometres from where the Cheshires were last in action. The Battalion war diary describes the billets as being *a position almost in the front line, outposts in touch with enemy.*

By the next morning it was clear that the Germans had again retreated and, at 7am, the Battalion moved off to regain contact with them. Their final objective was the village of Helghin, some ten miles away, on the River Scheldt. They were soon in contact with the German rear guards who, with support from their machine gunners, made determined stands at Ruddervoorde and Meuleken but were overcome by the Cheshires attacking from the flanks. The Germans fell back to positions on a ridge south west of St Genois, where they had established machine gun nests protected by thick barbed wire. The high ground allowed them to dominate the surrounding area and the German field artillery soon came into play. The advance was held up for the night.

> *Fighting a war with civilians about is a poor game. As the Boche*
> *artillery turned first on to one farm and then on to another, it was*
> *sad to see the little groups of old men and women struggling across*
> *the fields to get away from it all. And in the bad light they ran the*
> *risk of being mistaken for the enemy. On the other hand, they seem*
> *overjoyed to see us and, in the middle of a show, the troops were*
> *often given hot coffee! I had a cup this afternoon brought by an old*

woman while I was sitting at the side of the road, waiting for our left to clear the enemy from a sunken road. During the evening, a direct hit on a house which a little while before had been my Headquarters.

(Lieutenant Colonel Arthur Newth, diary entry)

The next morning Second Lieutenant Oswald Warrilow went forward to reconnoitre the enemy positions. Born in Staffordshire in 1898, he worked as a bank clerk before receiving his commission in 1917. He commanded the advanced patrols, supported by C Company in the assault, assembling them under the heavy machine gun and artillery fire. The other companies were be held in reserve. The Battalion war diary succinctly notes that the men *stormed and captured the ridge.* There were, however, a number of individual acts of bravery, described in the Battalion's history. Company Sergeant Major William Seaton took a Lewis gun team across the open ground under heavy machine gun fire to establish a position in a farm from where fire could be brought on the machine gun that was holding up the advance. Company Sergeant Major Fred Mitchell, from Mossley, also drove out the occupants of a machine gun post. Sergeant Charles Bowden, who previously served with 16th Cheshires before it was disbanded, rushed a machine gun post, capturing one of the team. Sergeant Frank Collier [96] was awarded the Distinguished Conduct Medal in 1916. He went forward on the left flank of the attack and, when the advance was held up, he and his officer spotted an enemy machine gun post on the roof of a farm. He went back, under heavy fire, and organised a fighting patrol from his platoon, bringing them forward and succeeding in clearing the Germans from the farm. It was an action that saw him awarded the Military Medal, which was also awarded to the other men mentioned. The history of the Battalion indicates that Oswald Warrilow was awarded the Military Cross but it has not been possible to confirm that from official records.

The advance continued with the final objective, Heughin, being taken next morning.

Civilians were occupying the farms and houses in the area through which we had advanced and our troops were warmly welcomed everywhere. Belgian flags were flying and bells ringing half an hour after the enemy had been forced to evacuate each place. The casualties amongst the civilians were promptly attended to by our medical staff. (Battalion war diary)

Sergeant George Jackson. He had joined the territorials in 1913, going overseas with the battalion in November 1914. Jackson was wounded in October 1916 and, on recovery, was transferred to 1st Cheshires. He was killed in action serving with them on 27 September 1918. Jackson is remembered on the war memorial at Godley Hill Road, Hyde.

The graves of Harold Pilling, from Nelson and Eric Winstanley, from Liscard. Two of the last four of the 6th Cheshires to be killed in action. Photos: British War Graves Project.

Casualties had, again, been relatively light. Twenty nine were wounded, of whom two would later die. Four men were killed outright. They were Company Sergeant Major William Marsh and Privates Harold Pilling, James Simpson and eighteen year old Eric Winstanley. Their comrades might be starting to think that the end of the war was in sight; but they could not have known that these four men would be the last members of the Battalion to be killed in action.

With the gains secured, the Cheshires moved back to billets at Petit Tourcoing where, for several days, they remained on alert ready to move back into action at an hour's notice.

In the summer of 1918 the world was suffering an influenza pandemic. It was a particularly virulent form which came to be known as Spanish flu and, in a time before anti-biotics, it would kill many millions of people between 1918 and 1920. It appeared to affect young men disproportionately and the armies of both sides suffered heavily, with men first displaying symptoms of flu which then rapidly became pneumonia. The pandemic hit the Cheshires on 22 October, with many reporting sick, including Colonel Newth, who had to spend several days in bed. By the 24th, over a hundred men had caught the flu. There was a death the next day but it was not the flu that killed twenty five year old Robert Cawley. The lance corporal came from Gee Cross, Hyde, where he had worked as a sewing machine fitter, joining the Battalion in 1910. His local newspaper reported he had been taken ill, dying of heart failure.[97]

Lance Corporal Robert Cawley. Died of natural causes on 25 October.

When the Battalion returned to the front line, on 26 October, they found it was still on the banks of the River Scheldt. The next day a patrol attempted to cross on a raft but failed when they found the Germans had thrown barbed wire defences into the water. Another attempt was made to cross by boat but it sank. At that point Second Lieutenant Fred Dearden swam across and reconnoitred the enemy positions, getting back under machine gun fire. He originally enlisted in the 21st Manchesters, one of the Regiment's Pals battalions and was awarded a Military Medal for an act of bravery in early 1917. He was commissioned in June 1918 and was posted to the Cheshires. He was awarded the Military Cross for this latest bravery.

On the 29th Second Lieutenant Frank Green also went into the river with the intention of swimming across, dragging a raft behind him attached by a wire round his waist. About halfway across he got into difficulties, becoming entangled in the wire and in the German barbed wire. Seeing this, Private John Glennon, a labourer from Birkenhead, went in, even though he was unable to swim. He managed to get to Green, freeing and rescuing him under machine gun fire that the Germans had opened when they had heard the commotion from the British held river bank. It was an act of courage for which Glennon received both the Military Medal and the Albert Medal, the equivalent of the George Cross.

On 31 October the Battalion received information that the Germans had withdrawn from the opposite bank and arrangements were made for the Cheshires to cross. However, it quickly became evident that the enemy still held a number of outposts strongly. During the evening of 1 November the Battalion withdrew to billets at Belleghem, south of Courtrai, where they remained until the 9th. That day they marched to what the war diary describes as the 'shattered village' of Moen, where they 'celebrated' the

Anseroeul.

fourth anniversary of the Battalion's arrival in France. The following day there was a march to Anseroeul, where the Cheshires were the first British troops to enter the village, with all ranks receiving a very warm welcome from the locals.

They left the village at 10.30am, on 11 November, making their way towards Fourquepire. Shortly after departing they heard that an Armistice had been signed and that hostilities would end at 11am. The war diary records the news was received *with acclamation by the troops and inhabitants and everywhere along the route the troops received a magnificent welcome from the liberated villagers.*

All they could do now was hope that peace really had come. Some must have reflected back over those four years, thinking of friends and relatives who had died. Some 6000 men had passed through the ranks of the Battalion and its two home service counterparts. Nearly 750 had been killed or died of wounds and over 4000 had been wounded or reported sick.

They were ordinary men who had lived through very extraordinary times.

Private George Dale, died on 3 November, possibly a victim of Spanish flu. The twenty year old lived in Congleton, where he work at a laundry. He is remembered on two war memorials in the town.

Joseph Daniels, a stonemason from the Wallasey area. Died of pneumonia on 7 November.

CHAPTER 10

The Men of 1919

After joining in the celebrations along the march, the Battalion reached Fourquepire late on 11 November and remained there until the 15th. The days were spent cleaning up and engaging in some training. There was then a two day march, via Moen, to Belleghem, where they remained until the end of the month. Training continued here, along with educational classes and lectures, intended to keep the men occupied. The divisional commander inspected the Brigade on the 25th, presenting medals to two officers awarded the Military Cross and ten men awarded the Military Medal.

The Cheshires left on the 29th. Ahead of them lay several days of marching, stopping overnight at Linselles and Le Provert before reaching what the war diary describes as the 'shattered' village of Lestrem, where they found shelter as best they could amongst the ruins. It was Colonel Newth's last day in command.

> *Brigadier tells me that Stanway is returning and will have to take over command. He has applied for me to be appointed to command the 2/23rd Londons. It is hard lines my having to give up the 6th Cheshires after all these months, but these things will occur. I finished the march with the Battalion and got the officers together after tea to say goodbye. Went to Hazebrouck in the lorry attached to us, caught a returning freight train to St Omer, a hospital train from there to a halt two kilos outside Boulogne, thence a car to the Quay, where I arrived half an hour before the leave boat was to sail.* (Lieutenant Colonel Arthur Newth, diary entry, 1 December 1918.)

The next night was spent in the asylum at St Venant, near the town of

'The shattered' village of Lestrem.

A Company, photographed in 1918.

Battalion NCOs, 1918. James Clarke DCM, sits fourth from right, front row. Photo: Richard Clarke.

The senior NCOs of one of the companies, 1918. Photo: Richard Clarke.

Several of the officers, 1918. It is not known why the face of one man appears to have been defaced. Photo: Regimental Museum.

The Battalion's officers, 1918. Photo: Regimental Museum.

Béthune. The patients had long since been removed and the building had served as a CCS as well as billets, coming under fire from German heavy artillery from time to time. Their final destination, Wardrecques, south east of St Omer, was reached on the 4th and they were met there by Lieutenant Colonel Stanway, who was returning to duty having recovered from the effects of being gassed in September 1917. The Cheshires stayed here for the remainder of the month. It was a time for sports, educational lectures, interspersed with the occasional working party, undertaking salvage of useful equipment from the trench lines.

Back home in Stockport arrangements were being made for the Battalion colours to be brought to France.

The ceremony of handing to an escort the colours of the 6th Cheshire Territorials was witnessed today by a large crowd. A military and civic procession took place at St George's Church, where the colours have rested since the Battalion went to France in 1914, and it included a considerable number of men who had served with the Battalion in France and two former commanding officers, Colonel Sykes and Colonel Heywood. At the church the colours were handed

The colours party, about to leave Stockport for France. Photo: Stockport Express

over to Captain Yorston MC and Captain H Wood. The company afterwards returned to the Town Hall, the procession being headed by a band and, from the steps of the Town Hall, the Mayor wished bon voyage to the escort party. (*Manchester Evening News*, 11 December 1918)

Yorston and Wood had served overseas, the latter as the Battalion Quartermaster. They were accompanied by Company Sergeant Major William Seaton and Sergeants Harry Butterworth and George Hobson, all of whom had been awarded gallantry medals. They arrived at Wardrecques on Sunday, 15 December, in time for divine services. The next day there was a Brigade football competition, the Cheshires beating a side from Brigade HQ 4 - 0. There was even more success on the 20th, when the team beat the Londons 12 – 0. Over recent days a number of soldiers who had been miners in civilian life returned to Britain to resume their employment. For the first time during their overseas service, Christmas Day festivities were enjoyed by the Battalion in the comfort of warm billets.

The Battalion left Wardreques on 2 January 1919, marching towards Dunkirk, which they reached on the 4th. Here they undertook various working parties, including building a new camp at Malo les Bains, just outside Dunkirk. They occupied the camp from the 13th, remaining there until 20 March. The main duties were acting as guards at the docks.

There was also time for sports, education classes and entertainment. The men attended two concerts in the YMCA hut, organised by Miss Lena Ashwell. In her younger days she had been an actress, before moving into stage management and opening her own theatre in 1907. She had organised many concerts for the troops and, by the end of the war, had over twenty performance groups in France and Belgium.

On 18 March, men from the Battalion, under the command of Captain Charles Seel, took part in a ceremonial parade on Place St Jean Bart in Dunkirk. Two days later the Cheshires marched into Dunkirk to catch a train to Étaples, from where they marched to Le Touquet, taking up billets at the Lewis Gun School. Mornings were spent undertaking drill, whilst the afternoons were devoted to sports.

Malo les Bains. The effects of German shelling in August 1918.

Lena Ashwell.

Company Sergeant Major Gordon Crosbie..

In early April news reached the Battalion that an old comrade had died, aged just twenty one. In civilian life, Gordon Crosbie lived in Hyde and worked as a cotton piecer at Hyde Spinning Ltd. He enlisted in March 1915, going overseas a year later. In August 1916, he was wounded in the arm and leg and had been in Britain until October 1918. In late November, after the Armistice, he was promoted to company sergeant major and posted to 1st Cheshires, then in Belgrade. He is believed to have caught the Spanish flu and was ill for fifteen days before he died on 30 March from pneumonia.

The Cheshires formed part of a Guard of Honour at Boulogne for Field Marshal Sir Douglas Haig on his departure from France, on 4 April 1919. He took command of the British Expeditionary Force in December 1915 and oversaw its eventually successful progress since then. On 13 May the men made the short march to a new camp at Étaples, where their daily duties were as guards.

On 13 June Lieutenant Colonel Stanway left the Battalion to return to Britain; his successor, Lieutenant Colonel R W Bradley, arriving to take command on 21 June. After spending some time in Britain, Stanway went to India where, in 1920, he took command of a mixed group of troops tasked with putting down a mutiny by men from the Connaught Rangers. The next year he secured a temporary transfer to the Indian Army and, between 1929 and 1933, was Commandant of a depot of the Railway Reserve Regiment, receiving an OBE in 1930 for his work with ex-

Colonel Stanway in Lahore. Photo: Jon Thornley

servicemen. From 1933 he was Director of Military Prisons in India, a post he held until retirement in 1936. Stanway returned to Britain; but in 1938 he and his wife, Emily, emigrated to South Africa, setting up home in Durban. He died there in 1961.

Captain Sydney Yorston commanded a small party from the Battalion that took part in the Allied Peace Celebrations in Paris on 14 July. He was accompanied by Captain James Hughes, a former civil servant from Dublin, who served throughout the war with the 11th Cheshires until it was merged with the 6th Battalion. Also in the party were Regimental Quartermaster Sergeant Harry Cooke, who had been with the Battalion since its creation in 1908; Company Sergeant Major John Donovan, another ex-11th Battalion man; and Sergeant Frank Collier, one time Battalion wag and holder of two gallantry medals.

The days continued as before until 31 August, when the final entry in the war diary notes that Second Lieutenant John Mackenzie and 141 other ranks left for Boulogne for service in the Black Sea, as part of the Army of Occupation. Over the previous months small groups had left to return to Britain for demobilisation and there was now only a small cadre of troops under Lieutenant Colonel Bradley's command. The cadre left

The parade at Stockport town hall. Photo: Stockport Express

France shortly after, arriving in Britain on 6 September. They arrived at Stockport station on the 12th and, led by the Battalion's band, marched to the Town Hall, where they were formally welcomed by the Mayor and the Town Clerk. The return was celebrated by a dinner at the Armoury. The history of the Battalion, published in the 1930s, describes that a *joyous re-union took place, tempered by thoughts of the gallant lads who had marched away, never to return.*

Now back in civilian clothes, the men tried to return to the normality of their prewar lives. They went back to work. They got married – the local marriage registers between 1919 and 1922 are full of men who had served in the war. They had children. And, in due course, they died. For most of them, their lives returned to relative obscurity. For some, their injuries affected them for the rest of their lives – men with amputated limbs could not easily return to work in the cotton mills. For others, the rigours of service affected their health and shortened their lives. For example, Henry Hibberd, a brass foundry worker from Stalybridge, was a prewar territorial and went overseas with the Battalion in November 1914. He was one of the Battalion transport troops and was gassed in 1918 when, reportedly, he put on his horses' gas masks before his own. He died from the effects of gas on 31 May 1919 and is buried at St Paul's Churchyard in the town.

For others the effects of the war on their health cannot now be known. Thomas Wedderspoon had served with Henry Hibberd, joining the Battalion's Stalybridge Company in 1909. He left in 1916, when his contracted time expired. It is not known how he spent the subsequent years but, in 1920, he was at Prestwich Asylum, presumably as a patient. His death, aged 77, is registered in that area in 1969, suggesting he may have spent many years as a patient.

As described in Chapter 8, Arthur Stansfield had been wounded and taken prisoner in 1917. He was discharged from the army on 1 February 1919 as no longer physically fit for service. He had actually been back in Britain for over twelve months as part of a prisoner exchange arrangement, which allowed men who were no longer fit enough to fight to be repatriated.

> *When the German sergeant came and told me I was to get ready to be exchanged, I could not believe it, but he fetched the interpreter who convinced me. I was carried to the door and saw a private motor car which took me to the hospital exchange centre. Here I was examined and passed for England. I started from this hospital on the journey on New Year's Day 1918, a day I shall never forget as long as I live. The journey on the train to Rotterdam passed without incident and we were transferred to the hospital boat and set sail for England, landing at Boston, Lincolnshire. My troubles came on again however, having another four operations under different conditions.* (Private Arthur Stansfield)

Records suggest that Stansfield got married in 1926. His injuries meant he was unable to return to his job at the tobacco company but was employed as a telephone operator until retirement. He is believed to have died in 1975.

There were other difficulties to be faced. Robert Seery worked as a baker's vanman in Stockport before the war. His marriage with Lilian was always difficult. She had been a heavy drinker and, when he joined the army, in July 1915, she started drinking again and went about with other men. When he returned home in March 1919 he found that she was missing. He reported this to the police, who traced her to Bath, where she had entered into a bigamous marriage. She was tried for the offence, refusing to question the witnesses or present any defence. Unsurprisingly, the jury found her guilty. The judge commented

> *You are a wicked, bad woman. You were convicted on the clearest evidence. The policeman who arrested you told me you treated the matter as a joke. You will find it is not a joke. Your sentence will be nine months hard labour.*

Seery divorced her, remarrying in 1921. He and his new wife, Eugenie, had a long and, hopefully, happy life together, until she died in 1957. Seery died in 1964.

Private Albert Lane married Mabel in 1917. He was then serving with the Cheshires but, in the latter part of the war, served with the Manchester Regiment. Once home, in 1919, the couple moved from Stockport to Doncaster where, in 1924, he deserted her, only to bigamously marry again the next year. His past caught up with him and he was brought before Stockport Magistrates Court where he declared that *I will have nothing more to do with my first wife. I am going to stand by the second.*[98] He was committed for trial at Durham Assizes. The outcome is not known.

He was not the only ex-Cheshire to face court proceedings in the years after the war. Alwyn Johnson served as a second lieutenant with the Battalion from January 1917 until around the spring of 1918. In 1933, he received a sentence of nine months' imprisonment with hard labour in respect of several charges of obtaining money by false pretences. He managed to persuade several clergymen to cash forged cheques. In mitigation, he claimed it was 'through drink'.

Walter Lees Birch also found himself before the court in 1923 because of alcohol. He had served with the 2/6th and 3/6th Battalions between 1915 and 1916, before going overseas, as a lieutenant, in January 1917. The case presented to Blackburn Police Court was that he had been speeding and driving on the wrong side of the road. A police car chased him and, when stopped, Birch said to the constable, *I have a right to go faster than you and it is sometimes safer to drive on the wrong side.* The magistrates disagreed, noting he had seventeen previous motoring convictions and fined him £20. In 1930, still serving as a major with the Territorials, he was brought before a court martial for an unknown offence and was dismissed from the army.

As far as is known, Albert Cook lived an honest life until his later years. He served with the Battalion as a second lieutenant for about six months, from September 1917, until he is thought to have been wounded during the German offensive of March 1918 and returned to Britain. On 23 October 1918 he was at Fort Horsted in Kent when he had an accident at night, falling into the moat and breaking his shoulder. It is not known if it was connected with early celebrations of his promotion to lieutenant three days later. He left the army in 1920 and, as was the custom, was permitted to use his rank for social

Walter Birch. Photo: Regimental Museum

purposes. In due course he set up in business as an estate agent until, in 1959, he was convicted of several charges of fraud – he had stolen money entrusted to him by clients as deposits on house purchases. He received a two year prison sentence. The War Office regarded this as "dishonourable conduct" and deprived him of use of the honorary rank.

There were, of course, success stories in the post war period. Ralph Huffam came from Cheadle Hulme and, before the war, worked as a technical manager. Most of his service was with the two home service battalions; when he went overseas in June 1917 he was attached to the 13th and 10th Cheshires. He was with the 10th Battalion during the German offensive in 1918 and was awarded a Military Cross for collecting stragglers and organising them into a company that checked the enemy advance. He left the army in 1919 and got married to Nora the following year. By 1951 he was a director on the board of Unilever Ltd – the multi-national manufacturer of soaps, detergents, margarines, etc.

Lieutenant Colonel Arthur Newth also became a company director, serving on the board of Harris & Hassall Ltd from 1929. This was a

Bristol based company that first made cars and, later, bodies for buses. He remained as a territorial officer, serving as a brigadier in the Second World. Newth died in 1978.

Captain Leo Ruddin was awarded the Military Cross for his bravery on 31 July 1917. He was shot in the leg that day and returned home for treatment and did not serve overseas again. Returning to south Manchester later in the year, he married his fiancée, Dorothy. Before the war he studied law and worked as an articled clerk for a solicitor. When he left the army in 1919, Ruddin resumed his studies and, in due course, qualified as a solicitor, opening a successful practice, with offices in Manchester and Wilmslow.

Vernon Spinks had joined the Battalion in the late spring of 1916, shortly after receiving his commission. His service was fairly brief and on 10 July 1916 he reported sick with what was diagnosed as shellshock. He returned to Britain for treatment and, as far as is known, did not return to overseas duty but did serve at home with the 2/5th Cheshires and 2/22nd Londons. After the war he resumed a career with the civil service with some success. He had previously worked for the Inland Revenue but, in the mid 1920s, was an immigration officer, based at Dover. He got married in the Kent area in 1925. A quarter of a century later, he had been promoted to be the Assistant Chief Inspector of the Home Office's Immigration Branch and received an OBE in 1950. He is believed to have retired to Battle in Sussex, where he died in 1973.

Frank Naden had many years experience as a territorial soldier. He had left the Battalion in April 1918 when wounded by shrapnel. Treated in Manchester, he quickly returned to duty and was promoted to lieutenant colonel and put in command of a battalion of the Black Watch and then 7th Royal Irish Regiment. His bravery in command of both units saw him awarded two bars to the Distinguished Service Order he had been awarded on 31 July 1917 when commanding the Cheshires. After the war he retained his connection with the territorials and, on 25 October 1922, he was summoned from Stockport's Armoury to the Town Hall. There he was met by the Chief Constable, Inspector Robbie, and the assistant town clerk, Frank Knowles. His expertise was required to help examine arms etc., which had been

Lieutenant Colonel Frank Naden.

found in the possession of an arrested Irishman. But, as they were doing so, a detonator exploded, injuring all four men. They needed treatment at Stockport Infirmary but none were detained. Frank Naden died in 1954. His medals are believed to have remained with his family until 2016, when they were sold at auction for £15,500.

In Burnley, the parents of Lieutenant George Cowpe, who was killed on 31 July 1917, were joined by his fiancée, Mabel Proctor, in looking at a practical way of remembering him. They decided to donate the significant sum of £1500 to the Victoria Hospital as an endowment in perpetuity for three cots in the children's ward. There were to be other memorials to him. In 1918 the family privately published a selection of his letters (from which extracts have been used in this book). He had been a keen cricketer and a competition was established in the Burnley area for the George Bleazard Cowpe Cup; and, in 1920, a stained glass window was unveiled in his memory at the local Wesleyan Chapel.

As the men settled back into civilian life, communities across Britain started to consider ways of remembering their dead neighbours, family members, colleagues, friends, etc. They would usually decide on some form of permanent memorial – perhaps a plaque in a church or school, perhaps a stone construction with the names embossed on brass plaques, located on the village green. Manchester University has two memorials that remember George Cowpe – one is at the old School of Technology building on Whitworth Street, later UMIST, where he studied textile science. It consists of three wooden panels with gold lettering, designed by Henry Cadness, Principal of the Manchester School of Art and made by John Lenegan, a teacher of wood carving at the School. It was unveiled in 1921.

There was no organised national movement for remembrance but communities got together independently to raise money for a war memorial. The town of Hyde has nine separate memorials and rolls of honour on streets and in churches. One of them, in Newton, recognises the sacrifice not just of the men who died but also of their families and gives thanks for those who returned. Local war memorials remain at the heart of Britain's continuing remembrance of those who lost their lives serving their country.

In Belgium, France and the other theatres of the war, men are buried in cemeteries maintained by the Commonwealth War Graves Commission. Originally called the Imperial War Graves Commission, it was founded in 1917. The guiding principle for the Commission is that all casualties are treated equally. There is no distinction between ranks. There is no distinction between cause of death – the man who had served throughout the war only to be killed in the final days is treated the same as the raw recruit who died of an illness days after joining up. The war cemeteries are often in now peaceful, rural locations and they can appear somewhat incongruous in the modern landscape, albeit a constant reminder of the past. In Belgium and France the land for the cemeteries has been given by the respective governments in perpetuity. Within the walls of the cemetery, there are no differences between the shape of the British headstones and the general is as likely to be buried next to a private as to another officer. There are other features, common across most cemeteries. There is grass and the gravestones are in narrow flowerbeds, planted wherever conditions permit, with varieties grown in Britain. Cemeteries with over 1000 burials have a 'Stone of Remembrance', designed by the famous architect, Sir Edwin Lutyens. It is 3.5 metres long and 1.5 metres high, inscribed 'Their Name Liveth for Everymore'.

Nearly all cemeteries with over forty burials have a 'Cross of Sacrifice'. It is a large stone Christian cross which sits on an octagonal base, with a bronze long sword mounted on it, designed by Sir Reginald Blomfield. After he left the army, Lieutenant Bob Morton returned to his craft as a stonemason, working for J & H Pattison in Trafford Park. In later life he became the firm's works manager. In his radio interview on 11 November 1983, he recalled that

> I did the Imperial War Graves Commission war memorials – Ramla, Haifa, Basra, Jerusalem, Falklands Islands, Taranto Italy – and all of them in stone. What they call the Blomfield Cross. There's one of those in every cemetery throughout the whole world and we supplied them to the Commission. We didn't fix them – they got the natives to do the labouring and they had one or two specialists from the Imperial War Graves……All these cemeteries and they are beautifully looked after and during the whole of the last war – Hitler's war – they kept on with their duties and the German cemeteries were looked after by their people, too, in friendliness. They didn't fall out or anything and nobody bothered with them – they left them to it, which was rather nice………I – or we – our firm had to give a price for the Menin Gate. You've heard of the Menin Gate in Ypres? It's a new gate. There used to be in the old days the ramparts at Ypres and there used to be a gate. Well, this is a war memorial gate to all the people in the [Ypres] Salient who never came back. There was a heck of a lot.

The Menin Gate commemorates 54,395 men. Morton's recollection is slightly wrong. These are not "all" the men who never came back from the fighting in that area, but only those who have no known grave – and even then not all. Thousands more are buried in the many war cemeteries around Ypres. The number includes 129 who had served with the 6th Battalion. Another 113 are commemorated on other memorials to the missing in Belgium and France.

On 29 July 1928 the Battalion unveiled its own memorial at Stockport Armoury. It was dedicated by Reverend Thorpe, vicar at St George's Church. The actual unveiling was not undertaken by a local 'worthy' but by Mary Spilsbury. Mrs Spilsbury's two sons, Samuel and William, were both killed on 31 July 1917. She was supported by a Mrs Oldham and a Mrs Phillips who had, presumably, also lost sons during the war. Bob Morton had known both men from school days.

Many men who had served in the war wanted to forget their experience as best they could and would never speak of their time in uniform. For others, the shared experience and camaraderie was important to them. In

The unveiling of the memorial at Stockport Armoury by Mrs Mary Spilsbury, 1928.

The ceremony of unveiling the memorial at Stockport Armoury, 1928.

The memorial at the Armoury. 'To the glory of God and in honour of the officers, NCOs and men of the Sixth Battalion the Cheshire Regiment who laid down their lives in the Great War 1914 – 1918.'

September 1924 sixteen of them formed the 6th Cheshire's Old Comrades Association. Its main object would be to *cement and retain the esprit de corps* of the war period. There would also be a benevolent fund *to assist, as far as possible, any of our members who, through sickness, are in need of help and assistance to put them on their feet.*

The membership quickly rose to around 250. Bob Morton was elected as Chairman, a position he held throughout the Association's existence. The Secretary was ex-sergeant Thomas Knott, a pre-war member of the Battalion who had left the army in 1917 due to illness. The Treasurer was H Pearson, possibly James Henry Pearson, who had been a Company Quartermaster Sergeant with the Battalion. The Honorary President was Colonel George Heywood, who commanded the 6th Cheshires from the autumn of 1914 until the spring of 1916. By the time the Association was formed the 6th Battalion had ceased to exist as a separate infantry unit and the local territorial unit had become the 60th (Cheshire & Shropshire) Medium Brigade, Royal Artillery and Heywood was its Honorary Colonel. Around this time he moved to Herefordshire but retaining his interest with the Association.

The Association had an annual subscription of two shillings, regardless of the previous rank of the member and met monthly, initially at the Windsor Castle Hotel on Stockport's Castle Street, before moving to the Armoury in 1930. There were other fund raising opportunities to help build up the benevolent fund. A draw was held, with prizes being donated by local businesses. It raised £43. Badges and ties, in Regimental colours, were produced and sold. Colonel Frank Naden gave permission for the Armoury to be used for a dance in 1925, which raised £16. That year, the Stockport War Memorial building was opened officially by the Duke of Gloucester and Association members provided the guard of honour. In later years Bob Morton organised an annual concert by the 'Premier Optimists' at Stockport's Garrick Hall. It was always well attended and was the Benevolent Fund's main source of income. The troupe put on other performances to help local groups several times a month. On at least one occasion, they performed at Stockport Workhouse on Christmas Night. Morton also bought a bottle of port, to be kept at Stockport Armoury with the intention that the last surviving member could claim it. It is understood to be still in the possession of the Regimental Association in remembrance of the men who served.

There were other social events and, from time to time, members of the Association and their wives would be entertained in Colonel Heywood's

PROGRAMME.

:: PART I. ::

1. We introduce ourselves ... THE COMPANY

2. A Weather Forecast (not guaranteed)
THE COMPANY

3. A Song of Zummerzet ... FRED REDFERN

4. EDITH WRIGHT will sing.

5. A Non-Stop Number ... ... CONCERTED

6. HAL LOW in his Latest Creation.

7. Bass Songs ... ... HARRY DAVIES

8. A "Busking" Episode...BOB MORTON & HAL LOW

9. PEGGY DISNEY will Entertain.

10. A Dancing Drama ... ... THE COMPANY

INTERVAL.

:: PART II. ::

11. "A Moving Wait"
PEGGY DISNEY & BOB MORTON

12. FRED REDFERN will sing.

13. BOB MORTON will "bob on."

14. "Clerical Errors" ... . MALE TRIO

15. WILLY WOOD and the Piano.

16. "My boy, Billy" ... EDITH WRIGHT & PARTNER

17. "Dignity and Impudence"
BOB MORTON & FRED REDFERN

18. HAL LOW has a few words.

19. EDITH WRIGHT will again sing.

20. FINALE ... ... "And so to bed"

This Programme is subject to slight alteration.

The Premier Optimists programme for 1924/25.

SEASON 1924-25.

.. THE ..

Premier Optimists

The Popular .. ..
Pierrot Entertainers,

PRESENT THEIR NEW SEASON'S

"POT-POURRI"

A Cabaret Burlesque.

Some Sense, but mostly Nonsense.

Programmes - One Penny each

F. WALTERS & Co., Printers, Rivers Street, Leicester.

Members of the Old Comrades Association pay their respects at Hereford's war memorial.

large home at Caradoc Court, Ross on Wye. During one visit in the 1930s the party travelled by train to Hereford, where they were collected by buses. A wreath was laid at the city's war memorial before moving on to Heywood's home for lunch. The newspaper report of the day records that lunch was served in a large marquee. Afterwards some of the visitors went on a tour of the Wye Valley, whilst others remained behind to play skittles, bowls and clock golf. Later in the afternoon tea was served and brief speeches made and Thomas Knott presented Colonel and Mrs Heywood with an inscribed brass tray, by way of thanks. By then, branches had been established in Hyde and Stalybridge, as well as the original Stockport branch, but it seems no branch was ever formed in Glossop. The Association held an annual dinner on 11 November each year.

On a more sombre note, the Association organised annual pilgrimages to the battlefields, each year laying a wreath at a cemetery where their comrades were buried. The first trip was in 1929 and twelve members travelled. Before they left the wreath was put on display and members of the public were invited to purchase British Legion poppies and place them

The Old Comrades Association lay their wreath at Tyne Cot in 1929 or 1930..

Thiepval Memorial to the Missing. Inauguration ceremony, 1931.

in the wreath's outer rim. It was reported that many hundreds responded. The wreath was laid at Tyne Cot Cemetery, under the Cheshire Regiment's panels on the memorial to the missing. Like the Menin Gate, this memorial at the back of what is the War Graves Commission's largest cemetery commemorates men who have no known grave – in this case, nearly 35,000 men killed in the Salient after 16 August 1917.

Mill Road Cemetery. To the left is the area of the Schwaben Redoubt, attacked by the Battalion in 1916.

The visit the following year saw twenty six men travel and the wreath was again laid at Tyne Cot. In 1931 numbers had increased to forty and the plan was to lay the wreath at the Thiepval Memorial, which commemorates over 72,000 of the missing from the Somme battles. However, when they arrived, they found that it was still under construction and so decided to lay the wreath at the nearby Mill Road Cemetery, which is near to the Battalion's attack on St Pierre Divion in the autumn of 1916. Seven members of the Battalion are buried there, including Howard Bryant and Allen Newton, mentioned in Chapter 7. The planned visit for 1932 had to be cancelled, because of *difficulties in travel, both at home and abroad and the impossible situation of the rate of exchange.*[99]

When war was again declared in 1939, the 6th Cheshires were reformed, under the command of Lieutenant Colonel Sydney Astle. As a young man, Astle had served with the Battalion as a lieutenant, being awarded a

The Stalybridge branch of the Old Comrades Association, dedicating a new standard at Holy Trinity Church, 1 July 1933. Photo: Tameside MBC Image Archive

July 1925. The Battalion colours are escorted to St George's Church. Bob Morton carries the colours. Photo; Jon Thornley

Military Cross for bravery in 1918. The Battalion saw action in Egypt and Italy before finally disbanding in 1946.

The Old Comrades Association continued in existence in the postwar period but time was taking its toll on the number of members and its last meeting was held in July 1974. Throughout its existence, members had held an annual parade, which they called 'St Julien Day', in recognition of their attack on 31 July 1917, which was the Battalion's costliest in terms of casualties. They would form up in the drill room at the Armoury, turning towards the war memorial and coming to attention, in respect for those who had not returned home, and the Mayor would lay a wreath. The men would then march to St George's Church for a service before holding a short service and wreath laying ceremony at Stockport's war memorial, at the art gallery. At the 1925 parade, when the Battalion was disbanded as an infantry unit, the colours were deposited at St Georges Church. Bob Morton led the parade, carrying the flag.

It is a tradition still maintained by the Stockport Branch of the Regimental Association. In 2009 many of its members had been on a two day visit to the battlefields, returning on 1 August. They paraded next

July 1925. Bob Morton leads the parade, carrying the Battalion colours.

morning and, after the service at St George's, a wreath was laid at the war memorial in its grounds, before going to the Armoury for a lunch attended by Stockport's Deputy Mayor.

The last words lie with ex-Lieutenant Bob Morton. During his radio interview in 1983, when he was aged 90, he was asked *Was it worth it? All those people dead, wounded, maimed, widowed, destruction, all that money?*

He replied *I don't think you thought about it, because it was so vast. I mean, you'd just go barmy if you did.*

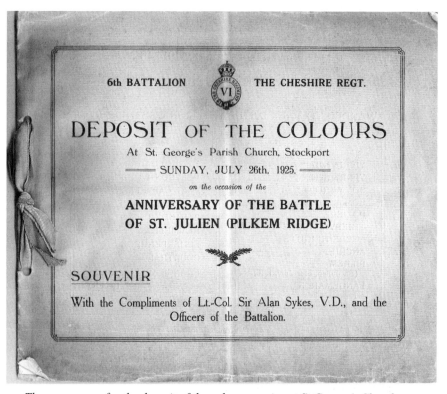

The programme for the deposit of the colours service at St George's Church.

Notes

1   *Luton Times,* 22 May 1908.
2   *Hyde Reporter*, 24 October 1914.
3   National Archives, WO95/1572.
4   Brockbank's diary is held by the Cheshire Regiment Museum and Archives and extracts are used with permission.
5   *War History of the 6th Battalion, Cheshire Regiment.* C Smith, 1932.
6   *Manchester Evening News*, 23 November 1914.
7   *Stockport Advertiser*, 4 December 1914.
8   *Stockport Express*, 10 December 1914.
9   *Northampton Mercury*, 4 December 1914.
10 *North Cheshire Herald*, 20 February 1915.
11 *Stalybridge Reporter*, 12 December 1914.
12 *Stalybridge Reporter*, 26 December 1914.
13 *Stalybridge Reporter,* 2 January 1915.
14 *Glossop Chronicle*, 1 January 1915.
15 *Manchester Evening News*, 29 December 1914.
16 *Glossop Chronicle*, 15 January 1915.
17 *Ashton Reporter*, 13 February 1915.
18 *Cheshire Observer*, 9 January 1915.
19 *Stockport Express*, 14 January 1915.
20 *Ashton Reporter*, 2 January 1915.
21 *Hyde Reporter*, 6 March 1915.
22 *Stockport Advertiser*, 8 January 1915.
23 *Stockport Advertiser*, 9 October 1914.
24 *Stalybridge Reporter,* 28 November 1914.
25 *Manchester Evening News*, 27 January 1915.
26 *North Cheshire Herald*, 10 April 1915.
27 *Bath Chronicle*, 25 March 1916.
28 *Stockport Express*, 21 January 1915.
29 *North Cheshire Herald*, 23 January 1915.
30 *Ashton Reporter*, 6 March 1915.
31 *Hyde Reporter*, 30 January 1915.
32 *Ashton Reporter*, 23 January 1915.
33 *Dundee Evening Telegraph*, 16 February 1915.
34 *Ashton Reporter*, 6 March 1915.

35 *Hyde Reporter,* 6 March 1915.
36 *North Cheshire Herald*, 13 March 1915.
37 *North Cheshire Herald*, 18 March 1916.
38 *Stockport Express*, 24 June 1916.
39 *North Cheshire Herald*, 1 May 1915.
40 *North Cheshire Herald*, 5 June 1915.
41 *Stockport Advertiser*, 2 July 1915.
42 *Stalybridge Reporter*, 1 April 1916.
43 *Winston Churchill as I Knew Him*, Violet Bonham Carter, 1965.
44 *Ashton Reporter*, 13 March 1915.
45 *Ashton Reporter*, 24 April 1915.
46 *Ashton Reporter*, 24 April 1915.
47 *Stockport Advertiser*, 26 April 1915.
48 *Ashton Reporter*, 24 April 1915.
49 *Stockport Advertiser*, 14 May 1915.
50 *Stockport Advertiser*, 29 October 1915.
51 *North Cheshire Herald*, 8 January 1916.
52 Dickinson's diary is held by the family and extracts are used with permission.
53 *Stalybridge Reporter*, 11 March 1916.
54 Whizz bangs – slang for smaller calibre German artillery shells. Rum jar –
trench mortar shell shaped like the jar in which the rum ration was stored. It was
packed with bits of metal.
55 *Glossop Chronicle*, 19 May 1916.
56 *Stalybridge Reporter*, 13 May 1916.
57 *Manchester Evening News*, 7 July 1916.
58 Tins of corned beef and hard army 'dog biscuits'.
59 Information supplied by Kevin Shannon, author *The Lion & The Rose. The 4th
Battalion Kings Own Royal Lancaster Regiment 1914-1919.*
60 *Stalybridge Reporter*, 29 July 1916.
61 *Glossop Chronicle*, 4 August 1916.
62 *North Cheshire Herald*, 6 September 1916.
63 *Cheshire Daily Echo*, 8 September 1916.
64 *Stalybridge Reporter*, 11 November 1916.
65 George Bleazard Cowpe, *Memories and Letters 1916-1917.*
66 *North Cheshire Herald*, 23 September 1916.
67 Morton was interviewed on 11 November 1983 by Piccadilly Radio, now
Key103. Extracts from the transcript are included with permission of Key103 and
the Morton family. Minor amendments have been made for clarity.
68 *Hyde Reporter*, 14 October 1916.
69 *Glossop Chronicle*, 13 October 1916.
70 *Stalybridge Reporter*, 3 February 1917.
71 Lieutenant Frank Naden.
72 *Cheshire Daily Echo*, 10 November 1916.
73 *The History of the Cheshire Regiment in the Great War*, Arthur Crookenden.
74 *North Cheshire Herald*, 9 December 1916.
75 Dodge was evacuated back to Britain suffering with shellshock, in particular
with sleep problems. He did not return to overseas duty and was invalided out of the

army in December 1918. He is believed to have died in 1980, in the Stockport area.
76 Brockbank returned to live in South Manchester where, in 1925, he married
Helen Norris. The couple would have two children. They moved to North Wales,
where he worked as a technical representative for Staveley Coal & Iron Ltd. During
the Second World War, he put on uniform again and became a captain in the Home
Guard. He is believed to have died in the Colwyn Bay area in 1976.
77 *North Cheshire Herald*, 2 December 1916.
78 1597 Frank Collier
79 *Stockport Advertiser*, 1 December 1916.
80 *Stalybridge Reporter*, 2 December 1916.
81 Family history websites suggest Platt died in 1985.
82 *Stockport Advertiser*, 2 March 1917.
83 *Stalybridge Reporter*, 3 March 1917.
84 *Glossop Chronicle*, 12 July 1917.
85 *North Cheshire Herald*, 18 July 1917.
86 Arthur Stansfield's papers are held by the Imperial War Museum and a statement
given after his repatriation to Britain as a prisoner of war is held by the National
Archives. Extracts from his papers are used with the permission of the family.
87 Morton recalled the soldier's name as Bob Harrison but it has not been possible
to identify a man with this name serving with the battalion at the time.
88 Returning prisoner of war statement.
89 King's wound was serious and he was repatriated to Britain, via the Netherlands,
on 19 July 1918. His comments are taken from a statement given on his return.
90 *Dundee Evening Telegraph*, 13 May 1930.
91 *The 25th Division in France & Flanders*, M Kincaid-Smith, 1919
92 Extracts from the diary from *War History of the 6th Battalion Cheshire
Regiment*, 1932.
93 *Glossop Chronicle*, 6 September 1918.
94 Wrongly identified as Arthur Dixon in the 1932 Battalion history.
95 The awards to these men were noted in the 1932 Battalion history. It has not
been possible to find the awards to Archer and Burgess listed in the *London Gazette*.
96 Wrongly identified as Fred Collier in the Battalion history published in 1932.
97 *North Cheshire Herald*, 9 November 1918.
98 *Hartlepool Northern Daily Mail*, 25 July 1929.
99 *History of the Battalion* published in 1932.

Index

(Note: Ranks are usually those at first mention in the text)